in italiano

A Handbook for Comparison and Contrast

for English-Speaking Students

Written by
Laura Alcini - Marilyn Melchiori Rossi

3. 2. 1.
1997 96 95

INDICE GENERALE INDEX

FOREWORD

Aims of the Text

The study of the Italian language is complex and difficult for native speakers of English, given the differences in the grammatical structures and the phonics of the two languages.

In Italiano: A Handbook for Comparison and Contrast for English-Speaking Students proposes to address in a concise but exhaustive manner the principal difficulties which native speakers of English encounter in the study of Italian. This *Handbook* is the result of a constructive and indispensable collaboration between two teachers: one Italian, whose academic background is English; and the other American whose academic background is Italian. Given our reciprocal areas of expertise, we have been able to develop, from two completely different points of view, an entire analysis of the differences and similarities between these two languages.

In developing this text, we have kept in mind the diverse motivations which foster the study of Italian. Thus, it is intended for the following: those who, as native speakers of English, want to begin the study of Italian; and those who, with some previous knowledge as a basis, want to strengthen certain aspects of the grammar and / or the spoken language. It should be welcome news that this text is appropriate for use both in high schools and in colleges and universities. Further, our text is intended for those who, although not native speakers of English, speak English as a second language in their native countries and who may use it as a medium for beginning the study of Italian. Finally, although the text may not and cannot substitute for a native speaker of Italian, it can serve as an aid and as a stimulus as well to those who, not being able to take an Italian course either in Italy or in their own countries, may want to "become familiar" with this language as "self-taught" students.

Description of the Text

A Handbook for Comparison and Contrast was developed by us as an integral part of the multi-media course *In italiano*, written by Professors Angelo Chiuchiù, Fausto Minciarelli, and Marcello Silvestrini; and as we have elaborated upon the original text, we have paid close attention to the glottodidactic criteria which are at the basis of the abovementioned course. At the same time, we have kept in mind our own experiences in the teaching of Italian to English-speaking students, making clear examples of this in every section of the text.

Our *Handbook* consists of six parts: *Pronunciation Guide*; *Grammar in Contrast*; *Take a Look at the Everyday Language*; *Exercises*; *Answer Key*; and *Vocabulary*.

The first of these six sections is the **Pronunciation Guide**, and in it we have given

i

simple explanations of pronunciation, given the noted phonetic differences between English and Italian. We have also given some essential rules which are necessary for an English speaker. After each phonetic explanation, there are some sample words for the student to use in order to practise the application of these rules to spoken Italian.

In the second section, **Grammar in Contrast**, we have emphasised, by means of the grammatical boxes seen in the 24 units of the course *In italiano*, the differing morphological and lexical structures which normally create marked difficulties in learning a second language. In the third section, **Take a look at the Everyday Language**, we have retained the idiomatic material found in the original 24 units and have divided each into two parts. The first is called **What's Different**, and in it we have discussed idiomatic expressions and catch phrases which make up a significant part of the spoken language and which rarely appear in grammar texts. These phrases have also been analyzed from a "contrastive" point of view, and in doing so we have tried to find for each one the corresponding English phrase without resorting to a literal translation. The second aspect of this section is called **How to Say It** ; and in this part, using the same method of the first part, we have highlighted some of the most important linguistic functions.

In the fourth section, **Exercises**, we have provided some practice exercises which are different from those found in *In italiano*. Essentially, these address all the most serious grammatical problems encountered by English-speaking students. The accompanying **Answer Key** comprises the fifth section of the text. As the last section of our *Handbook*, we have included a **Vocabulary** in which are listed in Italian and in English all the words which appear in the original course *In italiano*.

Description of the Method

It seems appropriate to us at this point to cite, however concisely, the principal theories which support the development of this text. The title, **A Handbook for Comparison and Contrast**, practically summarizes the method which we have adopted, namely, a contrastive method which in the development of teaching materials considers the diverse needs which we have personally observed among our students in class. Ours is a method which makes contrastive analyses not as mere theoretical examples but as a study developed in order to help students avoid making errors in language transfer and language interference. In addition, the process of translation from Italian to English should be seen as another means by which to reach the aims cited previously.

In closing this introduction, we would like to thank all those who have encouraged us in the sometimes difficult development of this text. We hope that it will be useful and that it will foster a great degree of enthusiasm for the study of Italian throughout the English-speaking world.

Laura Alcini
Marilyn Melchiori Rossi

Perugia September 1, 1989

Credits

Laura Alcini graduated from the University of Rome "La Sapienza" with a *Laurea* in British and American Language and Literature. She is currently teaching Italian language and Translation at the Università Italiana per Stranieri of Perugia. Marilyn Melchiori Rossi, a 1986 Rockefeller Fellow, graduated from the University of Massachusetts at Amherst with a B.A. in Classics and an M.A.T. in Italian. She is currently teaching Latin and Italian at West Springfield High School, West Springfield, Massachusetts.

PRONUNCIATION GUIDE

Alfabeto   **Alphabet**

The Italian alphabet consists of twenty-one letters.

Letters   *Names of Letters*

Letters	Names of Letters
a	a
b	bi
c	ci
d	di
e	e
f	effe
g	gi
h	acca
i	i
l	elle
m	emme
n	enne
o	o
p	pi
q	cu
r	erre
s	esse
t	ti
u	u
v	vu
z	zeta

The five letters which remain from the English alphabet are usually seen in foreign words which are borrowed in Italian and which, therefore, have not changed their original spellings. The 'j' is also seen in some unusual Italian spellings, i.e. Jesi, Lido di Jesolo.

j	i lunga
k	cappa
w	doppia vu
x	ics
y	ipsilon

In using the following guide to the pronunciation of Italian, it is important that you listen very carefully to the teacher's pronunciation and that you try repeatedly to duplicate the sounds which he produces.

Vocali   Vowels

The sounds of the vowels listed below correspond to the English sounds described after each vowel. Practice each vowel sound by repeating the words provided.

The vowel	*corresponds to the English*	*as in*
a	a	father
e (closed)	a	way, day, pay
e (open)	a	bet, set, get
i	i or ee	machine or beet
o (closed)	o	no, so, stow
o (open)	o	or, for, nor, bore
u	oo	food, brood, moon.

Pronunciation exercises for practice.

a   - sala, pasta, insalata, lago, fontana, alta

e (closed) - mele, pere, neve, candela, ridere, vedere

e (open)   - festa, bene, gente, sedia, treno, medico

i   - libri, quaderni, simili, minimi, italiani, americani

o (closed) - sto, sono, volo, solo, cotone, dolore

o (open)   - porta, storia, cosa, no, donna, mobile

u   - fungo, lungo, fulmine, luna, unico, futuro.

Consonanti   Consonants

The sounds of the consonants listed below correspond to the English sounds described after each letter or combination of letters. If no English equivalent is given, you may infer that the sound of the Italian consonant is the same as it is in English. In both instances, words for practice will be given after each consonant or combination of letters.

b - This letter is pronounced as it is in English:

- *banana, basilica, bello, brutto, febbraio, bar.*

c - The 'c' has several different sound combinations. If it is followed by an 'a', an 'o', or a 'u', it has the sound of the English 'k', a 'hard c' sound.

- *caffè, carica, comodo, articolo, curva, acustica*

  If it is followed by an 'e' or an 'i', it has the sound of the English 'ch', a 'soft c' sound.
- *cena, cento, aceto, ciao, cibo, amici.*
- If it is followed by 'he' or 'hi', it again has the sound of the English 'k'.
- *che, banche, perché, chiesa, chissà, chiacchierata.*

d - This letter is pronounced more sharply in Italian than it is in English. To pronounce it correctly, you should place the tip of your tongue behind your top front teeth.
- *dente, dentista, dove, sedia, sedano, siedono.*

f - The letter 'f' is pronounced the same in both English and Italian. The important thing to remember is that it represents the two English spellings 'f' and 'ph'. Thus, the English <u>fortunate</u> and <u>pharmacy</u> are <u>fortunato</u> and <u>farmacia</u> in Italian.
- *favoloso, Franco, fotografia, geografia.*

g - The 'g' also has several different sound combinations. If it is followed by an 'a', an 'o', or a 'u', it has the sound of the English 'g' heard in <u>go</u>, a 'hard g' sound.
- *gamba, gatto, gonna, longobardo, gusto, ragù.*
- If it is followed by an 'e' or an 'i', it has the sound of the English 'g' heard in <u>George</u>, a 'soft g' sound.
- *gennaio, gettone, eleggere, gita, giro, festeggiare.*
- If it is followed by 'he' or 'hi', it again has the hard sound of the English 'g' heard in <u>go</u>.
- *spaghetti, lunghe, righe, laghi, cataloghi, funghi.*
- There are two other Italian sound combinations for the letter 'g' which look strange to native speakers of English. One is 'gn'. It is best duplicated by using the sound heard in <u>canyon</u>, which is represented by the 'ny'.
- *bagno, legno, lasagne, gnocchi, signora, ragno.*
- The other is very difficult to reproduce exactly as the Italians do. It is 'gli', and it is easier to say if it is part of a word rather than an isolated word, which it also can be. It is best duplicated by imitating the sound heard in <u>million</u> or <u>cotillion</u>, which is represented by the 'll'. It is really important to remember that there is usually no type of 'g' sound in 'gli'.

- *famiglia, glielo, gli, aglio, meglio, meraviglia.*
- You will see that Italian has very few exceptions to its rules of pronunciation. However, the 'gli' combination offers some exceptions. In the following words, the 'gli' combination is pronounced as in English.
- *anglicanesimo, anglicano, glicemia, glicerina, negligente, negligenza.*

h - This letter is silent. It is seen in foreign words, but it remains silent.
  - *harem, hockey, hotel.*
- It alters the sounds of the letters 'c' and 'i' or 'e' and 'g' and 'i' or 'e', as seen above. It is also used to distinguish graphically words which sound alike.
- *o,* or; *ho,* I have
- *a,* at, to; *ha,* he has
- *anno,* year; *hanno,* they have

l - This letter is pronounced as it is in English.
- *lacrima, legge, libero, lira, luglio, lunedì*

m - This letter is pronounced as it is in English.
  - *madre, macchina, meccanico, mille, mondo, museo*

n - This letter is pronounced as it is in English.
- *nascita, negozio, nero, noia, nonno, notte*

p - This letter is pronounced as it is in English.
  - *pace, padre, pezzo, pericolo, poesia, pure*

q - In Italian, as in English, the 'q' is always followed by a 'u'. It also has the same 'kw' sound.
- *qualche, qualcuno, questo, quello, qui, quindi*
- The same 'kw' sound can also be heard in Italian in the 'cqu' letter combination.
- *acqua, acquatico, acquistare*

r - The 'r' in Italian is always trilled. This sound may be heard in British English but not in American English.
- *radio, rapido, re, regola, riguardare, rumore*

s - The 's', as well, has several different sound combinations. The first two described here are 'sc' followed by 'e' or 'i'. In each example, the 'sc' has the sound of the English 'sh'.

- *scegliere, scena, scendere, sci, scienza, sciopero*
- The next two are 'sch' followed by 'e' or 'i'. In each example, the 'sch' has the sound of the English 'sk'.
- *schema, scherzare, pesche, schifo, dischi, fiaschi*
- The 's' can also have the sound of the English 's' heard in <u>mouse</u>.
- *santo, scalino, secolo, sfortuna, sicuro, sole*
- The 's' can sometimes have the sound of the English 's' heard in <u>rose</u>. It always has this sound when followed directly by 'b', 'd', 'g', 'l', 'm', 'n', 'r', and 'v'.
- *rosa, tesoro, sbaglio, sdegno, sguardo, slancio, smettere, snello, sregolato, svanire*

t - This letter is pronounced as it is in English.
- *tana, tardi, tedesco, tempio, tiranno, trasformare*

v - This letter is pronounced as it is in English.
- *vacanza, vero, via, voce, volpe, vulcano*

z - The 'z' in Italian has two different sounds. One is like the 'ts' heard in the English <u>lets</u>.
- *forza, terzo, zio, pizza, zitto*
- The other is like the 'ds' heard in the English <u>weds</u>.
- *zero, zeta, zingaro, zona, zoo, zucchero*

Finally, all consonants except 'h' can be doubled in Italian. This does not change any of the above pronunciation rules. In only means that the consonant sounds are said more deliberately; in essence, you must pronounce each one, so the sound is more emphatic.
- *babbo, accanto, addormentare, affitto, ballare, mamma*

Capitalization and Punctuation

Many of the rules of capitalization in English do not exist in Italian. The following words are not capitalized in Italian as they are in English.

1. days of the week - *lunedì*

2. months of the year - *gennaio*

3. titles: Mr., Mrs., Miss. Dr., etc. - *il signor Puccini*

4. words in a title, except the first word - *I promessi sposi*

5. proper adjectives, except when they are used as plural nouns - *La moda france-se è nota.*

6. the pronoun I - *io*

7. Unlike English, in Italian the pronouns *Lei* and *Loro* (formal you) are usually capitalized.

Segni d'interpunzione

,	virgola
;	punto e virgola
:	due punti
...	puntini
.	punto
!	punto esclamativo
?	punto interrogativo
" "	virgolette
( )	parentesi tonde
[ ]	parentesi quadrate
-	trattino
—	lineetta

Stress and Accents

Accento tonico

Most words in Italian are stressed on the next-to-the-last (penultimate) syllable. Many words are stressed on the last (ultimate) syllable. If they are, they are written with an accent above the last vowel.

- città, università, perché, tassì, però, virtù

Some words are stressed on the antepenultimate syllable, and a few are even stressed on the syllables before that.

- umile, medico, parlano, ditemelo, mostragliela

Accenti

Written accents, usually grave (\\) but sometimes acute(/), in Italian words are always used for a specific reason and, therefore, cannot be omitted. In the following examples, whether an accent is written or not is the difference in the definition of a word.

dà	he gives	da	from
è	he is	e	and
tè	tea	te	you
sì	yes	si	himself
però	however	pero	peartree

1 GRAMMAR IN CONTRAST

Page 12 - Box 1/2

1) In Italian, nouns ending in **-o** are generally masculine (with a few exceptions); nouns ending in **-a** are generally feminine (with a few exceptions). Most masculine nouns end in **-o** in the singular and form their plural by changing the **-o** to an **-i**, such as: "post<u>o</u> → post<u>i</u>" ("place → places"). Most feminine nouns end in **-a** and form their plural by changing the **-a** to an **-e**, such as: "ragazz<u>a</u> → ragazz<u>e</u>" ("girl → girls").

2) Unlike the English **Definite Article** (invariable in gender and number). **L'Articolo Determinativo Italiano** agrees in gender and number with the noun which it accompanies. **Il** is the definite article used before masculine singular nouns beginning with a consonant: "<u>il</u> posto" ("the place"). **I** is the definite article used before masculine plural nouns beginning with a consonant: <u>i</u> posti" ("the places"). **La** is the definite article used before feminine singular nouns beginning with a consonant: "<u>la</u> ragazza" ("the girl"). **Le** is the definite article used before feminine plural nouns beginning with a consonant "<u>le</u> ragazze" ("the girls").

3) Unlike the English **Adjective** (invariable). **L'Aggettivo Italiano** agrees in gender and number with the noun it accompanies. A masculine singular adjective ending in **-o** accompanies a masculine singular noun in **-o**, and a masculine plural adjective ending in **-i** accompanies a masculine plural noun in **-i**, as in the sentences: "Il ragazzo è americano → I ragazzi sono americani" ("The boy is American → The boys are American").

   A feminine singular adjective ending in **-a** accompanies a feminine singular noun in **-a**, and a feminine plural adjective ending in **-e** accompanies a feminine plural noun in **-e**, as in the sentences: "La ragazz<u>a</u> è svizzera → Le ragazz<u>e</u> sono svizzere" ("The girl is Swiss → The girls are Swiss").

Page 12 - Box 3

1) **Il Presente (The Present Tense)** of the verb **essere (to be)** is irregular: "(Io) sono" ("I am"); "(Tu) sei" ("You are"), etc.

2) In Italian, **Il Pronome Soggetto (The Subject Pronoun)** is very often omitted and for this reason it is placed in parentheses in the following sentences: "(Io) sono di Boston" ("I am from Boston"); "(Tu) sei a casa" ("You are at home"), etc.

3) In Italian, a sentence is made negative by placing the adverb <u>non</u> before the verb "Sono in Italia / Non sono in Italia" ("I am in Italy / I am not in Italy").

4) In the sentence "Io sono **di** Zurigo" ("I am from Zurich"), the preposition **DI** follows the verb **essere (to be)** instead of preposition "from" used in English.

| **Page 13 - Box 1** |

1) **Il Pronome Interrogativo (The Interrogative Pronoun) chi** is used to refer to persons: "Chi è Paul?" ("Who is Paul?").

2) **L'Articolo Indeterminativo Italiano (The Indefinite Article)** also varies according to the gender and to the first letter of the noun which it accompanies. The indefinite article **UN** is used before masculine nouns beginning with a vowel or a consonant: "<u>un</u> ragazzo" ("a boy"). The indefinite article **UNA** is used before all feminine nouns which do not begin with a vowel: "<u>una</u> ragazza" ("a girl").

3) The preposition **DI** plus the definite articles <u>dei</u>, <u>delle</u>, etc. ("some") espresses an indefinite plural which is generally omitted in English. This construction is called **Articolo Partitivo (Partitive):** "Paul e Robert sono dei ragazzi americani" ("Paul and Robert are American boys"). Note that the partitive may be omitted in Italian as well.

1) **L'Avverbio Interrogativo (The Interrogative Adverb) Dove** indicates place and translates the English **where**; "Dove è Marianne?" ("Where is Marianne?").

2) Unlike English, the italian sentence "Paul è in treno" ("Paul is on the train") requires the simple preposition **IN.**

1 TAKE A LOOK AT THE EVERYDAY LANGUAGE

1. - Io sono italiano. *Anche tu* sei italiano?
   - Sì, *anch'io* (sono italiano).
2. - Io sono in Italia per studiare la lingua italiana. E tu?
   - *Anch'io* (sono in Italia per studiare la lingua italiana).
3. - Perché sei *in Italia*?
   - *Sono qui* per lavoro.
4. - Sei in Italia *per lavoro*?
   - Sì, sono qui *per questo*.
5. - Perché siete *a Firenze*?
   - Siamo *qui* in vacanza.
6. - Siete qui *in vacanza*?
   - Sì, siamo qui *per questo*.
7. - È straniera la ragazza?
   - Sì, sono *tutte e due* straniere.
8. - Sono stranieri?
   - Eh sì, sono *tutti e due* stranieri.

Il tabellone elettronico

A   WHAT'S DIFFERENT

1) The Italian sentences "Io sono italiano. *Anche tu* sei italiano? - Sì, *anch'io* (sono italiano)" correspond to the English "I'm Italian. Are you Italian, *too*? - Yes, I am". In this case, the adverb **anche** is necessary in Italian but is not translated in English.

2) The Italian sentence "S*ono qui per*..." expresses a reason for being in a place and corresponds to the English sentence "*I'm here for*...". "Sono qui per lavoro" translates "I am here for my job".

3) In order to express the idea of being in a city, Italian uses the preposition **a** while English uses **in** in front of the name of a city. Thus, the sentence "Perché siete *a Firenze*?" translates "Why are you *in Florence*?".

4) The Italian sentence "Siamo qui **in vacanza**" corresponds to the English sentence "We are here *on vacation*".

5) The Italian forms **tutti e due** and **tutte e due** correspond to the English **both of them** (or **they both**). So, "Sono stranieri? - Eh sì, sono *tutti e due* stranieri" translate "Are they foreigners? - Yes, *both of them* are foreigners" (or "Yes, they both are").

Interpellare		– Scusi, questo posto è libero? – Senta, sono liberi questi posti?		
Identificare	Chiedere e dire il nome	– Chi è Lei? – Chi sei tu?	⇨	- Sono Paul.
		– Come si chiama Lei? – Come ti chiami tu?		- Mi chiamo Paul.
	Chiedere notizie	– Di dove è Lei? – Di dove sei tu?		- Io sono di Boston.
	Presentare qualcuno	– Lui è Paul. – Lei è Marianne.		
	Rispondere alla presentazione	– Piacere! – Molto piacere! – Piacere, io sono Sandra Rivelli.		

B | HOW TO SAY IT

1) In Italian, in order to ask someone something (Interpellare) the expression **"Scusi"** (**"Excuse me!"**) must be used in formal situations before you actually ask the question. Likewise, the expression **"Scusa"** (**"Excuse me!"**) must be used in informal situation. The expression **"Senta"** (**"Listen"**) can also be used in formal situations, and the expression **"Senti"** (**"Listen"**), in informal situations.

2) In order to ask someone his name and to say one's own name (Chiedere e dire il nome), you must first be aware of whether you are in a formal or informal situation. In formal situations you should use the interrogative pronoun **chi?** (**who?**), plus the third person singular of the verb **essere** (**to be**), plus the subject pronoun **Lei** (**you**). "Chi è Lei? - Sono Paul" translate "Who are you? - I'm Paul". In informal situations you should use the interrogative pronoun **chi?** (**who?**), plus the second person singular of the verb **essere** (**to be**), plus the subject pronoun **tu** (**you**). "Chi sei tu? - Sono Paul" translate "Who are you? - I'm Paul". Another way to ask someone his name can be seen in the following sentences. "Come si chiama Lei?" translates "What is your name?" and is used in formal situations. "Come ti chiami tu?" translates "What is your name?" as well, but is used only in informal situations. The answer for either situation could be "Mi chiamo Paul" which translates "My name is Paul".

3) In order *to ask information (Chiedere notizie)*, you must also use two different expressions. In formal situations you say, "Di dove è (Lei)?" which translates "Where are you from?". In informal situations you may say, "Di dove sei? - Sono di Boston" which translate "Where are you from? - I'm from Boston". Unlike English, Italian uses the preposition **di** with the verb *to be* instead of the preposition **da**.

4) In order *to introduce someone (Presentare qualcuno)*, you must remember that in Italian, as in English, the easiest way to introduce someone is by using the verb **essere** (**to be**). "Lui è Paul. Lei è Marianne" correspond to "This is Paul. This is Marianne".

5) In order *to respond to an introduction (Rispondere alla presentazione)*, you must remember that in Italian the most common way to respond to an introduction is to say "Piacere!" or "Molto piacere!" each of which corresponds to "It's (very) nice to meet you!". For example, "Piacere, io sono Sandra Rivelli" is used in order to say "It's nice to meet you. I'm Sandra Rivelli".

2   GRAMMAR IN CONTRAST

Page 30 - Box 1

1) **Il presente (The present tense)** of the verb **avere (to have)** also is irregular:"(Io) ho molti amici" ("I have many friends"); "(Tu) hai una bella casa" ("You have a nice house").

Page 30 - Box 2

1) In Italian, nouns which end in **–e** in the singular may be either masculine or feminine; the **–e** changes to **–i** in the plural. "Il professore è italiano → I professori sono italiani" ("The teacher is Italian → The teachers are Italian").

2) The Italian adjectives which end in **–e** have only one form for the masculine and feminine singular. Also, they have only one form for the masculine and feminine plural; in the plural they change the final **–e** to an **–i**. "La stazione è grande → Le stazioni sono grandi" ("The station is big →The stations are big").

Page 31 - Box 1

1) **Il Pronome Interrogativo (The Interrogative Pronoun) Che cosa** is used to refer to things and translates the English **what**.

    "Che cosa è? E' il libro di Daniela" ("What is this? It is Daniela's book").

Page 31 - Box 2

1) In Italian all three forms **che cosa**, **che** and **cosa** indicate objects and correspond to the English **what**. "Che c'è sul banco?" ("What is on the desk?").

2) **C'è** and **ci sono** translate the English **there is** and **there are**. "Ci sono dei giornali" ("There are some newspapers").

3) The indefinite pronouns **niente/nulla** have the same meaning. They refer to things and correspond to the English **nothing**. Note that unlike English, sentences in Italian may contain two negative words. "Non c'è niente" ("There isn't anything").

Page 31 - Box 3

1) The sentence "Che giorno è oggi?" translates the English "What day is it today?"; the answer is "Oggi è..." ("Today is..."). Note that all Italian names of the days are masculine except "la domenica" ("Sunday").

2 TAKE A LOOK AT THE EVERYDAY LANGUAGE

1. - Chi è il professore della mia classe?
   - *Ogni* classe ha due insegnanti.
2. - Quante ore di lezione ci sono?
   - Ogni settimana ci sono venti ore di lezione.
3. - Ha il passaporto?
   - *Ecco* il passaporto.
4. - E per il permesso di soggiorno?
   - *Ecco qui* l'ufficio di polizia.
5. - *Ecco fatto*, i documenti sono pronti.
6. - Questo *che cosa è?*
   - È l'indirizzo del mini-appartamento.
7. - Questi *che cosa sono?*
   - Sono i documenti.
8. - Ha il passaporto?
   - Sì, *ce l'ho.*
9. - Ha anche il numero di telefono?
   - No, il telefono *non ce l'ho.*

- Quante ore di lezione ci sono?
- Ogni settimana ci sono venti ore di lezione.

A WHAT'S DIFFERENT

1) In Italian, as in English, the indefinite adjective **ogni** (**each**, or **every**) is always followed by a singular noun. "*Ogni classe* ha due insegnanti" translates "*Each class has two teachers*".

2) The adverb **ecco** translates the English phrases **here is; there is; here are** or **there are.** Thus, "Ecco il passaporto" means "Here is my passport". **Ecco** may also be followed by adverbial particles such as **qui** (**here**) or **là** (**there**). "Ecco qui l'ufficio di polizia" means "Here is the police station". The form **Ecco fatto** corresponds to the English ***That's done*** or **It's done.**

3) The interrogative sentences ***Che cosa è?*** (**What is this?** or ***What is that?***), and

Che cosa sono? (**What are these?** or **What are those?**) are used to refer to things or objects.

4) In Italian, the particle **ce** has many different grammatical functions. Note that in the above sentences there is the simple question "Ha il passaporto?" (Do you have your passport?), and it is followed by the quick response "Sì, ce l'ho" (Yes, I have it). The pronoun **lo** refers to the passport; however, **ce** does not refer to any specific word in the original question. Yet, its function is important because it emphasizes and stresses the idea of ownership. The use of such forms as **ce l'ho** or **non ce l'ho** may be compared with the English use of "got" when it follows and emphasizes the verb *to have: "I have got..." or "I haven't got...".*

Chiedere il permesso	— È permesso? — Posso entrare? — Posso sedermi? — Si può?
Concedere il permesso	— Avanti! — Prego! — Si accomodi / Accomodati!
Ringraziare	— Grazie! — Grazie tante! — Grazie mille!

B   HOW TO SAY IT

1) In Italian, in order *to ask permission to do something (Chiedere il permesso),* you may use the verb **potere** (**can/may**) followed by an infinitive "Posso entrare?"; "Posso sedermi?" ("Can/May> I come in?"; "Can /May> I sit down?") or the impersonal form "Si può?" ("May I?"). There are also other ways to ask whether you may enter a place. You can ask either "Si può?" ("May I?") or the more specific question "E' permesso?" ("May I come in?").

2) There are not only several ways to ask permission, but also several ways by which your request might be granted. In order *to grant permission (Concedere il permesso),* you may use several expressions. "Avanti!" ("Come in!") or "Prego!" ("Please, come in!") are both typical answers to the questions explained above. The expressions "Si accomodi!" (formal) and "Accomodati!" (informal) ("Please, sit down!"; "Have a seat!"; or "Take a seat!") are used to invite someone to sit down.

3) In order *to thank someone (Ringraziare),* you may use many idiomatic expressions: "Grazie!", "Grazie tante!", or "Grazie mille!" ("Thanks!", "Thanks a lot!", or "Thank you so/very> much!").

19

3 GRAMMAR IN CONTRAST

LE TRE CONIUGAZIONI: indicativo presente

Page 48 - Box 1/2/3

1) Infinitives of Italian verbs end in **-are** or **-ere** or **-ire**. According to these endings, Italian verbs are organized into three conjugations. First conjugation verbs end in **are**: *aspettare* (to wait); second conjugation verbs end in **ere**: *prendere* (to take); third conjugation verbs, in **ire**: *partire* (to leave).

   All regular verbs which belong to the same conjugation are conjugated like the model verb of that conjugation. The present tense of a verb is formed by adding the different endings to the stem.

   "Io aspetto una lettera" ("I'm waiting for a letter"); "Tu prendi un caffè" ("You are having a coffee"); "Noi partiamo oggi" ("We are leaving today").

2) Note that such verbs as *mangiare* (to eat) and *cominciare* (to begin) have only one **-i** in the second person singular and in the first person plural.

   "(Io) mangio" ("I eat"); "(tu) mangi" ("you eat"); "(noi) mangiamo" ("we eat").

3) The Italian **Presente Indicativo (Present Indicative)** translates not only the English simple present but also the emphatic "I do..." and the progressive "I'm...". "Io aspetto una lettera" ("I wait for a letter"; "I do wait for a letter"; "I'm waiting for a letter").

4) Unlike English, no auxiliary verb is needed in Italian to form a negative sentence; instead, the negative of a verb is formed just by placing **non** before it.

Page 49 - Box 1

1) Note that some verbs of the third conjugation **-ire** like **finire** (to finish) place **-isc-** between the stem and the ending in the first, second, and third persons singular and in the third person plural. "Io finisco il lavoro" ("I'm finishing my job"). The verb *finire* may also be followed by the preposition **di** + **infinitive** as in the sentence "Finisco di studiare" ("I'm finishing my studying").

1) The definite article **l'** is used before masculine and feminine singular nouns which begin with a vowel: "l'amico" ("the friend"); "l'amica" ("the friend"). The definite article **gli** is used before masculine plural nouns which begin with a vowel: "gli amici" ("the friends"). The definite article **le** is used before feminine plural nouns which begin with a vowel: "le amiche" ("the friends").

2) The indefinite article **un** is used before masculine singular nouns which begin with a vowel: "un uomo" ("a man"); "un libro" ("a book"). The indefinite article **un'** is used before feminine singular nouns which begin with a vowel: "un'amica" ("a friend"). The partitive **degli** is used before masculine plural nouns which begin with a vowel: "degli amici"; and the partitive **delle** is used before feminine plural nouns: "delle amiche" ("some friends").

3) Note that the plural of **amico** is **amici** (friends), and the plural of **amica** is **amiche** (friends).

   The plural of **uomo** (man) is **uomini** (men).

3 TAKE A LOOK AT THE EVERYDAY LANGUAGE

1. - <u>Che cosa *fai*</u>? Lavori?
   - No, frequento l'università. E Lei che cosa *fa*? Insegna ancora?
   - No, non insegno più, sono in pensione.
2. - <u>Che cosa *facciamo*</u> stasera?
   - Andiamo al cinema.
3. . <u>Che cosa *fai*</u> adesso?
   - Non vedi? *Faccio* gli esercizi per domani.
4. - <u>Come *stai*,</u> Mario?
   - Bene, grazie. E Lei?
   - <u>Non c'è male</u>, grazie.

- Che cosa *facciamo* stasera?
- Andiamo al cinema.

A | WHAT'S DIFFERENT

1) The verb **fare** translates both of the English verbs **to make** and **to do**: "*Che cosa fai?* Lavori?" - "No, frequento l'università". ("*What do you do?* Do you work?" - "No, I'm attending university" or "No, I'm going to college").

2) Unlike the English, the present indicative in Italian is used to express an action which is going to happen in a short time; so, the present indicative often translates the English present progressive: "*Che cosa facciamo* stasera?" - "Andiamo al cinema". ("*What are we doing* tonight?" - "We are going to the movies/cinema"). "*Che cosa fai* adesso?" ("*What are you doing* now?").

3) The verb **stare** is used instead of "essere" in the sentence "*Come stai?*" ("*How are you?*"). The Italian sentence "*Non c'è male*, grazie" answers this question and corresponds to the English "*Not bad,* thanks".

Salutare e rispondere al saluto	— Buon giorno, Professore! — Buon pomeriggio, signor Rossi! — Buona sera, signora Rossi! — Ciao, Mario! — Salve, ragazzi!
Prendere commiato	— Ciao! — Arrivederci! — ArrivederLa, Professore! — Ci vediamo domani! — A domani! — A presto!
Sospendere la comunicazione	— Aspetta! — Aspetti un momento, signora! — Un momento! — Un attimo, per favore!

B | HOW TO SAY IT

1) In Italian, in order *to say hello or to greet someone and to respond to a greeting* (*Salutare e rispondere al saluto*), you may use the following expressions: "Buon giorno, Professore!" ("Good morning, professor!"); "Buon pomeriggio, Signor Rossi!" ("Good afternoon, Mr. Rossi!"); "Ciao, Mario!" ("Hello, Mario!"); "Salve, ragazzi!" (Hi, guys!").

2) In order *to say good-bye* (*Prendere commiato*), you may use the following expressions: "Ciao!" ("Bye!") and "Arrivederci!" ("See you soon/again, Sir/Madam!") in formal situations. The forms "Ci vediamo domani!" and "A domani!" correspond to the English form "See you tomorrow!"; and the form "A presto!", to the English "See you soon!" or "See you later".

3) In order *to interrupt a conversation* (*Sospendere la comunicazione*), you can use the informal "Aspetta!" ("Wait!") and the formal "Aspetti!" ("Wait, Sir/Madam!") or "Aspetti un momento, Signora!" ("Wait a moment, Madam!"). The Italian forms "Un momento!", "Un attimo, per favore!" correspond to the English form "Just a moment, please!".

23

4   GRAMMAR IN CONTRAST

Page 72 - Box 1

1) Unlike English, the Italian **Aggettivo Possessivo (Possessive Adjective)** is almost always preceded by the definite article. Both article and adjective agree in number and gender with the noun they modify: "il mio libro" ("my book"); "la mia macchina" ("my car").

2) Note that unlike English, the Italian possessive adjective agrees with the noun it modifies and not with the owner; so **suo** may translate both **his** and **her**: "il suo appartamento" ("his/her apartment").

3) The possessive adjectives have the same endings (-o, -a, -i, -e) as adjectives which end in -o in the masculine singular, with the exception of "Loro" and "loro" which are invariable.

4) Note that the four adjectives **tuo**, **vostro**, **Suo** and **Loro** translate the English **your**: "il tuo / il vostro / il Suo / il Loro libro" ("your book").

   Suo and *Loro* (your) are usually written with a capital letter to distinguish them from *suo* (his/her) and *loro* (their).

Page 72 - Box 2

Page 73 - Box 1

1) As in English, Italian possessive adjectives also omit the article before the names of relatives *when they are singular and unmodified*. Note that only with the possessive form **loro** is the article not omitted.

Page 73 - Box 2

1) **Di chi** corresponds to the English **of whom?/whose?**.

   For the answer, two forms are possible: "Di chi è questa penna?" ("Whose pen is this?") "È la mia" or "È mia" ("It is mine").

Page 74 - Box 1/2/3

1) The verbs **volere** (to want, to wish); **potere** (to be able, can, may) and **dovere** (must, to be obliged, to have to...) are irregular. Note the following examples.

a) "Voglio imparare bene l'italiano" ("I want to learn Italian well").

b) "Posso già capire un giornale italiano" ("I can already understand an Italian news-spaper").

c) "Devo decidere subito" ("I have to decide right now").

Page 75 - Box 1

1) The verb **andare** (to go) is irregular in the present indicative: "*Vado a casa*" ("I'm going home"); "*Vai* a scuola" ("You are going to school").

2) The preposition **a** is used without any article before **casa** (home); **scuola** (school); **lezione** (class); **teatro** (theatre); **letto** (bed), as in the sentence: "Vado a casa" ("I'm going home").

3) The preposition **a** + the definite masculine article **il** becomes **al**, and it is used before masculine nouns, as in the sentence: "Vado *al* cinema" ("I'm going to the cinema"; "I'm going to the movies").

   The preposition **a** + the definite feminine article **la** becomes **alla**, and it is used in front of feminine nouns, as in the sentence: "Vado *alla* stazione" ("I'm going to the station").

4) The preposition **in** is used without any article before the following nouns: **banca** (bank), **biblioteca** (library), **classe** (class), **città** (city, town), **campagna** (country, countryside), **chiesa** (church), **piscina** (pool), **ufficio** (office), **albergo** (hotel), **farmacia** (drugstore), as in the sentence: "Vado *in* biblioteca" ("I'm going to the library").

   Note that the preposition **in** is also used before nouns ending in –**eria** like: **gelateria** (icecream shop), **libreria** (bookshop), etc., as in the sentence: "Vado *in pizzeria*" ("I'm going to the pizzeria").

   The prepositions **a** and **in**, when they are used with the verb *andare* (to go), both translate the English preposition **to**.

Page 76 - Box 1

1) In Italian, the preposition **a** is always used before names of cities, and the preposition **in** before names of countries and provinces.

   "Vado *a* Roma" ("I'm going to Rome"). "Vado *in* Australia" ("I'm going to Australia").

2) The verb *andare* (to go) requires the preposition **a** when it is followed by an infinitive. "Vado **a** studiare" ("I'm going to study").

3) In the idiomatic sentence "Vado *da* Maria" ("I'm going to Mary's"), the preposition **da**

is used to express a location. In this case, it translates the English preposition **to**; the word "casa" ("house") is only implied (Vado a casa di Maria), as in the English sentence: "I'm going to Mary's" (I'm going to Mary's house).

Page 76 - Box 2

1) Both the sentences "Vengo a lezione **con** la macchina" and "Vengo a lezione **in** macchina" have the same meaning and correspond to the English ("I come to class by car"; "I get to class by car").

2) The idiomatic expression "Vengo *a piedi*" corresponds to the English ("I'll walk").

Page 77 - Box 1

1) The sentence **Da dove vieni?** corresponds to the English sentence "Where do you come from?".

   Da dove viene? is the polite form of the same question.

2) The preposition **da** denotes the place of origin. Its spelling does not change when it is followed by the names of cities: "Vengo da Londra" ("I come from London").

   It combines with the definite article with names of countries: "Vengo dal Giappone" ("I come from Japan").

Page 77 - Box 2

1) In the Italian sentences "Quando vai a casa? **Ci** vado subito" ("When you are going home? I'm going there right now"), the use of **Ci** is idiomatic; and it means "there", in the sense of "in that place".

Page 77 - Box 3

1) The idiomatic expression **Quanto fa?** corresponds to the English "How much is...?". In Italian the verb used for mathematical operations is the verb **fare**.

Page 78-79

1) Both the sentences **Che ora è?** and **Che ore sono?** are used to ask the time, and they correspond to the English sentence "What time is it?".

2) Cardinal numbers are used to express time, and they are preceded by the definite feminine article **le**, as in the sentence: "Sono le tredici" ("It is one o'clock p.m.").

3) Except for **l'una** (one o'clock a.m.), **mezzogiorno** (noon), **mezzanotte** (midnight), the verb is always plural: "*Sono* le due" ("It is two o'clock").

4) **E** is used for any amount of time past the hour: "È l'una **e** un quarto" ("It is quarter past one"). **Meno** is used for time before the hour: "Sono le due **meno** un quarto" ("It is quarter to two"; "It is quarter of two").

5) For the sentence "Sono le ore tredici e quarantacinque minuti" ("It's a quarter to/of two"), three other forms are possible:

   a) È l'una e tre quarti.

   b) Sono le due meno un quarto.

   c) Manca un quarto alle due.

4 TAKE A LOOK AT THE EVERYDAY LANGUAGE

1. - Se _per te_ va bene, vengo domani.
   - D'accordo.
2. - Ci vediamo _verso_ le nove?
   - No, facciamo verso le otto e mezzo.
3. - Chiara, _vorrei_ parlare con te di alcune cose!
4. - Perché non chiedi a tuo nonno?
   - Sì, _è una buona idea_!

- Ci vediamo _verso_ le nove?
- No, facciamo _verso_ le otto e mezzo.

A   WHAT'S DIFFERENT

1) The Italian form **D'accordo** is used when you agree with what someone says, and it corresponds to both of the English forms **O.K.** and **all right**. "Se _per te_ va bene, vengo domani". - "_D'accordo_" ("I'll come tomorrow if it's O.K. _with you_". - "_O.K._"). In this same sentence, note that the Italian preposition **per** is actually translated by the English preposition **with**.

2) In Italian, the word **verso** has many different meanings. In the sentence "Ci vediamo _verso_ le nove?", **verso** changes the sentence from meaning "See you at nine o'clock" to a more general sense of "See you at _around_ nine o'clock".

3) The Italian conditional is often used, as is the English conditional, to ask someone something in a polite way; and, in this case, it is followed by an infinitive. "Chiara, _vorrei_ parlare con te di alcune cose!" ("Chiara, _I would like_ to talk with you about a few things").

4) The Italian sentence "_È una buona idea_!" translates in English "_It's a good idea_!". Unlike English, however, the Italian sentence doesn't require the subject pronoun 'it'.

28

Interpellare per telefono	— Pronto, sono Silvia, c'è Chiara? — Pronto, con chi parlo, scusi? — Pronto, parlo con Chiara?		
Rispondere per telefono	— Pronto, sì, sono io. — Pronto, qui parla casa Rossetti.		
Accordo/disaccordo	– Ci vediamo alle 9, siamo d'accordo?		– D'accordo, alle 9.
	– Ci vediamo alle 9,		– Mi dispiace, ma alle 9 non posso.
	– Non possiamo dimenticare Giovanni e Mirco.		– Si, è vero. – Proprio così. – Certo. – Certamente. – Hai ragione. – Sono pienamente d'accordo.
	– Vuoi invitarli?		– Non sono d'accordo. – Fai male. – Sono contraria.

B   HOW TO SAY IT

1) In Italian, in order *to call someone up (Interpellare per telefono),* you must use the expression **Pronto!** which corresponds to the English **Hello!**. So, the Italian sentence "Pronto, sono Silvia, c'è Chiara?" may be translated "Hello, this is Silvia; is Chiara there?".

2) In order *to answer the phone* (*Rispondere al telefono),* you must use the expression "Pronto!" ("Hello!"). The Italian sentence "Pronto, sì, sono io" is translated in English by "Hello, yes it's me". The sentence "Pronto, qui parla casa Rossetti" must be translated "Hello, this is the Rossetti residence".

3) In Italian, the commonest way *to show agreement (Accordo)* is to say "D'accordo" which corresponds to the English "Yes, O.K.". The sentences "Ci vediamo alle nove. Siamo d'accordo?" may be translated "See you at nine o'clock, O.K.?". A negative answer to the above question could be "Mi díspiace, ma alle nove non

posso" which can be translated "I'm sorry, but I can't make it at nine o'clock".

4) In Italian, in order *to say that you are in close agreement with someone's opinion,* you could say any of the following: "Sì, è vero", "Proprio così", "Certo", "Certamente", "Hai ragione", "Sono pienamente d'accordo". These forms correspond to the English expressions "Yes, it's true", "Right", "Sure", "Surely", "You're right", "I'm in complete agreement".

5) On the contrary, in order *to show that you are in disagreement with someone's opinion* (*Disaccordo*), you may say any of the following: "Non sono d'accordo", "Fai male", "Sono contrario/a". These correspond to the English expressions "I don't agree", "You're wrong", "I disagree".

5   GRAMMAR IN CONTRAST

| Page 100 - Box 1/2 |

| Page 101 - Box 1 |

1) The Italian **Passato Prossimo (Present Perfect)** indicates an action or state completed in the recent past. "Ieri sono andato ad Assisi" ("Yesterday I went to Assisi").

   It translates the English present perfect.

2) The Italian Passato Prossimo is formed by an auxiliary verb, either **avere** (to have) or **essere** (to be), plus the past participle of the main verb. With most verbs the auxiliary verb is the present tense of **avere**; with some verbs the auxiliary verb is the present tense of **essere**. The general rule is that verbs which may have a direct object (transitive verbs) use the auxiliary **avere** to form the present perfect tense.

   "Ieri ho mangiato al ristorante" ("Yesterday I ate at the restaurant").

   Verbs which do not have a direct object (most, not all, intransitive verbs) use the auxiliary **essere** to form the present perfect tense: "Ieri sono arrivato tardi" ("Yesterday I arrived late").

3) **Il participio passato** .**(The past participle)** is formed by dropping the infinitive endings and adding **–ato** to verbs of the first conjugation: "comprare" ("to buy") →**comprato** ("bought"); **–uto** to most verbs of the second conjugation: "vedere" ("to see") →**veduto** ("seen"); **–ito** to most verbs of the third conjugation: "preferire" ("to prefer") →**preferito** ("preferred").

4) Many past participles are irregular, especially in the second conjugation: decidere →deciso (decided), chiudere →chiuso (closed), fare →fatto (made), leggere →letto (read), prendere →preso (taken), etc.

5) Note that for verbs conjugated with **avere**, the past participle is invariable: "Lui ha mangiato/Lei ha mangiato" ("He/She ate or He/She has eaten"). On the contrary, for verbs conjugated with **essere**, the past participle always agrees in number and gender with the subject: "**Lui** è andat**o** / **Lei** è andat**a**" ("He/She has gone").

| Page 101 - Box 2 |

1) **Ogni** (every/each) and **qualche** (some) are invariable adjectives. The noun which **each** modifies is always singular: "ogni mattina" ("every morning"); "ogni giorno" ("every day"); "qualche volta" ("sometimes"); "Ogni mattina vado a lezione" ("Every morning I go to class").

Page 102 - Box 1

1) The singular definite article **lo** and the indefinite article **uno** are used before masculine nouns which begin with "z" or "s" plus another consonant: "lo *sbaglio*" ("the mistake"), "lo *scolaro*" ("the pupil"). **Gli** is the plural definite article used before these nouns: "gli sbagli" ("the mistakes"). **Degli** is the partitive used before these nouns as well.

Page 102 - Box 2/3/4

Page 103 - Box 1/2/3

1) The following groups of nouns do not change in the plural:

   a) nouns ending in an **accented vowel**: la città - le città (the city/the cities)

   b) nouns ending in **-i**: la tesi - le tesi (the thesis/the theses)

   c) nouns ending in a **consonant** (generally foreign words): Il bar/i bar (the bar/the bars)

   d) **abbreviated nouns**: la foto - le foto (the photo-the photos)

   e) feminine nouns ending in **–ie**: la specie - le specie (the species). Exceptions: la superficie - le superfici; la moglie - le mogli (the surface-the surfaces; the wife-the wives)

   f) **monosyllabic nouns**: il re - i re (The king-the kings)

Page 103 - Box 4

1) The most common Italian prepositions: **di** (of), **a** (to, at), **da** (from, by), **in** (in), **con** (with, by), **su** (on), when used together with the definite article, form contractions as seen above. Generally, they combine with the article and become a single word, except for **(con)**, where both forms are possible: **col** or **con il**; but the separate form **con il** is preferred.

5 TAKE A LOOK AT THE EVERYDAY LANGUAGE

1. - Prendi *qualcosa* con me?
   - <u>No</u>, grazie, <u>non prendo</u> *nien-te*.
2. - C'è *qualcosa* in frigorifero?
   - C'è *solo* <u>un po'</u> di formaggio.
3. - Hai *qualcosa* da dire?
   - <u>No, non ho</u> *niente* da dire.
4. - Vieni *solo* tu a ballare?
   - No, <u>ci</u> viene anche mia sorel-la.
5. - Hai comprato *soltanto* <u>delle paste?</u>
   - Sì, *solo* <u>delle paste.</u>
6. - Dove siete arrivate?
   - Siamo salite *fino alla* <u>Rocca.</u>
7. - *Fino a* <u>che ora</u> hai dormito?
   - Ho dormito *fino alle* <u>cinque.</u>
8. - Hai fatto il viaggio con lei?
   - Sì, *fino a* <u>Firenze.</u>
9. - Che cosa hai comprato?
   - Ho comprato *qualche* souvenir
10. - Chi hai invitato?
    - Ho invitato *qualche amico*.
11. - La tua giornata è stata interessante; la mia, *al contrario*, noiosa.
12. - Luisa è uscita, io *invece* no.
13. - *Appena* (siamo) arrivate, abbiamo visitato la Basilica di San Francesco.
14. - Vengo <u>da te</u> *appena* posso.
15. - Sono uscito *appena* (ho) pranzato.

- Prendi *qualcosa* con me?
- No, grazie, non prendo *niente*.

A | WHAT'S DIFFERENT

1) In Italian, the indefinite pronoun **qualcosa** translates the English indefinite pronoun **something**. Note that in the answer to the question "Prendi *qualcosa* con me?" ("Are you having *anything* with me?") two negative words are needed to make the answer negative. "No, grazie, non prendo niente" translates "No, thank you, I'm not

having anything". So, unlike English, in Italian two negative forms are possible in the same sentence.

2) The form **un po'** corresponds to the English forms **a little** or **a little bit**. The sentences "C'è qualcosa in frigorifero" - C'è solo *un po'* di formaggio" can be translated "Is there anything in the refrigerator? - There's only *a little bit* of cheese".

3) Often the Italian preposition **da** has the same role as the preposition **to** in English, especially when it follows the indefinite pronoun *niente* ("*nothing*") and it precedes an infinitive. "*Non ho niente da dire*" can be translated either by "*I have nothing to say*" or by "*I don't have anything to say* ".

4) The adjectives **solo** and **soltanto** have the same meaning and translate the English **only** or **just**. The question "Vieni *solo* tu a ballare?" is phrased in a manner which is used very frequently in Italian; however, if it were translated exactly, it would sound very awkward in English. So, a corresponding sentence could be "Who is going dancing, *just* you?". It is really important to note the differing use of the verb "venire" in Italian and the corresponding use of the verb "to go" in English. To continue, in the answer to the abovementioned question, "No, *ci* viene anche mia sorella" ("No, my sister is going, too"), the particle **ci** has the same sense as the English **there** (meaning, **in that place**), even if it does not need to be expressed in English.

5) In the sentence "Hai comprato solo *delle paste*?" ("Did you *only buy pastries*?" or "Did you *buy just pastries*?"), the Italian partitive **delle** has the same meaning as **some** in English. Note that the word "some" is not necessarily expressed in English.

6) In Italian, the compound preposition **fino a** has two different meanings:

   a) It can express distance, as in the sentence "Siamo salite *fino alla* Rocca" which translates "We went *up to* the Rocca".

   b) The English compound preposition **up to** has only a limited meaning, so it cannot be used to translate **fino a** in a sentence such as "Hai fatto il viaggio con lei?" - Sì, *fino a* Firenze". Rather, in this sentence, **fino a** must be translated **as far as**. For example, "Did you travel with her? - Yes, *as far as* Florence".

   c) It can also express time, as in the sentence "Ho dormito *fino alle cinque*" which translates "I slept *until/till* five o'clock".

7) Unlike the English, the Italian indefinite adjective **qualche (some)** is always followed by a singular noun. "Ho comprato *qualche* souvenir" ("I bought *some* souvenirs").

8) The Italian phrase **al contrario** translates the English phrase **on the contrary**. "La tua giornata è stata interessante; la mia, *al contrario*, è stata noiosa" ("Your day has been interesting; mine, *on the contrary*, has been boring").

9) The Italian **invece** translates the English **instead** or **on the other hand**. For example, "Luisa è uscita, io invece no" ("Luisa left; I, on the other hand, did not").

10) The Italian **appena** translates the English **as soon as** or **just as soon as**. For example, "*Appena* (siamo) arrivate, abbiamo visitato la Basilica di San Francesco" ("*As soon as* we arrived, we visited the Basilica of Saint Francis"). Further, the sentence "Vengo *da te* appena posso" can be translated "I am coming/I'll come *to your* house as soon as I can". In this sentence the Italian preposition **da** has a special idiomatic use which corresponds to the English words **to (someone's) house**.

Saluti, convenevoli	— Ciao, Pat, come stai? — Ciao, Pat, come va?	— Non c'è male e tu? — Bene, grazie e tu? — Benino e tu? — Male.
Ammirazione	— La città?	— Bellissima!
	— Il panorama?	— Che bello! — Stupendo!
	— I dipinti?	— Fantastici! — Magnifici! — Che belli!

B | HOW TO SAY IT

1) In Italian, the most common informal forms used to exchange *greetings (Saluti e convenevoli)* are "Ciao, come stai?" or "Ciao, come va?". These forms correspond to the English "Hi! How are you?" or "Hi! How's it going?". An answer to these greetings could be "Non c'è male, e tu?"; "Bene, grazie, e tu?"; "Benino, e tu?"; "Male" which correspond to the English "Not bad, and you?"; "Fine, thanks, and you?"; "Pretty good, and you?"; "Not good".

2) In order *to express admiration (Ammirazione)*, you may use any of the following expressions: "Bellissima!" ("Very/really beautiful!"); "Che bello!" ("How beautiful!"); "Stupendo!" ("Wonderful!"); "Fantastici!" ("Fantastic!"); "Magnifici!" ("Magnificent!"); and "Che belli!" ("How beautiful!").

6   GRAMMAR IN CONTRAST

Page 123 - Box 1

1) The Italian **Futuro Semplice (Future Tense)** has endings which are identical for all conjugations. The future tense of regular verbs is formed by dropping the final "e" of the infinitive and adding the endings: **ò - ai - à - emo - ete - anno**. In the first conjugation the vowel **a** of **-are** changes to **e** (cantare →canterò) before the endings of the future tense are added: "Domani telefonerò" ("Tomorrow I'll phone/call up").

2) Note that the preposition **fra** is also used in expressions of *time*: "fra poco" ("in a short while"), "fra pochi minuti" ("in a few minutes").

Page 123 - Box 2

1) In Italian, a number of common verbs are irregular in the future stem. Some verbs are irregular because the conjugation vowel is dropped before the future endings are added: avere - **avrò**, andare - **andrò**, sapere - **saprò**. In other verbs the conjugation vowel is dropped and the remaining "r" is doubled: tenere - **terrò**, rimanere - **rimarrò**, venire - **verrò**. "Verremo qui l'anno prossimo" ("We'll come here next year").

Page 124 - Box 1

1) The verbs ending in **–ciare** and **–giare** change **ia** to **e** before the endings of the future tense are added: cominciare - comincerò, mangiare - mangerò. The verbs ending in **-care** and **-gare** change **a** to **he** before the endings of the future tense are added: dimenticare - dimenti**he**rò, pagare - pag**he**rò. This last form is needed in order to maintain the hard sound of the consonants "c" and "g".

2) The verb *cominciare* requires the preposition **a** when it is followed by an infinitive: **cominciare a** (to begin to), as in the sentence: "Comincerò a girare il mondo" ("I'll begin to travel").

Page 124 - Box 2

1) The Italian **Futuro anteriore (Future Perfect)** is formed by the future tense of the auxiliary verb and the past participle of the main verb. In Italian, the future perfect is used to express an action that will have taken place before another action in the future: "Quando *avrò finito* gli esami, *farò* un bel viaggio" ("When I have finished the

examinations, I shall take a nice trip"). In English the present perfect is used instead of the future perfect tense in this type of sentence.

Page 124 - Box 3

In general, in Italian the future tense is used to express:

A) *A future action:* "Tomorrow I shall phone the agency to book a ticket".

B) *An order:* "Now you'll do everything that is necessary, and so you will not go out".

C) *Uncertainty* or *doubt:* "What time is it? I don't have my watch, but it must be 12." In this case the future is used to express what is probable in the present. This use has no equivalent in English; rather, the adverb "probably" is used to express the same doubt.

Page 125 - Box 1/2/3/4/5

1) Feminine nouns and adjectives ending in the singular in **–ca** and **–ga** form their plural in **–che** and **–ghe**.

2) Masculine nouns and adjectives ending in the singular in **–co** and **–go** form their plural in **–chi** and **–ghi**; if **–co** and **–go** are preceded by a vowel, they generally form the plural in **-ci** and **–gi**: amico - amici (friend-friends); however, there are some exceptions: antico - antichi, (ancient).

3) Nouns and adjectives ending in **–cia** and **–gia** form their plural in **–cie** or **–gie** if the **–cia** and **–gia** are preceded by a vowel: ciliegia - ciliegie (cherry/cherries); valigia - valigie (suitcase-suitcases).

   They omit the **-i** in the plural if the **–cia** and **–gia** are preceded by a consonant: pronuncia - pronunce (pronunciation-pronunciations); pioggia - piogge (rain-rains).

4) Nouns and adjectives ending in **–cia** and **–gia** always form their plural in **–ie** when the **i** in **–cia** and **–gia** is stressed: farmacia - farmacie (drugstore-drugstores); bugia - bugie (lie-lies).

Page 126 - Box 1

1) The expressions "Siamo nel mese di agosto" or "Siamo in agosto" translate the English sentences "We are in the month of August" or "It's August".

6 TAKE A LOOK AT THE EVERYDAY LANGUAGE

1. - Anna e Doris sono due ragazze: *l'una* è italiana, *l'altra* è tedesca.
2. - Quale pasta vuoi? Questa alla crema o questa al cioccolato?
   - *L'una e l'altra.*
3. - Faremo due gruppi di studenti: *gli uni* andranno a visitare il museo, *gli altri* la cattedrale, ma tutti dovranno essere qui a mezzogiorno.
4. - Ho <u>preso *in affitto*</u> una camera al centro.
   - Ah sì? Quanto *paghi d'affitto*?
5. - Io ho <u>dato *in affitto*</u> il mio appartamento.
6. - Le due ragazze *sono diventate* amiche.
7. - Non ti piace questo vino?
   - No, è cattivo, *è diventato aceto.*
8. - Pierino, che cosa farai quando sarai grande?
   - *Voglio diventare* un ingegnere.
9. - *Questa volta* vengo con te, ma *la prossima volta* andrò al cinema con mio fratello.
10. - A quest'ora torni a casa? *E' la prima e l'ultima volta che* ti faccio uscire.

A | WHAT'S DIFFERENT

1) The Italian forms **l'uno.../l'altro...** and **l'una.../l'altra...** correspond to the English **one... the other**. In Italian, as in English, the first pronoun must be followed by its own verb; the second pronoun, however, may be followed by its own verb, or the sense of its verb may be implied. Likewise, in the plural, **gli uni.../gli altri...** and **le une.../le altre...** correspond to the English **some... others**. The use of verbs with these plural forms is the same as it is for the singular forms. "Anna e Doris sono due ragazze: *l'una* è italiana, *l'altra* è tedesca". ("Anna and Doris are two girls: *one* is Italian, *the other* is German"). An example of the plural use is as follows: "Faremo due gruppi di studenti: *gli uni* andranno a visitare il museo, *gli altri* la cattedrale, ma tutti dovranno essere qui a mezzogiorno" ("We shall make two groups of students: *some* will go to visit the museum, *others* the cathedral, but everyone will have to be here at noon").

2) All the Italian forms **l'uno e l'altro, l'una e l'altra; gli uni e gli altri**, and **le une e le altre** correspond to the English **both** or **both of them**. "Quale pasta vuoi? Questa alla crema o questa al cioccolato? - *L'una e l'altra*". ("Which pastry do you want? This cream one or this chocolate one? - *Both* [of them]").

3) In Italian, the word **affitto** has many different uses:

   a) *Prendere in affitto*, which may be translated by the English "*to rent* ". "*Ho preso in affitto* una camera al centro" ("*I rented* a room in the center of town").

   b) *Pagare una certa somma d'affitto*, which may be translated by *"to pay a certain amount for rent"*. "Quanto paghi *d'affitto*? ("How much do you pay *for rent*?").

   c) *Dare in affitto*, which may be translated by *to rent*. "*Io ho dato in affitto* il mio appartamento" ("*I have rented* my apartment").

4) The Italian verb **diventare** also has many different uses:

   a) It is used, as in English, to mean **to become**. "Le due ragazze *sono diventate* amiche" ("The two girls *became/have become* friends"). Also, "Pierino, che cosa farai da grande? - Voglio *diventare* ingegnere" ("Pierino, what do you want *to be* (or, *become*) when you grow up? - I want *to be/become* an engineer").

   b) It is also used with the meaning of **to turn into**. "Non ti piace questo vino? - No, è cattivo, è *diventato* aceto" ("Don't you like this wine? - No, it's bad, *it has turned into* vinegar").

5) The Italian form **questa volta** corresponds to the English form **this time**, while the form **la prossima volta** corresponds to the English **next time.** "*Questa volta* vengo con te, ma *la prossima volta* andrò al cinema con mio fratello" ("*This time* I'm coming with you, but *the next time* I'll go to the movies with my brother"). The fragment **"E' la prima e l'ultima volta che..."** may be translated **"This is the first and last time that...".** "*E' la prima e l'ultima volta che* ti faccio uscire" ("*This is the first and last time that* I'm letting you go out").

Interpellare per lettera	— Cara Anna, ... — Gentile signora, ... — Gentile signore, ... — Spettabile ditta, ...
Prendere congedo per lettera	— Cari saluti. — Con i migliori saluti. — Cordiali saluti. — Un abbraccio. — Baci.
Trasmettere i saluti	— Saluta Roberto. — Tanti saluti a Roberto.
Intenzione, voglia, decisione di fare	— Ho voglia di tornare in Italia. — La prossima estate tornerò in Italia. — Ho deciso di tornare in Italia. — Ho intenzione di tornare in Italia.
Rinuncia (negazione della decisione)	— Penso che non tornerò in Italia. — Ho deciso di non tornare. — Non ho voglia di tornare. — Non mi va.

B | HOW TO SAY IT

1) There are some special functions which we have to use in order to write a correct letter. In Italian, in order *to write an appropriate salutation in a letter* (*Interpellare per lettera*), you must change the format in accordance with the different kinds of letters. So, the form "Cara Anna..." ("Dear Anne...") has a very informal meaning, as in English and may be used when writing to friends or relatives. The forms "Gentile signora" and "Gentile signore" ("Dear Madam" and "Dear Sir") are considered polite and only somewhat formal. The form "Spettabile ditta" ("Dear Sirs" or "Gentlemen") is used only in a formal business letter.

2) In order *to write an appropriate closing to a letter* (*Prendere congedo per lettera*), you also have to change the format. So, the forms "Cari saluti" ("Fond regards"), "Un abbraccio" ("A hug"), and "Baci" ("Kisses") are very informal and are used with friends and relatives. The form "Con i migliori saluti" ("With best regards") is a little more formal, while the form "Cordiali saluti" ("Sincerely yours") is somewhat formal.

3) In order *to ask someone to give your regards to some other person* (*Trasmettere i saluti*), you may use sentences such as "Saluta Roberto" ("Say hello to Robert for me") and "Tanti saluti a Roberto" ("Give my regards to Robert"). Please note that the translation offered for each of the above can be used interchangeably, for there is really not much distinction at all between them.

4) In order *to show your intention, desire, or decision to do something* (*Intenzione, voglia, o decisione di fare*), you may say the following: "Ho voglia di tornare in Italia" ("I want to return to Italy"); "La prossima volta tornerò in Italia" ("I've decided to return to Italy"); "Ho intenzione di tornare in Italia" ("I intend to return to Italy").

5) In order *to reconsider or alter a decision or to change your mind about something* (*Rinuncia o negazione della decisione*), you may use sentences such as: "Penso che non tornerò in Italia" ("I think that I won't return to Italy"); "Ho deciso di non tornare" ("I've decided not to return"); "Non ho voglia di tornare" ("I don't want to return"); "Non mi va" ("I don't want to").

7   GRAMMAR IN CONTRAST

Unit 7

Page 148 - Box 1

1) The Italian **Pronomi Riflessivi (Reflexive Pronouns)** are **mi** (myself), **ti** (yourself), **si** (himself, herself, yourself); **ci** (ourselves), **vi** (yourselves), **si** (themselves, yourselves).

2) Unlike English reflexive pronouns, Italian reflexive pronouns usually precede the verb, as in the sentence "*Mi* sveglio tardi la mattina" ("I wake up late in the morning").

3) Reflexive verbs are frequent in Italian but rare in English, so the Italian reflexive verbs are not always translated literally in English, as in the sentence: "Ti svegli tardi la mattina" ("You wake up late in the morning").

Page 148 - Box 2

1) Reflexive pronouns can also follow an infinitive. In this case, they are attached to the infinitive which first drops the final "e". "Preferisco svegliar**mi** presto la mattina") ("I prefer to wake up early in the morning").

2) When the verbs **dovere, potere, volere,** and **sapere** are followed by reflexive verbs, the reflexive pronoun may be attached to the infinitive of the reflexive verb. Both "Devo svegliar*mi* alle 7 domani" and "**Mi** devo svegliare alle 7 domani" translate ("Tomorrow I must wake up at seven o'clock").

3) Many verbs that are reflexive in form are not reflexive in meaning. They take the same pronouns as the reflexive verbs: "Vogliamo fermarci qualche giorno in questa città" ("We want to stop for a few days in this city").

Page 149 - Box 1/2

1) In the passato prossimo (present perfect) reflexive verbs always take the auxiliary **essere**, and the past participle always agrees in gender and in number with the subject. "Ci siamo alzati/e molto presto" ("We got up very early").

2) When the verbs **dovere, potere,** and **volere** are followed by reflexive verbs, two forms are possible in the compound tenses:

a) "**Mi** sono dovuto alzare" ("I had to wake up").

b) "Ho dovuto alzar**mi** " ("I had to wake up").

In the first form (a), the past participle always agrees with the subject.

Page 150 - Box 1/2

1) Unlike English, negative sentences in Italian may contain two negative words: **non...mai** (never), **non...nessuno** (nobody, not...anybody), **non...niente** (nothing), **non...nulla** (nothing). Negative sentences usually have two parts. **Non** is placed before the verb, and the **negative expression** after the verb: "**Non** vado **mai** al concerto" ("I never go to concerts").

2) **Nessuno** is the indefinite pronoun which refers to persons; **niente** and **nulla** are the indefinite pronouns which refer to things.

Page 150 - Box 3

1) In Italian, the *present tense* with the preposition **da** (since, for) is used to indicate an action which began in the past and is continuing in the present: "*Studio* l'Italiano *da* una settimana" ("I have been studying Italian for one week"); "Sono qui dal 1983" ("I have been here since 1983").

In this type of sentence, the English present perfect and present perfect progressive are used.

Page 151 - Box 1/2/3

1) Nouns and adjectives ending in **–io** form their plural in **–i** when the **-i** of **-io** is unstressed: un bravo figlio (a good son); dei bravi figli (good sons).

2) A number of masculine nouns ending in **–io** in the singular become **feminine** in the plural and have an irregular plural ending in **–a**: il paio - le paia (the pair - the pairs).

3) Nouns and adjectives ending in **–io** form their plural in **–ii** when the **-i** of **-io** is stressed: "Mio zio abita in America" ("My uncle lives in America"); "I miei zii abitano in America" ("My uncles live in America").

7 TAKE A LOOK AT THE EVERYDAY LANGUAGE

1. - Telefona sempre quando _mangi_ ?
   - Sì, telefona sempre _durante il pranzo_.
2. - Ti ricordi quante chiacchierate abbiamo fatto _durante le ore_ libere dal servizio?
3. - Hai una sigaretta?
   - No, _purtroppo_ le ho finite.
4. - Hai un foglio?
   - No, _mi dispiace_ li ho finiti.
5. - Ti trovi bene _nella tua ditta_?
   - Sì, _mi ci_ trovo bene.
6. - Come _ti_ trovi _a Milano_?
   - _Mi ci_ trovo bene.
7. - Da quanto tempo _sei_ qui?
   - _Sono qui da due giorni._
8. - Da _quanto tempo_ non _ci vediamo_?
   - Non _ci vediamo da tre anni._

- Ti ricordi quante chiacchierate abbiamo fatto _durante le ore_ libere dal servizio?

A | WHAT'S DIFFERENT

1) The Italian verb **mangiare** translates the English verb **to eat**. "Telefona sempre quando _mangi_?" ("Does he/she always call when you _are eating_ ?").

2) The Italian preposition **durante** translates the English preposition **during**. "Sì, telefona sempre _durante_ il pranzo" ("Yes, he/she always calls _during_ dinner). Unlike English, in the Italian sentence the articles are generally retained after "durante".

3) The Italian noun **chiacchierata** may correspond to the English **chat**. Generally, it is preceded by the verb "fare" which in this expression may be translated by the verb _to have_ in English. Thus, _fare una chiacchierata_ may be translated _to have a chat_ or, more loosely, _to talk about this and that_. "Ti ricordi quante _chiacchierate_ abbiamo fatto durante le ore libere dal servizio?" ("Do you remember how many _chats_ we had during our free time in the service?").

4) The Italian adverb **purtroppo** may correspond to the English **unfortunately**. "Hai

una sigaretta? - No, *purtroppo* le ho finite" ("Do you have a cigarette? - No, *unfortunately*, I've finished them" or "Unfortunately, I'm all out"). In this sentence, the direct object pronoun **le** (*them*), which refers to "sigarette" ("cigarettes"), and the past participle **finite** (finished) must always agree.

5) The Italian sentence **mi dispiace** corresponds to the English sentence **I'm sorry**. "Hai un foglio? - No, *mi dispiace* li ho finiti" ("Do you have a sheet of paper? - No, *I'm sorry*, I've used all of it"). Please note that you should not confuse "mi dispiace" ("I'm sorry") with "non mi piace" ("I don't like it"). For, the verb **dispiacere** is *NOT* the opposite of the verb **piacere**.

6) The Italian reflexive verb **trovarsi** corresponds to various English verbs. In the sentences "*Ti trovi bene* nella tua ditta? - Sì, mi ci trovo bene", it may be translated "*Are you doing well* in your company? - Yes, I'm doing well there". In this case, the particle *ci* means "there" (in that place) and stands for "ditta".

7) To express an action which started some time ago and is still continuing, Italians use the expression **Da quanto tempo...** plus a verb in the present indicative. Please note that this construction is totally different from the English which uses the present perfect indicative. So, a sentence such as "*Da quanto tempo sei qui?*" must be translated "*How long have you been here?*".

Ricordare	– Ti ricordi?	⇨	– Mi ricordo di tutto. – Adesso è tutto chiaro. – Non mi sono dimenticato niente.
Dimenticare	Ti ricordi?	⇨	– Non mi ricordo niente. – Non mi ricordo di niente – Buio completo.
Sorpresa	– Che sorpresa! – Ma che bella sorpresa! – Non credo ai miei occhi! – (Mi) sembra impossibile!		

B HOW TO SAY IT

1) In Italian, in order *to express the idea of remembering* (*Ricordare*), many expressions may be used. Note that the question "Ti ricordi?" has several possible responses: "- Mi ricordo tutto"; "- Adesso è tutto chiaro"; "- Non mi sono dimenticato niente". These correspond to the English "Do you remember? - I remember everything; - Now it's all clear; and I have never forgotten anything".

2) On the contrary, in order *to express the idea of forgetting* (*Dimenticare*), there are different expressions to use as well. Again, the question "Ti ricordi?" has several possible responses: "- Non mi ricordo niente" and "- Non mi ricordo di niente" (which are identical in meaning); and "Buio completo". These correspond to the English "Do you remember? - I don't remember anything; and I have absolutely no recollection". This last sentence only corresponds to the Italian "Buio completo". It is important to note that although "Buio completo" literally means "complete darkness", it does not at all have the same meaning as the English idiom which means that an individual has no idea that something had been happening.

3) In Italian, an expression of *surprise* (*Sorpresa*) may be seen in the following: "- Che sorpresa!"; "- Ma che bella sorpresa!"; "- Non credo ai miei occhi!"; and "- (Mi) sembra impossibile!". These can be translated by "What a surprise!"; "My, what a wonderful surprise!"; "I don't believe my eyes!"; and "It seems impossible (to me)!".

8 GRAMMAR IN CONTRAST

Page 171 - Box 1

1) The Italian **Pronomi diretti deboli o atoni (Direct Object Pronouns)** are closely related to the verb and may never stand alone.

    "Carlo **la** conosce bene" ("Charles knows her well").

    The direct object pronouns are **mi** (me), **ti** (you), **La** (you), **lo** (him, it), **la** (her, it); **ci** (us), **vi** (you), **li** (them), **le** (them).

2) Unlike English, the direct object pronouns always precede the verb in Italian: "Carlo **mi** capisce alla perfezione" ("Charles understands me perfectly").

3) The masculine singular direct object pronoun **lo** also means "ciò" (that, this, it) or "questa cosa" (this thing): "E' andato via il professore? - Non lo so" ("Did the professor go away? - I don't know").

Page 171 - Box 2

1) Just as the third person is used for the polite form of the subject pronoun **Lei** (you), so the third person **La** (you) is used as the polite form of the direct object pronoun. This form is often capitalized to distinguish it from **la** (her).

    "Cari studenti, mi capite? - Sì, **La** capiamo, professore" ("Dear students, do you understand me? - Yes, we understand you, Sir"). On the contrary, **ti** (you) is used for the informal form of the direct object pronouns: "Cari studenti, mi capite? - Sì, **ti** capiamo") ("Dear students, do you understand me? - Yes, we understand you").

Page 172 - Box 1

1) In Italian, in addition to the forms already studied, the direct object pronouns have other forms called **Pronomi Diretti Forti o Tonici**. These pronouns which are termed disjunctive in English are used when **they** are the emphasis of the sentence rather than the verb. The disjunctive pronouns must be used:

    a) Whenever a pronoun is the object of a preposition: "Studio **con lui**" ("I study with him").

    b) In a statement which places special emphasis on the direct object: "Chi cerca quel signore? - Cerca **me**" ("Whom is that man looking for? - He is looking for me").

3) I pronomi diretti forti (disjunctive pronouns) generally follow the verb: "Quel signore aspetta me" ("That man is waiting for me"). These pronouns are **me** (me), **te** (you), **lui** (him, it), **lei** (her, it), **Lei** (you); **noi** (us), **voi** (you), **loro** (them).

Page 172 - Box 2/3

1) When there is an infinitive preceded by a conjugated verb, two forms are possible:

a) Direct object pronouns follow the infinitive and are attached to it to form one word. "Posso aiutar*lo*" ("I can help him").

b) Direct object pronouns precede the conjugated verb which is followed by the infinitive. "**Lo** posso aiutare" ("I can help him").

Page 173 - Box 1/2

1) In Italian **ne** is the partitive pronoun. It may be translated in English by "some", "any", "some of it", "any of them", etc. In English these words can often be omitted, but in Italian **ne** may never be omitted.

2) Note that **ne** is often introduced by the interrogative adjective "quanto", "quanta"; "quanti", "quante" ("how much; how many").

3) As with the direct object pronouns, **ne** usually precedes the verb. "Quante sigarette fumi? - **Ne** fumo molte" ("How many cigarettes do you smoke? - I smoke a lot [of them]").

4) In the negative answer "Non **ne** fumo nessuna" ("I don't smoke any [of them]"), the partitive pronoun **ne** precedes the verb. The negative indefinite pronoun "nessuno,nessuna" ("nobody,none") follows the verb and agrees with its object. The negative adverb "non" ("not") is placed before the direct object pronoun.

Page 173 - Box 3

1) The adverb **ci** (here, to this place, there, to that place), already mentioned, can be preceded by *mi, ti* and *vi*. "Mi accompagni al Luna Park? - Sì, ti ci accompagno" ("Will you take me to Luna Park? - Yes, I'll take you there").

Page 174 - Box 1

1) The adverb **ci** may also be followed by **lo, la, La, li, le** and by the partitive pronoun **ne**. In this case, the adverb **ci** changes to **ce**. "Quando accompagni tuo figlio al cinema? - **Ce lo** accompagno dopo cena" ("When will you take your son to the

cinema? - I'll take him there after dinner").

2) When there is an infinitive preceded by a conjugated verb, two forms are possible:

   a) The adverb **ce** and the pronouns **lo, la, li, le** and **ne** follow the infinitive and are attached to it in order to form one word. "Quando accompagni tuo figlio al cinema? - Non puoi accompagnar**celo** prima di cena?" ("When will you take your son to the cinema? - Can't you take him there before dinner?").

   b) The adverb **ce** and the pronouns **lo, la, li, le** and **ne** precede a conjugated verb which is followed by an infinitive. "Quando accompagni tuo figlio al cinema? - Non **ce lo** puoi accompagnare prima di cena?" ("When will you take your son to the cinema? - Can't you take him there before dinner?).

Page 174 - Box 2/3

1) **C'è** (there is) and **ci sono** (there are) can be followed by the partitive pronoun **ne** (some, any). In this case, the adverb **ci** changes to **ce**.

The structure **ce n'è** (there is), **ce ne sono** (there are) is often introduced by the interrogative adjectives: *quanto / quanta; quanti / quante* (how much; how many). "Quanti libri ci sono? - Ce ne sono due" ("How many books are there? - There are two [of them]").

The adjectives **molto, molta; molti, molte** (much, a lot; many); **poco, poca; pochi, poche** (little, few); **tanto, tanta; tanti, tante** (so much; so many); **parecchio, parecchia; parecchi, parecchie** (rather a lot; several); **nessuno, nessuna** (no, not...any) always agree with the nouns which they modify. "Quanti libri ci sono? - *Ce ne* sono molti" ("How many books are there? - There are a lot [of them]").

2) The negative sentence "Quante signorine ci sono? - Non *ce n'è* nessuna" may be translated "How many girls are there? - There aren't any".

8 TAKE A LOOK AT THE EVERYDAY LANGUAGE

1. - Carlo, <u>prendi</u> un caffè?
   - Sì, <u>lo</u> prendo *volentieri*.
2. - Mi <u>accompagneresti</u> all'auto-bus?
   - Sì, ti accompagno *con piacere*.
   - Veramente non è un <u>sacrificio</u> per te?
   - No, lo faccio *volentieri*.
3. - *Fai presto* a <u>prepararti</u>?
   - Sì, faccio *in un attimo*.
4. - Ma, cara, non è ancora pronta la cena?
   - Un po' di pazienza, caro: la preparo *in un attimo*.
5. - Signore, <u>La prego, sa dirmi</u> do-v'è via Tacito?
   - Sei fortunato bambino, io vado *in quella direzione*, puoi venire con me.
6. - <u>Da che parte vai?</u>
   - *Sono diretto* alla posta.

- Ma, cara, non è ancora pronta la ce-na?
- Un po' di pazienza, caro: la preparo *in un attimo*.

A | WHAT'S DIFFERENT

1) In the sentence "Carlo, *prendi* un caffè?" the verb **prendere** corresponds to the English **to have** ("Carlo, *are you having* a [cup of] coffee?". In the answer to this question "Sì, *lo* prendo volentieri" ("Yes, I'll have *one* gladly"), the direct object pronoun **lo** refers to *caffè* (coffee).

2) The Italian expressions **volentieri** and **con piacere** show courtesy and may correspond to the English forms **willingly/gladly** and **with pleasure**.

3) The Italian verb **accompagnare** translates the English verb **to accompany**. "*Mi accompagneresti* all'autobus?" ("*Would you accompany me* to the bus?"). In this case, the verb is conditional in order to express a polite request.

4) The Italian form **in un attimo** corresponds to the English **in a moment** or **in a second**. "Fai presto a prepararti? - Sì, faccio *in un attimo*" ("Are you going to be

ready soon? - Yes, I'll be ready *in a moment* "). In this sentence the Italian reflexive verb **prepararsi** corresponds to the English verb **to get ready**, and the entire sentence "*Fai presto a prepararti* " translates the English sentence, as seen above, with a sense of the future.

5) In the formal sentence "Signore, *La prego, sa dirmi* dov'è via Tacito?" ("Sir, *please, can you tell me* where via Tacito is?") the polite direct object pronoun **La** is used together with the verb **pregare (to ask)** to express a very polite request (literally, I ask you); the verb **sapere** followed by an infinitive in this case corresponds to the English **can** and here expresses willingness; as in any other formal sentence, the verb is in the third person.

6) The expression **in quella direzione** translates **in that direction**.

7) The Italian expression **Da che parte...** may be translated in English by **toward what direction** or **where**; and the other expression **Sono diretto a...** by **I am headed toward....** "*Da che parte vai? - Sono diretto* alla posta" ("*Toward what direction*/Where are you going? - *I'm headed toward* the post office").

Proporre di fare insieme	– Prendiamo un caffè? – Perché non prendiamo un caffè?	
Scusarsi	– Mi scuso, – Domando perdono, – Vi prego di scusarmi, – Chiedo scusa,	ma devo proprio andare.
Rispondere alle scuse	– Si figuri, signora. – Figurati. – Niente.	
Porre un fatto come certo	– È chiaro che preferisci accompagnare lei. – È sicuro. – È evidente. – Sicuramente preferisci accompagnare lei. – Certamente.	

B | HOW TO SAY IT

1) In Italian, in order *to propose to do something together* (*Proporre di fare insieme*), you may use expressions such as:

"Prendiamo un caffè?   "Shall we have a cup of coffee?"

"Perché non prendiamo un caffè?"   "Why don't we have a cup of coffee?"

2) In order *to apologize to someone or to make one's excuses (Scusarsi)*, you may use the following expressions:

"Mi scuso."   "Excuse me."

"Domando perdono."   "I beg your pardon."

"Vi prego di scusarmi."   "Please excuse me."

"Chiedo scusa."   "I (must) ask you to excuse me."

3) On the contrary, in order *to respond to someone who is making his excuses (Rispondere alle scuse)*, you may use the following expressions:

"Si figuri."   "Not at all."

"Figurati."   "Don't mention it."

"Niente."   "It's nothing."

4) In order *to affirm or assert one's own opinion with absolute certainty (Porre un fatto come certo)*, you may use expressions such as:

"E' chiaro che preferisci   "It's clear that you prefer to accompany

. accompagnare lei."   her."

"E' sicuro."   "It's certain."

"E' evidente."   "It's evident."

"Sicuramente preferisci   "Surely you prefer

accompagnare lei."   to accompany her."

"Certamente."   "Certainly."

9   GRAMMAR IN CONTRAST

Page 193 - Box 1/2

1) The Italian **Imperfetto** may correspond to the English **Simple past** or **Past Progressive** and to the English form **"I used to..."**. The *Imperfetto* is a simple tense. To form the *Imperfetto* of regular verbs you drop **-re** from the infinitive and add the appropriate endings. "Ascolt*avo* la radio" ("I listened to the radio" / "I used to listen to the radio" / "I was listening to the radio").

The endings of the three conjugations (-are-ere-ire) are identical except that each conjugation retains its identifying vowel as the first vowel before the ending. Ascolt*avo* ("I listened to, I used to listen to, I was listening to"); legg**evo** ("I read, I used to read, I was reading"); dormivo ("I slept, I used to sleep, I was sleeping").

2) The verb *essere* is irregular in the imperfect: **ero** ("I was, I used to be"), as are the verbs *dire* (to say): **dicevo** (I said, I used to say, I was saying); *fare* (to do / to make): **facevo** ("I did, I used to do, I was doing / I made, I used to make, I was making"); and **bere** (to drink): **bevevo** ("I drank, I used to drink, I was drinking").

Page 193 - Box 3

1) The **Trapassato Prossimo (Past Perfect)** is a compound tense like the present perfect (passato prossimo). It is formed by the *Imperfetto* of the auxiliary verbs **avere** or **essere** plus *the past participle* of the main verb. "Il film *era* cominciato" ("The film had begun"); "L'assassino aveva ucciso" ("The murderer had killed").

2) The *Trapassato prossimo* (past perfect) is used, as in English, to refer to an action which had taken place prior to another action in the past. "Quando ho acceso il televisore, il film era cominciato da alcuni minuti" ("When I switched on / turned on the television, the film had begun a few minutes before").

Page 194 - Box 1/2/3

1) In Italian, the adverbs **troppo** (too, too much); **molto** (very); **parecchio** (quite, rather a lot); **tanto** (so, so much, a lot); **poco** (not very much, a little, not much) can modify *a verb*. "Ho studiato troppo" ("I studied too much"). They can also modify *an adjective*. "Questo vino è troppo caldo" ("This wine is too warm"). Finally, they can modify *an adverb*, too. "Ti sei alzata troppo presto" ("You got up too early"). In these three cases, they are invariable.

Page 194 - Box 4

1) In Italian, *troppo, molto, parecchio, tanto* and *poco* can also be adjectives, and as such they can modify a noun. "Ha parecchi soldi" ("He/she has quite a lot of money"). In this case, they agree in number and gender with the nouns which they modify.

Page 195 - Box 1

1) In Italian, the special forms of the adjectives **bello** (beautiful) and **quello** (that) are similar to those of the definite article. "Ho comprato un bel vaso" ("I bought a beautiful vase").

Page 195 - Box 2

1) The adjective *bello* has the above-mentioned special forms when it precedes a noun; but it is perfectly regular *bello, belli* when it follows a noun. "Ho visto in vetrina a Roma un vaso bello" ("I saw a nice vase in a shop window in Rome").

Page 196 - Box 1/2/3

1) Both the Italian verbs **sapere** and **conoscere** can be translated in English by the verb **to know**, but they are *not* interchangeable. **Sapere** means **to know a fact / to have knowledge of**. "Sapete a che ora parte il treno?" ("Do you know what time the train leaves?"). In this case, it is followed by a clause. **Sapere** also means **to know how / can**. "Sai parlare italiano?" ("Can you speak Italian?"). In this case, it expresses capability and is followed by an infinitive. **Conoscere** also means **to know** but in the sense of **to be acquainted with**. "Conosci l'Italia?" ("Do you know Italy?"). Also **conoscere** may be used in the sense of **to meet / to make the acquaintance of** "Avete conosciuto gli studenti della classe?" ("Did you meet the students in your class?"). Note that *conoscere* is always followed by a noun.

Page 197

1) In Italian, the **Imperfetto** is the tense used to describe something in the past or to refer to something which used to happen or was happening in the past. "Studiavo" ("I studied, I used to study, I was studying"). The present perfect, on the contrary, refers to a single completed action which happened at some definite time in the past. "Sono uscito" ("I went out").

2) **L'imperfetto** is used to express:

A) *A state of being in the past:*

"Stavo male" ("I felt bad").

B) *Simultaneous actions in the past:*

"Mentre mangiavo, guardavo la TV" ("While I ate, I watched TV").

C) *Actions that were either continuous or habitual:*

"Andavo spesso a teatro durante le vacanze" ("I used to go to the theatre often during vacation/holidays").

D) *An incomplete action going on while something else happened or was happening:*

"Quando sono entrato in camera, il nonno dormiva" ("My grandfather was sleeping, when I entered the bedroom"). In this case, the present perfect is used to describe the completed action.

3) Note that the **Imperfetto** often may translate the English **past perfect**: "Li conoscevo da molto tempo" ("I had known them for a long time").

9 TAKE A LOOK AT THE EVERYDAY LANGUAGE

1. - Sei uscito?
   - No, non *avevo voglia*.
2. - Vuoi leggere?
   - No, non *ho voglia di* leggere.
3. - Insomma che cosa vuoi fare stasera?
   - *Ho voglia di* andare al concerto.
4. - Quali film preferisci vedere?
   - *Vado pazzo per* i film gialli, per i film del brivido, per tutti quelli dove c'è suspense.
5. - Qual è la musica che ascolti volentieri?
   - La musica rock, folk, jazz, sinfonica, tutta la musica: *io vado pazzo per* la musica.
6. - Sai qual era il titolo del film e chi era il regista?
   - No, *non lo so*.
7. - Sai se la polizia è riuscita a scoprire l'assassino?
   - No, *non lo so*.

- Qual è la musica che ascolti volentieri?
- La musica rock, folk, jazz, sinfonica, tutta la musica: *io vado pazzo per* la musica.

A WHAT'S DIFFERENT

1) The Italian expression **aver(e) voglia di...**, followed by a noun or by an infinitive, corresponds to the English **to have the desire > for something/to do something**, and **to want > something/to do something**. The expression "non aver(e) voglia di..." expresses the opposite meaning and conveys the same negative idea in English. Also, **voglia** can be used alone with the various forms of avere, as seen in the sentence: "Sei uscito? - No, *non avevo voglia*" ("Did you go out? - No, *I didn't want to*").

2) The verb **preferire** corresponds to the English **to prefer**. The expression **vado pazzo per...** translates the English phrase **I'm crazy about...** or **I'm nuts about...**

"Quali film preferisci vedere? - *Vado pazzo* per i film gialli, per i film del brivido, per tutti quelli dove c'è suspense" ("Which/What kind of films do you prefer to see? - *I'm crazy about* mystery films, horror films, all the ones where there's suspense").

3) The verb **ascoltare** translates the English **to listen** or **to listen to**.

4) Consider the following sentences. "*Sai* qual era il titolo del film e chi era il regista? - No, *non lo so*" ("*Do you know* what the title of the film was and who the director was? - No, *I don't know*"); "*Sai* se la polizia è riuscita a scoprire l'assassino? - *No, non lo so*" ("Do you know whether the police have succeeded in discovering [who] the murderer [was]? - No, I don't know"). In the above sentences, the verb **sapere** means **to know** (a fact, a piece of information), which is different from what we explained in Unit 8.

Paura	— Non voglio vedere i film gialli. — Ho paura. — Tremo dalla paura — Ho una paura da morire! — Che paura! — Ho paura di vedere questi film del brivido.
Incoraggiare	— Niente paura! — Non bisogna avere paura. — Via! Un po' di coraggio!
Chiedere il perché di un fatto contenuto in un enunciato	— E perché? — Perché mai? — Per quale ragione? — Non ho capito perché?

B ‖ HOW TO SAY IT

1) In Italian, in order *to express fear* (*Paura*), you may say any of the following sentences (Note: Some of these sentences refer to the specific theme of this unit or to a similar personal situation):

"Non voglio vedere i film gialli."	"I don't want to see (any) mystery films."
"Ho paura."	"I'm afraid."
"Tremo dalla paura."	"I'm trembling with fear."
"Ho una paura da morire!"	"I'm scared to death!"
"Che paura!"	"I'm so afraid!"

2) In order *to encourage someone* (*Incoraggiare*), you may say any of the following sentences:

"Niente paura!"　　　　　　　　　　　　　"Don't be afraid!"

"Non bisogna avere paura."　　　　　　　　"There's no need to be afraid."

"Via! Un po' di coraggio!"　　　　　　　　　"Come on! Have a little courage!"

3) In order *to ask the reason for or the cause of a fact contained in a statement* (*Chiedere il perché di un fatto contenuto in un enunciato*), you may say any of the following sentences:

"E perché?"　　　　　　　　　　　　　　"And... why?"

"Perché mai?"　　　　　　　　　　　　　"Why ever?"

"Per quale ragione?"　　　　　　　　　　"For what reason?"

"Non ho capito perché!"　　　　　　　　　"I don't understand why!"

Note that the Italian *ho capito* which is actually in the present perfect has the sense of the English present tense.

10   GRAMMAR IN CONTRAST

Page 217 - Box 1/2

1) In the sentence: "Hai comprato il giornale? - Sì, *l'ho* compra*to*" ("Have you bought the newspaper? - Yes, I bought it"), the direct object pronoun precedes a compound tense. So, the past participle of the verb conjugated with *avere* (to have) must agree with the direct object pronoun in number and in gender.

Page 217 - Box 3

Page 218 - Box 1

1) The partitive object pronoun **ne** follows the same rule as the other object pronouns when it precedes a compound tense. "Quanti esercizi hai fatto? - **Ne** ho fatt**i** molt**i**" ("How many exercises did you do? - I did a lot").

2) As explained previously, unlike English, Italian negative words such as *nessuno,nessuna* must always be used in sentences with a negated verb. "Non **ne** ho fatto *nessuno*" ("I didn't do any").

Page 218 - Box 2/3

1) The verb **fare** (to do, to make) is used in a variety of Italian idiomatic expressions where English uses other verbs. "Che cosa fa tuo padre? - Fa il professore, l'ingegnere" ("What does your father do? - My father is a professor, an engineer"). "Fai bene/male a fare questa dieta" ("You are right/wrong to follow this diet"). "Faccio presto/tardi a preparare il pranzo / a finire questo lavoro" ("I will be quick/late in preparing lunch / in finishing this work"). "Fai tardi a scuola/al concerto" ("You'll be late for school/for the concert"). "Facciamo poco/molto sport" ("We play sports a little/a lot"). "Fanno una domanda al professore" ("They are asking the professor a question"). "Facciamo un esercizio" ("We are doing an exercise"). "Facciamo molti sbagli" ("We make a lot of mistakes"). "Faccio una passeggiata al centro" ("I am taking a walk to the center"). "Lui fa una festa" ("He is giving a party"). "Faccio il caffè" ("I am making coffee"). "Lei fa colazione al bar" ("She is having breakfast at the bar").

2) The Italian verb **fare** translates either the general meaning of the English **to do** "Che cosa fai / che cosa stai facendo?" ("What are you doing?") or the more concrete meaning of the English **to make** "Facciamo molti sbagli" ("We make many mistakes").

3) In Italian, the construction **fare + infinito** expresses the idea of *making, having, or letting someone do something*. "Fai entrare gli studenti" ("Let the students come in"); "Fai studiare i figli all'estero" ("Get your sons to study abroad"). It also expresses the idea of *having something done*. "Fai preparare le valigie" ("Have the suitcases packed").

10 TAKE A LOOK AT THE EVERYDAY LANGUAGE

1. - Ciao, cara. Che c'è _da mangia-_
   _re_ oggi?
2. - Hai un buon libro _da farmi_ leggere?
3. - Che cosa mi dai _da bere_?
4. - Ciao, cara. _Eccomi_ qua.
   - Finalmente, era ora!
5. - Dove sono i bambini?
   - _Eccoli_ là che giocano.
6. - _Eccoci_ arrivati finalmente a casa!
7. - E _che ci posso fare_! Tu non
   sopporti lei, io non sopporto lui.

il palco

A   WHAT'S DIFFERENT

1) In Italian, the preposition **DA** has several meanings. As seen in the case below, it may be followed by an infinitive. Thus, the form of **DA+ infinitive** may correspond to the English **to**, which is already contained in the idea of the infinitive. "Ciao, cara. Che c'è _da mangiare_ oggi?" ("Hi, Honey. What's there _to eat_ today?").

2) The Italian expression **Ecco** may be followed by the direct object pronouns. In this case, the form **eccomi** translates the English sentence **Here I am**. "Ciao, cara. _Eccomi_ qua!" ("Hi, Honey. _Here I am_ [here]"). So, the other forms _eccoti/eccolo/eccola/eccoci/eccovi/eccoli_ correspond to the English "_Here you_ (s.) _are_"; "_Here he is_"; "_Here she is_"; "_Here we are_"; "_Here you_ (pl.) _are_"; and "_Here they are_".

   The idiomatic sentence _Era ora!_, which appears in the answer to the abovementioned question, may be translated "_It's about time!_".

3) The Italian idiomatic sentence "_E che ci posso fare!_" corresponds to the English sentence "_And what can I do about it_ !". In the sentence "_Tu non sopporti lei, io non sopporto lui_ " ("_You can't stand her, I can't stand him_"), the verb **sopportare** translates the English **to stand**, in the sense of tolerating the presence of someone.

		non la sopporto. non la trovo simpatica.
Antipatia	— Ti ho detto tante volte che	non sto bene con lei. la detesto. non la posso vedere. è antipatica.
Simpatia	— Io la trovo simpatica. — Sto bene con lei. — Mi piace. — È simpatica.	
Pazienza, rassegnazione	— Ti è antipatica? Pazienza! Che ci posso fare?	
	— Non ha il resto?	— Non importa. — Fa lo stesso. — Non fa niente.

B HOW TO SAY IT

1) In Italian, in order to express *dislike* (*Antipatia*), you may use sentences such as:

Ti ho detto tante volte che:	I have told you so many times that:
non la sopporto.	I can't stand her.
non la trovo simpatica.	I don't find her likeable. / I don't think she's nice.
non sto bene con lei.	I don't get along well with her.
la detesto.	I detest her.
non la posso vedere.	I can't stand her.
è antipatica.	she is not nice.

2) On the contrary, in order to express *liking* (*Simpatia*), you may use sentences such as:

Io la trovo simpatica.	I find her nice. / I think she's nice.
Sto bene con lei.	I get along well with her.
Mi piace.	I like her.
E' simpatica.	She's nice.

3) In order to express *patience* and *resignation* (*Pazienza* e *Rassegnazione*), you may use sentences such as:

Ti è antipatica? Pazienza! Che ci posso fare? Do you dislike her? Patience! What can I do about it?

Or, in a shop, restaurant, or store:

Non ha il resto?	You don't have the change?
Non importa.	It doesn't matter.
Fa lo stesso.	Never mind.
Non fa niente.	It's nothing.

11 GRAMMAR IN CONTRAST

Page 239 - Box 1

1) In Italian the **Condizionale Semplice (Present Conditional)** is formed by taking the future stem and adding the endings **–ei** / **–esti** / **–ebbe** / **–emmo** / **–este** / **–ebbero.** The endings of the present conditional are the same for all verbs: telefon**are** telefonerei... ("I would phone/call up/call..."); scriv**ere** scriverei ("I would write..."); part**ire** partirei ("I would leave...").

2) In the conditional we find again the same irregularities which appear in the future: andare →andrei ("I would go..."); tenere →terrei ("I would hold...").

Page 240 - Box 1

1) The **Condizionale Composto (Past Conditional)** is formed with the present conditional of the helping verb and the past participle of the main verb. It is used like the corresponding tense in English. "Avrei studiato volentieri, ma stavo male" ("I would have studied gladly, but I didn't feel good").

Page 240 - Box 2

1) In Italian the conditional is used, as in English, to express:

   a) *Desire* or *request*: "Salve ragazzi, potrei farvi qualche domanda?" ("Hello boys/Hi guys, could I ask you some questions?").

   b) *Intention, doubt*: "Stasera potrei venire da te, ma non sono sicuro" ("This evening I might come to see you, but I'm not sure").

   c) *Personal opinion*: "Direi che sarebbe consigliabile rimandare a domani la partenza" ("I think that it would be advisable to put off the departure until tomorrow").

2) Unlike English the conditional is used in Italian to express what is reported by hearsay; this is a characteristic form of the journalistic style which expresses *uncertainty* or *probability* in reporting unsubstantiated news. "Il Primo Ministro non era presente alla cerimonia perché secondo i bene informati, sarebbe ammalato, avrebbe disturbi cardiaci" ("The Prime Minister was not at the ceremony because, according to well-informed sources, he is ill; he has cardiac problems").

Page 240 - Box 3

1) The Italian verb **volere** (*to wish / to want*) has a variety of uses. In this case, when it

follows the particle **ci**, it has an idiomatic use; and it means **essere necessario** (to be necessary), **occorre** (to be required). **Volerci** translates the English verb **to take**: "Ci vuole molto denaro per studiare all'estero" ("It takes a lot of money to study abroad"); "Ci è voluta un'ora per risolvere il problema" ("It took an hour to solve the problem"); "Ci sarebbero voluti molti soldi per fare il giro del mondo" ("It would have taken a lot of money to go on / to take a trip around the world").

Page 241 - Box 1

1) Nouns ending in **–ista** are of both genders: *questo pianista* (this pianist), *questa pianista* (this pianist). They have the some ending for masculine and feminine. In the singular their gender is shown by means of an article. In the plural they are regular and form the masculine plural in **–i**: *questi pianisti* (these pianists) and the feminine plural in **–e**: *queste pianiste* (these pianists).

11 TAKE A LOOK AT THE EVERYDAY LANGUAGE

1. - Sei *bravo* in matematica?
   - Abbastanza.
2. - Che sai di Antonio?
   - Adesso lavora con suo padre in officina; è serio, preciso.
     E' diventato davvero *un bravo ragazzo*.
3. - *Come mai* hai deciso di smettere di studiare?
   - Ho smesso *di studiare, perché non avevo voglia di* stare sopra i libri.
4. - A che ora *avete smesso di giocare* a poker?
   - Smesso? *Abbiamo* continuato a *giocare* fino alle quattro.
5. - Sai che Roberto *ha vinto una somma* favolosa alla lotteria?
   - Ah sì? *Beato lui* !

- Sei *bravo in* matematica?
- Abbastanza.

A │ WHAT'S DIFFERENT

1) The Italian adjective **bravo** often translates the English **good**, as in the sentence "Sei *bravo in* matematica?" ("Are you *good in* math?"). The answer to this question "*Abbastanza*" can be translated by the English "*Good enough*".

2) In the sentence "*Adesso* lavora con suo padre in officina; è *serio, preciso*. E' diventato *davvero* un bravo ragazzo" ("*Now* he's working with his father in a shop (or in an autoshop); he's *serious, precise*. He's *really* become a capable young man"), the adverb **adesso** translates the English **now**; while the adverb **davvero** translates the English **really, indeed**. The verb **lavorare** translates the English **to work** and the adjectives **serio** and **preciso** may correspond to the English **serious** and **careful** or **precise**.

3) The Italian expression *come mai...?* expresses the meaning of perché and, therefore, may be translated in English by "*why* ?" or by "*how come*?" "*Come mai hai deciso di smettere di studiare?*" ("*Why did you decide to stop studying?*" or "*How come you decided to stop studying?* "). Both the Italian verbs **decidere** (**to decide**) and **smettere** (**to stop**) are always followed by the preposition DI plus an infinitive; the Italian inifinitive, when preceded by a preposition, often is translated by the English gerund.

4) The idiomatic expression **stare sopra i libri** can be translated by the English idiom **to be sitting on top of my books** or **to be sleeping with my books**.

5) The Italian verb **continuare** (**to continue**) is generally followed by the preposition A plus an infinitive. "Abbiamo *continuato a giocare* fino alle quattro" ("*We continued playing* until 4 o'clock"). As seen in the sentence in part 3 above, Italian verbs followed by a preposition plus an infinitive often may be translated by the English gerund.

6) The verb **vincere** translates the English verb **to win**. "Sai che Roberto *ha vinto* una somma favolosa alla lotteria?" - "Ah sì? *Beato lui!*" ("Do you know that Robert *won* a fabulous sum/amount in the lottery?" - "Oh? *Lucky him!*").

Dare la parola	— Prego! — Dica pure! — Dica!
Precisare, spiegarsi	— Cioè... — Voglio dire... — Vale a dire... — Mi spiego...
Assicurarsi che ci si è spiegati	— Mi spiego? — È chiaro? — Capito? — Sono stato chiaro?
Desiderio	— Vorrei... — Mi piacerebbe...

B   HOW TO SAY IT

1) In Italian, in order *to invite* or *encourage someone to speak to you* (*Dare la parola*), you may use the following polite expressions, all of which you are likely to hear in any place of business.

"Prego!"	"Please!"
"Dica pure!"	"Please go on!"
"Dica!"	"Go on!"

2) In order *to state something precisely* or *to make oneself understood* (*Precisare, spiegarsi*), you may use any of the following:

"Cioè..."	"Namely...; that is..."
"Voglio dire..."	"I want to say..."
"Vale a dire..."	"It's worth saying..."
"Mi spiego..."	"I'm explaining (myself)...".

3) In order *to be certain that we have been understood* (*Assicurarsi che ci si è spiegati*), any of the following may be used.

"Mi spiego?"	"Am I making myself understood/clear?"
"E' chiaro?"	"Is it clear?"
"Capito?"	"Understood?"
"Sono stato chiaro?"	"Have I made myself clear?"

4) In Italian, as in English, the conditional expresses the idea of a *wish* (*Desiderio*). So, either of the following phrases may be used when we want to ask politely for something which we wish very much.

"Vorrei..."	"I would like..."
"Mi piacerebbe..."	"I would like...".

12 GRAMMAR IN CONTRAST

Page 265 - Box 1

1) In Italian, the pronouns **mi, ti, ci** and **vi** are used both as *direct* and *indirect* object pronouns. The third person **gli** (to him) is the masculine singular indirect object pronoun, and **le** (to her) is the feminine singular indirect object pronoun. Also, **gli** ("to them") is used for the masculine or feminine plural indirect object pronoun. For the third person plural, besides the most commonly used form **gli**: "Carlo **gli** scrive una lettera" ("Charles is writing them a letter"), there is the grammatically correct form: "Carlo scrive **loro** una lettera" ("Charles is writing them a letter"). In this case the pronoun **loro** (to them) must follow the verb.

2) Unlike English, the Italian **pronomi indiretti deboli (indirect object pronouns),** (except loro →to them), precede the verb. "Carlo *mi* scrive una lettera" ("Charles is writing me a letter"); "Carlo ti manda un pacco" ("Charles is sending you a parcel ").

3) In Italian, there is also a polite form for the third person singular indirect object pronoun **Le** (to you). This form is always capitalized to distinguish it from **le** (to her). "Carlo **Le** consegna le chiavi" ("Charles is giving you the keys").

4) It is useful to remember that not all verbs which take a direct object in English also take a direct object in Italian. Unlike English, verbs like **telefonare** (to call, to phone); **rispondere** (to answer, to respond); and **augurare** (to wish); require an indirect object.

Page 266 - Box 1/2

1) In Italian, unlike English, the verb **piacere** (to like) requires an indirect object: "Mi piace l'Italia" ("I like Italy"). So, the form "*piace*" (literally, "is pleasing") is used when what we like is singular; and "piacciono" (literally, "are pleasing") is used when what we like is plural; the indirect pronoun precedes the verb, with the one exception of *loro.*

2) *Piacere* is, therefore, used most frequently in the third person singular: "Gli,le piace..." ("He, she likes..."); "Le piace...?" ("Do you like...?") and plural: "Gli piace, piace loro ("They like..."); "Gli piace...?" ("Do you like...?". **What is the subject in English becomes an indirect object pronoun in Italian.** "Gli piacciono i dolci" ("He likes sweets"); "Le piacciono i fiori" ("She likes flowers").

3) The verb **piacere** (to like) takes the auxiliary **essere** in the present perfect and in the other compound tenses. Therefore, the past participle always agrees with the

subject, that is, the object in English. "Ci è piaciut*o* lo spettacol*o*" ("We liked the performance"); "Ci è piaciut*a* la visit*a* al museo" ("We liked the visit to the museum").

4) *Piacere* may also be followed by an infinitive: "Mi piace (di) viaggiare" ("I like travelling").

5) In Italian, the negative form of a sentence like "*Mi piace l'Italia*" ("I like Italy") is *"Non mi piace l'Italia"* ("I don't like Italy"). So, it is necessary to stress that the verb **dispiacere or rincrescere** is *not* "to dislike". Neither one is the negation of the verb *piacere*. Rather each has a different meaning: **"to be sorry"** or **"to regret"**. "Mi dispiace di partire" ("I'm sorry to leave"); "Ci è rincresciuto di partire" ("We were sorry to leave").

6) The verb **dispiacere** (to be sorry) takes an indirect pronoun, too. "Gli/le dispiace" ("He/She is sorry").

Page 266 - Box 3

1) In addition to the forms studied before, the *indirect object pronouns* have other forms called **Pronomi Indiretti Dativi forti**: **A me** (to me); **a te / a Lei** (to you); **a lui** (to him); **a lei** (to her); **a noi** (to us); **a voi** (to you); **a loro** (to them). These pronouns are not placed so close to the verb as are the indirect object pronouns (*pronomi indiretti dativi deboli*) seen in Unità 8. The emphasised indirect object pronouns are used when a special emphasis on the indirect object pronoun must be expressed. "A chi pensi? - Penso a te" ("Whom are you thinking of"? - I'm thinking of you"); "A chi presti la moto? A Rodolfo? - Sì, la presto a lui" ("To whom are you lending your motorcycle? To Rodolfo? - Yes, I'm lending it to him"). These pronouns are often seen as objects of prepositions, particularly the preposition **a** (to). These phrases usually follow the verb.

Page 267 - Box 1/2/3/4

1) In Italian, it is possible to join a direct object pronoun to an indirect object pronoun in a particular way. When in a sentence a verb has both a direct and an indirect object pronoun, the indirect object pronoun precedes the direct. "Carlo **mi** presta il vocabolario; **me lo** porta domani" ("Charles is lending me his dictionary; he'll bring it to me tomorrow"). In such a sentence the pronouns precede the verb in this order:

(a) *Indirect object pronoun* - (b) *Direct object pronoun* - (c) *Verb*. In this form, the **-i** of the indirect pronouns *mi, ti, ci,* and *vi* changes to an **-e** before the direct pronouns.

2) Note that the indirect object pronouns **gli** and **le, Le** become **glie-** before the direct object pronouns and combine with them to form one word. "Mario **gli** regala un

libro; **glielo** compra stasera" ("Mario is going to give him a book; he is going to buy it for him this evening").

3) The indirect object pronouns *loro* and *Loro* must *always* follow the verb. "Questo è il programma per i turisti svizzeri; lo consegnerò *loro* a cena" ("This is the program for the Swiss tourists; I'll give it to them at dinner"); "Questa è la stanza per Loro, signori; la preparerò *Loro* per mezzogiorno" ("This is your room, gentlemen; I'll prepare it for you for noon").

12 TAKE A LOOK AT THE EVERYDAY LANGUAGE

1. - La macchina <u>mi servirebbe</u> per domani, se non è *troppo disturbo* per te.
2. - Posso entrare? <u>Disturbo</u>?
   - Ti prego, entra, *tu non disturbi* mai.
3. - Non puoi smettere di fumare?
   - Scusa, smetto subito se il fumo *ti disturba*.
4. - *Ti dispiace* <u>passarmi</u> il sale?
   - Non mi *dispiace* <u>affatto</u>. <u>Eccoti</u> il sale.
5. - E' freddo qui. *Le dispiacerebbe* chiudere la finestra?
   - La chiudo subito, signora.
6. - *E' un mese che* non vediamo la nonna. Quando *andiamo a tro-varla*?
   - Andremo da lei domenica.
7. - <u>Allora</u>, la macchina, <u>gliela presto</u> o non gliela presto?
   - <u>Per me</u>, fai male a <u>prestarglie-la</u>, ma poi decidi tu, <u>tanto</u> *fai* sempre *come ti pare*!
8. - *Ti piace* quella ragazza?
   - No, *non mi piace*.

A | WHAT'S DIFFERENT

1) The Italian verb **servire** has many different meanings. When it is used together with the indirect object pronouns **mi** (to/for me); **ti** (to/for you); **gli** (to/for him); **le** (to/for her); **Le** (to/for you); **ci** (to/for us); **vi** (to/for you); **loro** (to/for them), it corresponds to the English verb **to need**, in the sense of **to serve a need**. So, a sentence such as "La macchina mi servirebbe per domani, se non è *troppo disturbo* per te" may be translated "*I need* my car by/for tomorrow, if it's not *too much trouble* for you". (The literal and clearly awkward translation of "La macchina mi servirebbe" is, "The car would serve [a need] for me"). In this sentence the noun **disturbo** may be translated by the English **trouble**.

2) The Italian word **disturbo** is not only a noun but also a verb, as in the sentence "Posso entrare? *Disturbo*?" ("May I come in? *Am I disturbing you*?"). In this case the verb **disturbare** translates the English verbs **to disturb**, **to bother**, or **to annoy**.

3) The Italian verb disturbare (to disturb, etc.) may also be used together with the direct object pronouns: **mi** (me); **ti** (you); **lo** (him); **la** (her); **La** (you); **ci** (us); **vi** (you); **li/le** (them). Note the sentence "Scusa, smetto subito se il fumo *ti disturba*" ("Excuse me, I'll stop right away if the smoke *is bothering you* "). *Smoke* is the subject of the second clause, and the verb "disturbare" requires the direct object pronoun "ti".

4) We have already seen the Italian verb **dispiacere**, which may correspond to the English verbs **to be sorry about something**, **to displease someone**, or **to mind**. So, a sentence such as "*Ti dispiace, passarmi* il sale?" may be translated "*Do you mind passing me* the salt?". In this sentence the verb **passare** (**to pass**) is followed by the indirect object pronoun **mi** (to me), which in Italian may be attached to the infinitive: **passarmi**. The pronoun may also precede the main verb, as, for example, *mi puoi passare*. In either case, the translation remains the same: "*Can you pass me...?*".

5) Please note that in a negative sentence, the Italian adverb **affatto** translates the English phrase **at all**. "Non mi dispiace affatto" ("It doesn't bother me at all"). In the same sentence "Non mi dispiace affatto. *Eccoti* il sale" ("It doesn't bother me at all. *Here it is*"), the adverb **ecco** is followed by the indirect object pronoun to ("to you"); this expression corresponds to the English expression **Here it is**.

6) The conditional form of the verb **dispiacere** is used, as in English, to ask someone something in a polite way. So, the formal expression **"Le dispiacerebbe...?"** corresponds to the English expression **"Would you mind...?"**. In Italian, there is also a similar, informal expression which is **"Ti dispiacerebbe...?" ("Would you mind...?")**. These expressions are usually followed by an infinitive in Italian, while they are followed by a gerund in English. "*Le dispiacerebbe chiudere la finestra?*" ("*Would you mind closing the window?*").

7) The Italian sentence "*E' un mese che non vediamo la nonna*" may be translated in English by either of the following sentences: "*We haven't seen our grandmother for a month*," or "*It's been a month since we've seen our grandmother*". In each of these sentences, the English verb in the present perfect tense (we have seen) corresponds to the Italian verb in the present tense (vediamo). In the following sentence, "Quando *andiamo a trovarla*?" ("When *are we going to go to see her*?"), the Italian expression **andare a trovare** corresponds to both English verbs **to go to see**.

8) In the sentence "*Allora*, la macchina, *gliela presto* o non gliela presto?" ("*OK then/All right then/So, am I going to lend my car to him/to her, or not?*"), the Italian adverb **allora** corresponds to the English **then**, or **so**. The verb **prestare** is translated in English by **to lend**. The form "gliela" is formed by joining the indirect object pronoun "gli" ("to him/to her"), plus the direct object pronoun "la" ("it"), which takes the place of "la macchina" ("the car").

9) In answering this question, you may attach the form **gliela** to the infinitive: "*Per me, fai male a prestargliela, ma poi decidi tu, tanto fai sempre come ti pare*" ("*To me you're wrong to lend it to him/her, but then you decide, in the end you always do what you want*"). In the abovementioned sentence, the expression **Per me** corresponds to the English **To me** or **According to me**. The form **tanto** corresponds to the phrase **in the end**. The expression **fai sempre come ti pare** corresponds to the English **you always do what you want**.

10) The Italian verb **piacere** (literally, *to be pleasing*) corresponds to the English **to like**, but it needs an indirect object pronoun. So, a sentence such as "*Ti piace quella ragazza?*" must be translated by "*Do you like that girl?*" (Literally, it is translated, "Is that girl pleasing to you?").

Chiedere un piacere	— Ciao, Carlo,	mi faresti un piacere? puoi farmi un piacere? me lo fai un piacere?
Risposta alla richiesta	— Certo! — Volentieri! — Se posso, volentieri! — Come no?! — Perché no?	
Possibilità	— Posso lasciartela sabato, se ti va bene.	
Impossibilità	— Impossibile! — Non è possibile! — Non ci pensare neanche!	
Tolleranza, permesso	— Per me va bene, ma sei sicuro che te la riporterà tutta intera? — Fa' pure, se vuoi. — Puoi farlo, se vuoi.	

B ☐ HOW TO SAY IT

1) In Italian, in order .*to ask a favour of someone* (*Chiedere un piacere*), you may use the following expressions:

"Mi faresti un piacere?"	"Would you do me a favour?"
"Puoi farmi un piacere?"	"Can you do me a favour?"
"Me lo fai un piacere?"	"Can you do me a favour?"

In this last sentence, the direct object pronoun **lo** is pleonastic; that is, it is part of the sentence, but its translation is superfluous.

2) In order *to answer this request* (*Rispondere alla richiesta*), the following expressions may be used.

"Certo!"	"Sure!"
"Volentieri!"	"Gladly!"
"Se posso, volentieri!"	"If I can, gladly!"
"Come no?!"	"Why not?!"
"Perché no?"	"Why not?"

3) In order *to express the possibility of doing someone a favour* (*Possibilità*), the expression "... se ti va bene" ("... if it's OK/all right with you") may be used. Consider the sentence "Posso lasciartela sabato, se ti va bene" ("I can leave it for you on Saturday, if it's OK with you").

4) On the contrary, *the impossibility of doing someone a favour* (*Impossibilità*) may be shown by the following expressions:

"Impossibile!"	"Impossible!"
"Non è possibile!"	"It's not possible!"
"Non ci pensare neanche!"	"Don't even think about it!"

5) In order *to express tolerance or permission* (*Tolleranza, permesso*) *toward someone who is going to do a favour for someone else*, you may use an expression such as "Per me va bene..." ("It's fine with me..."). Consider the sentence "Per me va bene, ma sei sicuro che te la riporterà tutta intera? (It's all right/fine with me, but are you sure that he will bring it back to you undamaged?"). You may also use the following expressions:

"Fa' pure, se vuoi."	"Go right ahead, if you want."
"Puoi farlo, se vuoi."	"You can do it, if you want."

13 GRAMMAR IN CONTRAST Unit 13

Page 284 - Box1/ 2

1) Even when the form *Indirect object pronoun + direct object pronoun* precedes a compound verb, the past participle of the verb must *always* agree with the direct object pronoun in number and in gender as usual. "Il pacco? Me l'ha mandat*o* a casa" ("The parcel? He sent it to me at home").

Page 285 - Box 1

1) The Italian Pronomi Indiretti Dativi forti are used:

   a) When a pronoun is the object of a preposition: "Vieni a cena *da noi?* - Sì, vengo *da voi*" ("Will you have dinner at our house? - Yes, I'll come to your house").

   b) When there is a special emphasis on direct or indirect objects: "Sei arrabbiato *con me?* No, non sono arrabbiato *con te*" ("Are you angry with me? - No, I'm not angry with you").

   c) When there are two or more direct or indirect objects: "Insomma, per chi è questo pacco, *per noi* o *per voi?* - Né *per voi,* né *per noi,* ma *per loro*" ("In short, whom is this parcel for? For us or for you? - It is neither for you nor for us, but for them").

Page 286 - Box 1

1) I numeri ordinali (Ordinal numbers) are regular adjectives which agree in gender and in number with the noun which they modify and usually precede these nouns. "E' la prim*a* volt*a* che vengo in Italia" ("This is the first time that I have come to Italy").

2) The first ten ordinal numbers have their own distinctive forms. After *decimo* ("tenth") the ordinal numbers are formed by dropping the final vowel of the corresponding cardinal number and adding **–esimo**. "Viviamo nel ventesimo secolo" ("We live in the 20th century").

3) The ordinal number always follows proper names: "Napoleone primo" ("Napoleon the First").

13 TAKE A LOOK AT THE EVERYDAY LANGUAGE

1. - *Siccome* cinque anni di galera non ti sono bastati, ti sei rimesso al "lavoro".
2. - *Siccome* non posso fumare, mi sono messo a masticare gomma americana.
3. - Mi racconti *per filo e per segno* quello che è successo sabato.
4. - Che cosa hai fatto di bello durante il tuo viaggio in Europa?
   - Adesso ti racconto tutto, *per filo e per segno*.
5. - *Senti* amico, *ti conviene* "cantare"!
   - Sì, se parlo il giudice sarà più comprensivo con me, *mi conviene dire* tutto quello che so.
6. - Perché parti oggi, non è presto?
   - *Senti*, il lavoro è finito, per domenica è probabile uno sciopero dei treni, dunque *mi conviene* partire oggi.
7. - E' stato il maggiordomo a darmi la pianta della villa.
   - Un uomo così fedele, e *chi l'avrebbe detto*!
8. - Adesso una pioggia così e un'ora fa c'era un sole stupendo: nessuno ci pensava, *chi l'avrebbe detto*!

Adesso una pioggia così e un'ora fa c'era un sole stupendo: nessuno ci pensava, *chi l'avrebbe detto*!

A WHAT'S DIFFERENT

1) The Italian conjunction **siccome** translates the English **as, since**, or **because**, as in the sentence "*Siccome* non posso fumare, *mi sono messo a* masticare gomma americana" ("*Since* I can't smoke, *I've started to* chew/chewing gum"). In the abovementioned sentence, the reflexive verb **mettersi**, followed by the preposition **a**, corresponds to the English verbs **to begin to...** or **to start to...**

2) The Italian idiomatic expression **per filo e per segno** corresponds to the English **in detail** or **thoroughly**, and it is generally preceded by the verb **dire** (**to say**) or **raccontare** (**to tell**). In Italian these verbs need an indirect object pronoun as in the sentence "*Mi racconti per filo e per segno* quello che è successo sabato" ("*Tell me in detail* what happened on Saturday").

3) The Italian idiomatic expression **Che cosa fai di bello**? corresponds to the English **What are you doing that's good/nice/enjoyable?** So the sentence "*Che cosa hai fatto di bello sabato e domenica?*" may be translated by "*What did you do* on Saturday and Sunday *that was nice*?*".

4) The Italian imperative form **"senti!"** has different meanings and uses. It may correspond to the English use of **"Listen!"** when it expresses intimidation or a threat, as in the sentence "Senti amico, *ti conviene 'cantare'!*" which may be translated "*Listen* buddy, *you had better talk*!". In this sentence the idiomatic expression **"ti conviene"** followed by an infinitive corresponds to the English expression **"you had better..."** followed by a form of the infinitive without expressing the "to"; for example, you had better (to) talk. In the same sentence the verb **"cantare"** (**"to sing"**) is used in an idiomatic way instead of saying parlare or confessare ("to talk or to confess"). Also, the Italian imperative **"senti"** has a milder use from the one described above. It may be used to draw someone's attention to a situation as in the sentence "*Senti*, il lavoro è finito, per domenica è probabile uno sciopero dei treni, dunque mi conviene partire oggi". This sentence may be translated "*Listen*, the work is finished; on Sunday there will probably be a train strike, so I had better leave today". In this sentence the conjunction **dunque** translates the English **so** or **therefore**.

5) The Italian verb **dare** (**to give**) often needs an indirect object pronoun. In the following sentence the pronoun is attached to the infinitive. "E' stato il maggiordomo *a darmi la pianta* della villa" ("It was the majordomo *who gave me the map* of the villa"). In this sentence the word **pianta** translates the English words **plan** or **map**.

6) The idiomatic expression **"Chi l'avrebbe detto!"** may correspond to the English **"Who would have thought it!"** as in the sentence "Un uomo così fedele, e *chi l'avrebbe detto!*" ("A man so faithful, and *who would have thought it!*").

7) The idiomatic expression **"nessuno ci pensava"** may be translated by the English **"No one could imagine it"**. It is seen in the sentence "Adesso una pioggia così e un'ora fa c'era un sole stupendo: *nessuno ci pensava, chi l'avrebbe detto!*" ("Right now it is raining so much and an hour ago it was so sunny: *no one could imagine it, who would have thought it!*").

Sapere, non sapere, chiedere informazioni	— Tu sai chi ha commesso il furto? — Dimmi tutto quello che sai! — Sai se ci sono dei complici?	— Non so niente!
Porre un fatto come facile	— E con i cani?	— Facile, semplice. — È stato facile. — Una cosa da nulla. — Nessun problema.

B HOW TO SAY IT

1) In Italian, in order *to express the idea of knowing (Sapere)* or *not knowing (Non sapere)*, or *seeking information (Chiedere informazioni)*, you may use sentences such as the following. Please note that these sentences are particular to the theme of Unità 13. "Tu sai chi ha commesso il furto? - Non so niente!" ("Do you know who committed the crime? - I don't know anything!"); "Dimmi tutto quello che sai! - Non so niente!" ("Tell me everything you know! - I don't know anything!"); "Sai se ci sono dei complici? - Non so niente!" ("Do you know whether there are any accomplices? - I don't know anything!").

2) In order *to affirm the easiness of an action (Porre un fatto come* facile), you may use expressions such as the following:

"Facile, semplice."   "Easy, simple."

"E' stato facile."   "It's been easy."

"Una cosa da nulla."   "It's nothing."

"Nessun problema."   "No problem."

14   GRAMMAR IN CONTRAST

Page 308 - Box 1/2/3

1) The endings of the **Imperativo Formale (Polite Imperative)** *Lei, Loro* (you) are as follows.

   a) For regular verbs ending in *–are*: **–i** in the singular: "Parl**i** ad alta voce!" ("Speak loudly!"); **–ino** in the plural: "Parl*ino* ad alta voce!" ("Speak loudly!").

   b) For regular verbs ending in *–ere* and *–ire*: **–a** in the singular: "Scriva questa lettera!" ("Write this letter!"); "Finis**ca** presto!" ("Finish soon!"); **–ano** in the plural: "Scrivano questa lettera!" ("Write this letter!"); "Finiscano presto!" ("Finish soon!").

2) The negative polite imperative is made by putting "non" before the verb: "Non parli ad alta voce!" ("Don't speak loudly"); "Non scriva questa lettera!" ("Don't write this letter!"); "Non finisca presto!" ("Don't finish soon!").

3) The imperative is used mainly to express:

   a) *An order.* "Si accomodi qui e attenda!" ("Take a seat here and wait!")

   b) *Advice.* "Mi ascolti, aspetti qualche giorno prima di partire!" ("Listen to me, wait a few days before leaving!").

   c) *An entreaty.* "Mi raccomando non mi faccia male!" ("Please, don't hurt me!").

   In the imperative the subject pronouns are omitted.

Page 308 - Box 4

1) With the polite form of the imperative *Lei, Loro,* object pronouns always precede the verb. "Inviti la professoressa, **la** inviti per telefono!" ("Invite the teacher, invite her by phone!").

Page 309 - Box 1

In Italian, the particle **ci** can have many different grammatical roles.

1) **Ci** = *noi stessi/e* (ourselves): "Vi lavate con acqua calda? - No, ci laviamo con acqua fredda" ("Do you wash yourselves with hot water? - No, we wash ourselves with cold water").

2) **Ci** = *a noi* (to us): "Perché chiami quel signore? - Perché ci indichi la strada" ("Why are you calling that man? - Because he'll point road out to us").

3) **Ci** = *a ciò, a questa o quella cosa* (about this, about that, about it): "Penserai a quello che ti ho detto? - Sì, ci penserò" ("Will you think about what I told you? - Yes, I'll think about it!").

5) **Ci** + essere = *esistere, trovarsi* (to exist / to be): "Mi racconti una fiaba? - Sì, c'era una volta una bimba piccola piccola..." ("Will you tell me a fable? - Yes. Once upon a time there was a little, little girl...").

6) **Ci** = *con questa / quella persona; con questa / quella cosa* (with this / that person; with this /that thing): "Perché non parli con il segretario? - Ci parlerò senz'altro" ("Why you don't talk with the secretary? - Of course, I'll talk with him").

7) **Ci** pleonastico (pleonastic): "Perché lo butti quest'accendino? - Non fumo più e non so cosa farci" ("Why are you throwing this lighter away? - I don't smoke any more and I don't know what to do with it").

8) **Ci** in locuzioni fisse (in fixed expressions), such as **volerci** (to take / to be necessary): "Quanto tempo occorre per riparare la macchina? - Ci vorranno due giorni" ("How long will it take to fix/repair the car? - It will take two days").

Page 310 - Box 1

In Italian the particle **ne** can also have many different grammatical roles.

1) **Ne** = *partitivo* (partitive): "Quanti romanzi hai letto in questo periodo? - Ne ho letti tanti" ("How many novels have you read/did you read during this period? - I have read many").

2) **Ne** = *di lui, di lei, di loro, di esso, di ciò, di questa/quella cosa* (of him, of her, of them, of it, of this/that thing): "Parlerai allo zio della mia proposta? - Sì, *gliene* parlerò" ("Will you talk to your uncle about my proposal? - Yes, I'll talk to him about it").

3) **Ne** = *da questo o quel luogo* (from this or that place): "E' tornato dagli Stati Uniti? - Sì, ne è ritornato ricco sfondato" ("Did he come back from the United States? - Yes, he came back awfully rich").

4) **Ne** = *pleonastico* (pleonastic). "Hai letto molti libri? - Sì, di libri ne ho letti tanti" ("Did you read many books? - Yes, I read a lot").

5) **Ne** = *in locuzioni fisse* (in fixed expressions): "Lasci questo paese? - Sì, me ne vado finalmente da qui, me ne ritorno a casa" ("Are you leaving/going to leave this country? - Yes, at last I'm leaving here, I'm going back home").

14 TAKE A LOOK AT THE EVERYDAY LANGUAGE

1. - *Mi raccomando*, dottore, non mi faccia male!
2. - Ecco le chiavi della macchina, ma, *mi raccomando* vada piano!
3. - Sono due notti che non dormo. *Non ne posso più dal dolore.*
4. - Sono stanco, sono stufo, *non ne posso più.*
5. - Vada nella stanza accanto, *è questione di* pochi istanti.
6. - Quanto tempo ci vuole per riparare questo orologio?
   - Bisogna vedere qual è il guasto: può *essere questione di* un'ora o *di* un giorno.
7. - Presto! La signora non si sente bene, *c'è bisogno di* un medico.
8. - Con i bambini *c'è bisogno di* tanta pazienza.

- Con i bambini *c'è bisogno di* tanta pazienza.

A | WHAT'S DIFFERENT

1) The idiomatic sentence **"mi raccomando"** may correspond to the English **"Please"**, and the polite imperative sentence **"non mi faccia male"** may be translated **"don't hurt me"**.

2) The idiomatic expression **"Non ne posso più"** may correspond to the English **"I can't stand it any more"**. This expression can be used in two different ways: independently, as in the above example; or followed by the preposition **da** plus a noun, as seen in the following example. "Sono due notti che non dormo. *Non ne posso più dal dolore*" must be translated "I haven't slept for two nights. *I can't stand the pain any more"*.

3) The idiomatic expression **"sono stufo"** may correspond to the English **"I'm fed up"**.

This expression can also be used in two different ways: independently, as seen in the above example; or followed by the preposition **di** plus a noun, or by an infinitive. This last way translates the English **"I'm fed up with..."**. So, a sentence such as "Sono stanco, *sono stufo, non ne posso più*" must be translated "I'm tired, *I'm fed up*, I can't stand it any more".

4) The expression **è questione di** may correspond to **it will only take...** as in the sentence "Vada nella stanza accanto, *è questione di pochi istanti* " ("Go into the next room, *it will only take a few minutes*").

5) The idiomatic expression **"Quanto tempo ci vuole..."** is generally followed by the preposition **per** plus an infinitive and corresponds to the English **"How much time does it take..."** "Quanto tempo ci vuole per riparare questo orologio?" (*"How much time does it/will it/would it take to* repair/fix this watch?").

6) The Italian word **Presto!** has many different meanings and uses. In this case it corresponds to the English **Quick!** as in the sentence "*Presto!* La signora non *si sente* bene, *c'è bisogno di* un medico" ("*Quick!* The/This lady doesn't feel good; *she needs* a doctor"). In the abovementioned sentence the reflexive verb **sentirsi** translates the English **to feel**, in the sense of one's health; and the expression **c'è bisogno di**... corresponds to the English **someone needs something** .

Raccomandare, pregare di fare o non fare	— Mi raccomando, — La prego,	dottore,	non mi faccia male!
Porre un fatto come necessario	— Signorina,	c'è bisogno di è necessario è indispensabile è bene	fare una radiografia.
Porre un fatto come non necessario	— Signorina,	non è necessario non bisogna non importa	far niente.

B HOW TO SAY IT

1) In Italian, in order *to ask strongly that someone do or not do something* (*Raccomandare, pregare di fare o non fare*), you may use the following polite expressions: "Mi raccomando" ("Please"), or "La prego" ("Please").

2) In order *to affirm that something is necessary* (*Porre un fatto come necessario*), the following expressions may be used.

"C'è bisogno di..."   "There is need of..."

"E' necessario..."   "It is necessary..."

"E' indispensabile..."   "It is indispensable..."

"E' bene..."   "It is well/good..."

They are generally followed by an infinitive, as in the sentence "Signorina, c'è biso-gno di fare una radiografia" ("Miss, it is necessary to take an x-ray").

3) On the contrary, in order *to affirm that something is not necessary* (*Porre un fatto come non necessario*), the following expressions may be used.

"Non è necessario..."	"It is not necessary..."
"Non bisogna..."	"There is no need..."
"Non importa..."	"It is not important..."

They also are generally followed by an infinitive, as in the sentence "Signorina, non è necessario far niente" ("Miss, it is not necessary to do anything").

15   GRAMMAR IN CONTRAST

Page 330 - Box 1-2

1) In Italian there are two different forms used for giving commands; that is, two types of imperatives: *Imperativo formale (Lei, Loro)* [Polite Imperative (you)] and *Imperativo informale (tu, noi, voi)* [Informal Imperative (you)]; both correspond to the form "you" in English.

2) As in the polite imperative, so in the **Imperativo Informale (Informal Imperative)** the subject pronouns are omitted. The forms of the *Informal Imperative* are identical to the present tense forms, except that in verbs of the first conjugation *(–are)* the *"tu"* (you) command is formed by changing the **–i** of the second person singular ending to an **–a**: "Parla ad alta voce!" ("Speak loudly").

3) The *negative form* of the informal imperative is formed by placing **non** before the **infinitive** for the second person singular: "**Non parlare** ad alta voce!" ("Don't speak loudly!"); and by placing **non** before the regular present tense for the first person and second person plural: "**Non** parliamo ad alta voce!" ("Let's not speak loudly!").

Page 330 - Box 3

1) Unlike the polite imperative which is usually preceded by the object pronouns, the informal imperative (tu, noi, voi) is generally followed by these pronouns. "Scrivi al professore. - *Scrivigli* oggi stesso!" ("Write to the teacher! - Write to him this very day!"). In this case, the pronoun is joined to the verb, and they form a single word.

2) The adverb **ci** also follows *the informal imperative forms*. "Se vuoi andare al centro, va**ci** con l'autobus!" ("If you want to go to the center, go there by bus!").

Page 331 - Box 1/2/3/4

1) Many of the more common verbs have irregular forms in the *polite Imperative* (Lei, Loro). "**Vada** a casa!", "**vadano** a casa!" ("Go home!"); "**Venga** a lezione domani!", "**Vengano** a lezione domani!" ("Come to class tomorrow!"); "**Dia** la precedenza!", "**Diano** la precedenza!" ("Give way!"); "**Stia** in fila!", "**Stiano** in fila!" ("Stay in line!"); "**Faccia** silenzio!", "**Facciano** silenzio!" ("Keep quiet!"); "**Dica** la verità!", "**Dicano** la verità!" ("Tell the truth!"); "**Abbia** pazienza con lui!", "**Abbiano** pazienza con lui!" ("Be patient with him!"); "**Sia** lì prima delle 7!", "**Siano** lì prima delle 7!" ("Be there before seven!").

2) Many of the more common verbs have irregular forms in the *Informal Imperative* (tu, voi), too:

"*Va* a casa!" ("Go home!")

"*Dà* la precedenza!" ("Give way!")

"*Sta in fila!*" *("Stay in line!")*

"*Fa* silenzio!" ("Keep quiet!")

"*Dì* la verità!" ("Tell the truth!")

"*Abbi* pazienza con lui!", "*Abbiate* pazienza con lui!" ("Be patient with him!")

"*Sii* lì prima delle 7!", "*Siate* lì prima delle 7!" ("Be there before seven!").

Page 332 - Box 1

1) *The informal imperatives of: dare* (to give), *dire* (to say, to tell), *fare* (to do, to make), follow the general rule when used with direct or indirect object pronouns; that is, the pronouns always follow the informal imperatives. Note that when a verb has two object pronouns, the indirect object pronoun precedes the direct object pronoun (*the opposite of English usage*), both follow the verb, and are joined to it to form one word. "Dammi un libro, dam*melo* subito!" ("Give me a book, give it to me at once!").

2) All pronouns double their initial consonant when they combine with the monosyllabic imperative forms of the verbs listed above: dà (give), dì (say - tell), fa (do - make): "*Dimmi* la verità, di*mmela*!" ("Tell me the truth, tell it to me!") [The pronoun *gli* is the only exception; it does not double its initial consonant].

3) The monosyllabic imperative forms of the verbs *andare* (to go) and *stare* (to stay) follow the same rule as *dare* (to give), *dire* (to say, to tell) and *fare* (to do, to make); but when they are followed by an infinitive, the pronouns may be attached either to the imperative or to the infinitive. "Sta*mmi* a sentire!" or "Sta a sentir*mi*!" ("Listen!").

Page 332 - Box 2

1) The peculiar verb **andarsene** corresponds to the English *to go away*. In the imperative forms (polite and informal) which have attached pronouns, this verb follows the general rules of the imperative + pronouns. "Non voglio ripeterlo, vat**tene**!"; "Non voglio ripeterlo, **se ne** vada!" ("I don't want to repeat it, go away!").

15 TAKE A LOOK AT THE EVERYDAY LANGUAGE

1. - Rallenta, è una s*tradaccia!*
   - E' veramente una brutta strada, piena di buche.
2. - E' brutto, *fuori moda, ti sta stretto.* Perché vuoi *mettere* questo *vestitaccio?*
3. - *Cerca l'ombrellone!* (L'ombrello grande per il sole)
4. - Ha un naso grande e grosso che *sembra* una patata.
   - Sì, ha un nasone veramente sproporzionato.
5. - Prendi anche il *cestino* per il picnic.
6. - Per un *bambino piccolino* come te, ci vogliono *calzine, scarpine, calzoncini, maglioncino* e *cappottino.*
7. - Ho dimenticato di portare il libro.
   - *Non fa niente,* useremo il mio.
8. - Qual è la ragazza che ti piace? *Questa qui* seduta davanti a me?
   - No, mi piace di più *quella lì* vicino alla porta.

- Ha un naso grande e grosso che sembra una patata.
- Sì, ha un *nasone* veramente sproporzionato.

A WHAT'S DIFFERENT

1) The Italian suffixes **-accio, -accia, -acci, -acce** negatively alter the meaning of the nouns to which they are attached, as in the example "Rallenta, è una *stradaccia*!" ("Slow down, it's an *awful road* !").

2) Also, note the sentences "E' brutto, *fuori moda, ti sta stretto.* Perché vuoi *mettere* questo *vestitaccio*?" ("It's ugly, *out of style, it's too tight.* Why do you want *to wear* this *ugly dress*?"). The expression **fuori moda** corresponds to the English **out of style**; the expression **ti sta...** corresponds to the English **it fits, or it suits...**; and the verb **mettere**, which is often used in common, everyday language, translates the English **to put on**, or **to wear**.

3) The Italian suffixes **-one, -ona, -oni, -one** alter the meaning of the nouns to which they are attached because they add a sense of increased volume or size, as in the example "Cerca *l'ombrellone*!" ("Look for the *big umbrella*!").

4) The Italian verb **sembrare** translates the English verb **to seem**. "Ha un naso grande e grosso che *sembra* una patata" ("He has a big, huge nose which *seems* like a potato").

5) The Italian suffixes **-ino, -ina, -ini, -ine** alter the meaning of the nouns to which they are attached because they add a sense of smallness. Note their use in the following sentences. "Prendi anche il *cestino* per il picnic" ("Take the *small basket* for the picnic, too"); "Per un bambino *piccolino* come te, ci vogliono *calzine, scarpine, calzoncini, maglioncino, e cappottino*" ("For a very *little boy* like you, you need your *little socks*, your *little shoes*, your *little pants*, your *little sweater*, and your *little coat* "). Please note that in the abovementioned sentence the last part of the word "bambino" ("child") must not be considered a sense-altering suffix; rather, it is the regular spelling of the word. The Italian expression **ci vuole** is followed by a singular noun; while **ci vogliono** is followed by a plural noun, and both correspond to the English **it takes...**

6) The idiomatic expression **"non fa niente"** translates the English **"It's nothing"**.

7) When using the following special forms of the Italian demonstrative pronouns **questo/a/i/e qui** or **quello/a/i/e/ lì**, you must not translate the extra forms **qui** or **lì** in English. So, a sentence such as "Qual è la ragazza che ti piace? *Questa qui* seduta davanti a me? - No, mi piace di più *quella lì* vicino alla porta" must be translated "Which one is the girl you like? *The/This one* seated in front of me? - No, I like *that/the one* near the door more".

Tollerare, permettere	— Possiamo portare le racchette?	▶	— Fate pure! — Per me va bene! — Fate come vi pare!
Avvertire, segnalare, mettere in guardia	— Stà attento a quella bicicletta! — Fa' attenzione a quella bicicletta! — Attento! Una bicicletta!		
Chiedere di fare o di non fare	— Per piacere, rallenta! — Ti dispiace rallentare? — Ti dispiacerebbe rallentare? — Non sorpassare quella macchina!		

B		**HOW TO SAY IT**	

1) In Italian, in order *to allow or to let someone (to) do something* (*Tollerare, permettere*), the following expressions may be used.

"Fate pure!"	"Go right ahead!"
"Per me va bene!"	"It's fine with me!"
"Fate come vi pare!"	"Do as you like!"

2) In order *to warn someone about something* (*Avvertire, segnalare, mettere in guardia*), the following expressions may be used.

"Sta attento a...!"	"Be careful about...!"
"Fa attenzione a...!"	"Pay attention to...!"
"Attento!"	"Watch out!"

3) In order *to ask someone to do or not to do something* (*Chiedere di fare o non fare*), there are several phrases which you may use to begin your request. The following examples use these phrases in a specific situation in which someone is being asked to slow down.

"Per piacere, rallenta!"	"Please, slow down!"
"Ti dispiace rallentare?"	"Do you mind slowing down?"
"Ti dispiacerebbe rallentare?"	"Would you mind slowing down?"
"Non sorpassare quella macchina!"	"Don't pass that car!"

16 GRAMMAR IN CONTRAST

Page 358 - Box 1/2/3

1) Unlike English, **Il Pronome Relativo (The Relative Pronoun) che** (that, who, which, whom) must be expressed in Italian; it is never omitted. **Che** is invariable; it refers to persons or things and can be used as the subject or direct object of a verb. "Mio figlio, che è nato nel 1973, si chiama Lorenzo" ("My son, who was born in 1973, is called Lorenzo"); "Le sigarette che fumi sono molto forti" ("The cigarettes you smoke are very strong").

2) I pronomi relativi (The relative pronouns) *il quale, la quale; i quali, le quali,* agree in number and in gender with the noun to which they refer. They are also used as subject or direct object of a verb. They may sometimes replace the relative pronoun *che* in subordinate clauses. "Accanto a me era seduto un signore **il quale/che** parlava da solo" ("A man was sitting next to me who was talking to himself").

Page 359 - Box 1/2/3

1) Il Pronome Relativo (The Relative Pronoun) **cui** (whom, which) is always used after prepositions, for example: **di cui, a cui, con cui, in cui** etc. The relative pronoun **cui** refers to persons or things, and it is invariable. "Non conosco la signora con cui stavi parlando ieri al bar" ("I don't know the lady with whom you were talking yesterday in the bar").

2) The relative pronouns *il quale / la quale; i quali / le quali* (whom, that, which) may also be used after prepositions instead of the relative pronoun *cui.* "Non conosco la signora **con cui (con la quale)** stavi parlando ieri al bar" ("I don't know the lady with whom you were talking yesterday in the bar").

3) The relative pronoun **cui** can be preceded by the definite articles. In this instance it has a specific possessive use and translates the English *whose.* "Quel signore, **il cui figlio (il figlio del quale)** studia in America, è mio zio" ["That man, whose son (the son of whom) is studying/studies in America, is my uncle"].

Page 360 - Bpx 1/2/3

1) In Italian, the pronoun **chi** is an interrogative; but it can also function as a relative pronoun which refers to persons. **Chi** is invariable and traslates the English forms "(he) who", "(she) who"; it is used especially in proverbs and sayings. "Chi trova un

amico, trova un tesoro" ("He / She who finds a friend, finds a treasure"). "Chi cerca, trova" ("He / She who seeks, finds"). In this use, the pronoun **chi** is used as the subject of the sentence, and it is always followed by a verb in the third person singular.

2) The relative pronoun **chi** can also be used as the object of a preposition. In this case, it corresponds to the English pronoun "whom". "Non fidarti di chi non conosci bene" ("Don't trust [anyone / someone] whom you don't know well").

3) The masculine singular form **colui che** (he who) and the feminine singular form **colei che** (she who) may be used instead of **chi** as the subject of a sentence or the object of a preposition. They are always followed by a verb in the third person singular. "Colui che dice questo sbaglia di grosso" ("He who says this is making a big mistake / a blunder"). The masculine and feminine plural forms **coloro che** (they who, those who), **le persone che** (people who) may also be used instead of **chi** as the subject of a sentence or the object of a preposition. They are always followed by a verb in the third person plural. "*Coloro che* dicono questo sbagliano" ("Those who say this are wrong"). "Non puoi fidarti delle *persone che* non conosci bene" ("You can't trust those whom you don't know well").

Page 360 - Box 4

1) The Italian relative pronouns **ciò che, quello che, quanto** correspond to the English "*what*", "*that which*" and are used just to refer to things. "Non capisco ciò che (quello che, quanto) ha detto" ("I don't understand what / that which he / she said").

16 TAKE A LOOK AT THE EVERYDAY LANGUAGE

1. - Vorrei un paio di scarpe nere.
   - *Ha* già *un'idea* del modello?
2. - Dove vuoi andare in vacanza?
   - Mah, *non ho* ancora *un'idea* precisa.
3. - Questa è un po' stretta. *In ogni caso* mi piace più il modello che ho provato prima.
4. - Arriverai domani o dopo domani?
   - Non lo so; ma *in ogni caso* ti telefonerò subito.
5. - Questa, signore, è la scarpa che *fa per* lei.
6. - Doppi servizi, garage, cantina, giardino e a questo prezzo; dove la troviamo un'altra casa come questa? Questa è la casa che *fa per* noi.
7. - *Mi dia retta*, signore, Lei acquista una scarpa alla quale non manca niente.
8. - E' ubbidiente questo cane?
   - *Macché*; lo chiamo, lo chiamo, e lui non mi ascolta; è un cane che non *dà* mai *retta*.

- E' ubbidiente questo cane?
- Macché; lo chiamo, lo chiamo, e lui non mi ascolta; è un cane che non *dà* mai *retta*.

A | WHAT'S DIFFERENT

1) The adverb **già** translates the English **already**, as in the sentence "Vorrei un paio di scarpe nere. - Ha *già* un'idea del modello?" ("I would like a pair of black shoes. - Do you *already* have an idea of the style?"). On the contrary, the adverb **ancora** translates the English **still/yet,** as in the sentence "Dove vuoi andare in vacanza? Mah, non ho *ancora* un'idea precisa" ("Where do you want to go for vacation? But, I don't have an exact idea *yet* ").

2) The Italian expression **in ogni caso...** translates the English **in any case** or **at any rate**, as in the sentence "Questa è un po' stretta. *In ogni caso mi piace di più* il modello che ho provato prima" ("This is a little tight. *At any rate, I like* the style which

I tried before *more*"). In the same sentence, the expression **mi piace di più** corresponds to the English expression **I like... more**. Please note that the verb *piacere* ("*to like*") is always preceded by an indirect object.

3) The Italian expressions **questo fa per...** and **questo non fa per...** are generally followed by the pronouns *me/te/lui/lei/Lei/noi/voi/loro*. They may còrrespond to the English expressions: **This is (not) good for whomever**; or, **This suits (does not suit) whomever**. So, a sentence such as "Questa, signore, è la scarpa che *fa per Lei*, may be translated "This, sir, is the shoe which *suits you* ".

4) The Italian verb **dare retta** corresponds to the English verb **to take advice** or **to pay attention**. So, the idiomatic polite expression **mi dia retta** translates the English **take my advice**, as in the sentence "*Mi dia retta*, signore, Lei acquista una scarpa alla quale non manca niente" ("*Take my advice*, sir, you are getting a shoe which is lacking nothing").

5) The very idiomatic form **"macché"** may be translated by **"Forget it!"**, as in the sentence "E' ubbidiente questo cane? - *Macché*; lo chiamo, lo chiamo, e lui non mi ascolta; è un cane che non mi dà retta" ("Is this dog obedient? - *Forget it*; I call him, and call him, and he doesn't listen to me; he's a dog who never pays attention to me").

Preferenza	— Preferisco — Preferirei — Mi piace più	il modello che ho provato prima.	
Accordo	— Mi sembra anche abbastanza elegante		— Sono d'accordo con lei, signore. — Pienamente d'accordo! — Certo, è così. — Ne sono pienamente convinto.
Disaccordo			— Non sono d'accordo con Lei, signore. — Per me non è così. — Non ne sono convinto.

B HOW TO SAY IT

1) In Italian, in order *to show preference* (*Preferenza*), the following verbs may be used.

"Preferisco."   "I prefer."

"Preferirei."   "I would prefer."

"Mi piace di più."   "I like... more."

2) In order *to express agreement* (*Accordo*) with someone's statement, the following expressions may be used.

"Sono d'accordo con Lei, signore." "I agree with you, sir."

"Pienamente d'accordo!"   "I totally agree."

"Certo è così."   "Sure, that's how it is."

"Ne sono pienamente convinto." "I'm totally/completely convinced of it."

3) In order *to express disagreement* (*Disaccordo*) with someone's statement, the following expressions may be used.

"Non sono d'accordo con Lei, signore." "I don't agree with you, sir."

"Per me non è così."   "I don't think so."

"Non ne sono convinto."   "I'm not convinced of it."

17 GRAMMAR IN CONTRAST

Page 383 - Box 1/2/3

1) **Il Congiuntivo (The Subjunctive)** occurs much more frequently in Italian than in English. With few exceptions it occurs only in subordinate clauses. "Mario pensa che →io non *parli* questa lingua" ["Mario thinks (that) I don't speak this language"]. In Italian, the subjunctive mood has four tenses and is used to express an action or a state, not as a factual, but as possible, probable, uncertain, or dependent upon another action either expressed or understood.

2) **Il Congiuntivo Presente (The Present Subjunctive)** *is commonly used:*

A) When in the main clause there are verbs expressing *personal opinions*. "Mario pensa che →Eva *parli* questa lingua" ["Mario thinks (that) Eva speaks this language"].

B) When in the main clause there are verbs expressing hope or will. "Mario spera che →voi finiate presto" ["Mario hopes (that) you'll finish soon"].

3) In the present subjunctive of regular verbs the first, second and third persons singular are identical in all conjugations. *Parlare*: che io parl*i* / che tu parl*i* / che lui, lei parl*i* / che Lei parl*i* (that I speak / that you speak / that he, she speak / that you speak); *Scrivere*: che io scriv*a* / che tu scriv*a* / che lui, lei scriv*a* / che Lei scriv*a* (that I write, that you write / that he, she write / that you write); *Partire*: che io part*a* / che tu part*a* / che lui, lei part*a* / che Lei part*a* (that I leave / that you leave / that he, she leave / that you leave). The endings of the first, second and third persons singular of regular verbs ending in **-are** are always **-i: parli**. The endings of the first second and third persons singular of verbs ending in **-ere** or **-ire** are always **-a: scriva, parta**.

The endings of the first and second persons plural are the same in all conjugations: **-iamo**, **-iate**.

The endings of the third person plural differ; each keeps the characteristic vowel of the singular forms: *-are* →**ino**; *-ere* → **ano**; *-ire* → **ano**.

4) The verbs *essere* and *avere* are irregular in the present subjunctive. "che tu *sia*" ("that you be/are"); "che tu *abbia*" ("that you have").

Page 383 - Box 4

1) Because of the relationship between two clauses, the tenses of the subjunctive are determined strictly by the tenses used in the main clause on which the subjunctive depends. When the verb of the principal clause is in the present tense, it may be followed by a Present Perfect Subjunctive (*Congiuntivo Passato*) if the action of the

subordinate clause is past in relation to the action of verb in the principal clause. "Antonio crede che → *lei sia partita*" ["Antonio believes (that) she has left"].

2) **Il Congiuntivo Passato (The Present Perfect Subjunctive)** is formed with the present subjunctive of the helping verb *essere* or *avere* plus the *past participle* of the main verb.

"Antonio crede che lei *sia partita*" ("Antonio believes she has left"); "Antonio crede che lei *abbia perso* il treno" ("Antonio believes she has missed the train").

| Page 384 - Box 1/2/3 |

1) The *subjunctive is used after verbs or phrases expressing:*

A) *Personal opinions*: *penso* ("I think"); *credo* ("I believe"); *suppongo* ("I suppose"); *ritengo* ("I think, I believe"); *mi pare, mi sembra* ("it seems to me"); *temo, ho paura* ("I am afraid"); *spero* ("I hope"). "Penso che lui *sia* a casa e *abbia* molte cose da fare" ("I think that he is at home and has a lot of things to do").

B) *Command*, wish or *preference*: *voglio* ("I want"), *desidero* ("I wish"), *preferisco* ("I prefer"). "Desidero che lui *sia* sempre gentile" ("I wish him always to be nice/kind").

2) If the verb of the principal clause has the same subject as the verb of the subordinate clause, the verb of the subordinate clause is not in the subjunctive mood, but in the infinitive mood. "Penso *di non avere* domande da fare" ("I don't think that I have questions to ask"). In this type of sentence, the present indicative in English translates the Italian infinitive.

| Page 384 - Box 4 |

| Page 385 - Box 1/2 |

1) The present subjunctive and the present perfect subjunctive are also used when in the principal clause there is an impersonal verb expressing *probability: può darsi, può essere* (may be, perhaps, it is likely). "Può darsi che domani *piova*" ("It is likely that it will rain tomorrow"); "Può essere che ieri sia andato a trovare Maria" ("It's likely that he went to see Maria yesterday"). Only the present subjunctive may be used if, in the principal clause, there is an impersonal verb expressing *necessity, need,* or *opportunity*: "Bisogna (,occorre, è necessario) che →tu venga da me appena possibile" ["It is necessary (that) you come to my house as soon as possible"]. These verbs may also be followed by an infinitive. "Bisogna fare questo in tempi brevi" ("This has to be done in a short time").

2) Note that the forms *può darsi* / può essere (maybe, perhaps, it is likely), followed by the present subjunctive, have the same meaning as the adverb *forse* (maybe, perhaps); but *forse* is always followed by an indicative tense. "Forse domani pioverà" ("Maybe it will rain tomorrow").

Page 386 - Box 1

1) In Italian, such impersonal expressions as **È facile** ("It is likely"), **È difficile** ("It is possible"), **È impossibile** ("It is impossible"), **È probabile** ("It is probable"), etc., are generally followed by a subjunctive tense. "È facile che loro siano a casa" ["It is likely (that) they are at home"]. The same expressions may also be followed by an infinitive, as in English. "È possibile imparare bene l'italiano in due mesi" ("It is possible to learn Italian well in two months").

2) The expressions **È ora** / **È tempo** ("It is time") may be followed by two different structures. One is the present subjunctive. "È ora che loro seguano i miei consigli" ["It is time (that) they take my advice"]. The other is the preposition **di** plus an infinitive. "È tempo di dire pane al pane e vino al vino" ("It is time to call a spade a spade").

Page 387 - Box 1/2/3/4

Page 388 - Box 1/2

1) In Italian there are some conjunctions and expressions which are generally followed by the subjunctive mood.

a) **Benché, sebbene, malgrado, nonostante, quantunque:**
   (Although; in spite of; even though)
   "Stasera andrò al cinema *benché* sia stanco morto"
   ("I'll go to the movies tonight, even though I'm dead tired").

b) **Purché, a patto che, a condizione che:**
   (Provided that; on the condition that)
   "Ti racconterò tutto *a patto che* tu non lo dica a nessuno"
   ("I'll tell you everything *on the condition that* you not tell [it to] anyone").

c) **Nel caso che:** (In case) "Devi andare dal dottore *nel caso che* domani non ti senta   meglio"
   ("You have to go to the doctor's *in case* you don't feel better tomorrow").

d) **Prima che** (Before) "Maria ti telefonerà *prima che* tu esca"
   ("Mary will call you *before* you go out").
   Prima may also be followed by the preposition **di** plus an infinitive. "Prendo

sempre un aperitivo *prima di* pranzare"
("I always have an aperitif *before* having lunch").

e) **Senza che** (Without) "Farà ciò che è necessario *senza che* io glielo chieda"
("He / she'll do what is necessary without my asking him / her").
Senza may also be followed by an infinitive. "Ha fatto di testa sua senza ascoltare   nessuno"
("He / she went his / her own way without listening to anybody").

f) **Affinché, perché** (In order to; in order that; so that)
"Andrò dai miei amici affinché / perché mi aiutino"
("I'll go to my friends' in order that they may help me / so that they may / can help me").
Note that this kind of dependent clause in Italian is usually introduced by the conjunctions *affinché* or *perché* followed by a subjunctive tense (present or past). The auxiliary verbs in English are *may* for the present subjunctive and *might* for the past subjunctive.
Affinché and *perché* may also be followed by an infinitive.
"Andrò dai miei amici per farmi aiutare"
("I'll go to my friends' to get help").

| Page 388 - Box 3/4 |

| Page 389 - Box 1/2/3/4 |

| Page 390 - Box 1/2 |

1) All the following verbs are irregular in the present subjunctive.

   a) First conjugation verbs **stare** (to stay); **dare** (to give); **andare** (to go); and **fare** (to do / to make).

   b) The three verbs **dovere** (Must, to be obliged, to have to...); **potere** (to be able / can / may); **volere** (to want / to wish) and other verbs belonging to the second conjugation: **togliere** (to take away / to remove); **porre** (to put / to place); **tenere** (to keep); **tradurre** (to translate).

   c) The third conjugation verbs **venire** (to come) and **uscire** (to go out).

17 TAKE A LOOK AT THE EVERYDAY LANGUAGE

1. - Che animale sarà? Quanto è *bellino*!
2. - È bella quella ragazza.
   - Proprio bella, bella, no; è *bellina*, *carina*, graziosa.
3. - *Chissà* che animale può essere?
4. - Sai se Luciano ha comprato i biglietti?
   - No, non lo so; *chi lo sa*? Forse sì.
5. - *Forse si è allontanato* troppo dalla sua tana.
   - Sì, *penso* proprio che *si sia allontanato* troppo.
6. - Allora *faremo così*: oggi lo portiamo a casa e gli diamo il latte; domani lo portiamo allo zoo.
7. - E per la cena *che si fa*?
   - *Facciamo così*: io preparo una pizza al pomodoro e mozzarella e tu vai a comprare due bottiglie di birra e un po' di frutta.

- E' bella quella ragazza!
- Proprio bella, bella, no:
  è *bellina*, *carina*, graziosa.

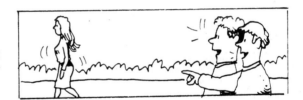

A │ WHAT'S DIFFERENT

1) The Italian adjectives **bellina** and **carina** may be translated by the English **pretty** and **cute**.

2) The expressions **chissà**; **chi lo sa?** have the same meaning, and they correspond to the English **who knows?** Consider the sentences "*Chissà* che animale può essere?" ("*Who knows* what animal it could be") or "Sai se Luciano ha comprato i biglietti? - No, non lo so; *chi lo sa*? Forse sì" ("Do you know whether Luciano has bought the tickets? - No, I don't know; *who knows*? Perhaps yes. [Maybe he has]").

3) The reflexive verb **allontanarsi** translates the English verb **to go away** or **to leave a place**.

4) In Italian, the impersonal expression **che si fa...?** is often used instead of **che facciamo? (What shall we do?)**, but it has the same meaning, as in the sentence "E per la cena *che si fa*?" ("And for dinner, *what shall we do*?"). The Italian expression **facciamo così** translates the English **Let's do this**.

Porre un fatto come facile, apparente, probabile, improbabile, possibile, impossibile,	– Sembra			
	–È	facile probabile improbabile possibile impossibile	che	sia un lupacchiotto. abbia una zampa rotta.
o necessario	– È necessario – Bisogna		portarlo da un veterinario.	
			che	lui lo porti da un veterinario.
Ammirazione	– Carino! – Bellino! – Quant'è bellino! Quant'è carino!			
Pietà, partecipazione	– Poverino! – Poveretto! Mi fa pena! – Che pena!			

B   HOW TO SAY IT

1) In Italian, in order *to affirm that a fact is easy; apparent; probable* or *improbable; possible* or *impossible* (*Porre un fatto come facile, apparente, probabile, improbabile, possibile, impossibile*), the following expressions may be used.

"Sembra che..."	"It seems that..."
"È facile che..."	"It is easy that..."
"È probabile che..."	"It is likely/probable that..."
"È improbabile che..."	"It is unlikely/improbable that..."
"È possibile che..."	"It is possible that..."
"È impossibile che..."	"It is impossible that..."

2) In order *to affirm that a fact is necessary* (*Porre un fatto come necessario*), the following expressions may be used.

"È necessario."	"It is necessary."
"Bisogna."	"It is necessary."

3) In order *to show admiration* (*Ammirazione*), the following expressions may be used.

"Carino!"	"Cute!"
"Bellino!"	"Lovely!"
"Quant'è bellino! Quant'è carino!"	"How nice it is! How cute it is!"

4) In order *to show pity for or involvement in someone's sorrow* (*Pietà, partecipazione*), the following expressions may be used.

"Poverino!"	"The poor man/guy!"
"Poveretto! Mi fa pena!"	"The poor man/guy! I feel bad, sorry, terrible, awful for him!"
"Che pena!"	"How terrible!" "How awful!"

18   GRAMMAR IN CONTRAST

Page 413 - Box 1/2

1) In the **Congiuntivo Imperfetto (Imperfect Subjunctive)** the endings are alike in all three conjugations except that each conjugation keeps its characteristic vowel **(-a - e - i)** before the endings. "Pensava che parla**ssi** bene" ["He thought (that) I spoke well"]; "Pensava che legge**ssi** molto" ["He thought (that) I read a lot"]; "Pensava che parti**ssi** in treno" ["He thought (that) I left by train"].

2) Some verbs are irregular in the imperfect subjunctive: **essere** (to be) / che io fossi; **dire** (to say, to tell) / che io dicessi; **dare** (to give) / che io dessi; **fare** (to do, to make) / che io facessi; **stare** (to stay, to be) / che io stessi; **porre** (to put) / che io ponessi; **tradurre** (to translate) / che io traducessi; **promuovere** (to promote) / che io promuovessi; **compiere** (to do) / che io compissi; **bere** (to drink) / che io bevessi.

3) **Il Congiuntivo Trapassato (The Past Perfect Subjunctive)** is formed with the imperfect subjunctive of the auxiliary verbs plus the past participle of the main verb. "Credevo che tutti avessero capito la lezione" ["I thought (that) everyone had understood the lesson"].

Page 414 - Box 1/2/3/4/5

1) The imperfect subjunctive and past perfect subjunctive follow the same verbs and expressions which the present subjunctive follows, namely: *clauses expressing personal opinions, hope, commands, wishes, preference.*

2) When the verb of the principal clause has the same subject as the verb of the subordinate clause, the verb of the latter is not in the subjunctive mood; rather an infinitive is used. "Speravo di superare l'esame di economia" ("I hoped to pass / that I passed the economics examination").

1) As with the present subjunctive and the present perfect subjunctive, the imperfect and past perfect subjunctive are also used after *impersonal forms* in the past tense such as *poteva essere* (maybe, perhaps, it was likely). "Poteva essere che stesse male" ("It was likely he was not well"). The imperfect subjunctive is also used when there is an impersonal verb expressing *necessity, need,* or *opportunity.* "Bisognava che io andassi alla posta a ritirare un pacco" ["It was necessary (that) I go to the post office to get / to collect a package / a parcel"].

2) The forms *poteva darsi / poteva essere* (maybe, perhaps, it was likely) also have the same meaning as the adverb **forse,** but forse is always followed by the indicative. "Forse stava male" ("Maybe he was not well").

1) As with the present subjunctive and the present perfect subjunctive, such impersonal expressions as **era facile** ("it was likely"), **era difficile** ("it was unlikely"), **era possibile** ("it was possible"), **era impossibile** ("it was impossible"), **era probabile** ("it was probable"), **era improbabile** ("it was improbable"), etc. are generally followed by an imperfect or past perfect subjunctive. "Era probabile che fossero a casa" ["It was probable (that) they were at home"]. The same expressions may also be followed by the infinitive, as in English. "Era meglio andare via subito" ("It was better to leave / to go away at once").

2) The expressions **era ora , era tempo** ("it was time...") may be followed either by an imperfect subjunctive: "Era ora che loro seguissero i nostri consigli" ("It was time (that) they took our advice") or by the preposition **di** plus the infinitive: "Era tempo di dire pane al pane e vino al vino" ("It was time to call a spade a spade").

1) As with the present subjunctive, the below-mentioned conjunctions and expressions are generally followed by the subjunctive mood. They are followed by an imperfect subjunctive or past perfect subjunctive when the verb of the principal clause is in the past tense:

a) **Affinché**, (perché) (in order that; in order to; so that): "Sono andata dai miei amici affinché (perché) mi aiutassero" ("I went to my friends' in order that they might help me").

Affinché, (*perché*) may be also followed by an infinitive. "Sono andato dai miei amici per farmi aiutare" ("I went to my friends' to get help").

b) **Prima che** (before): "Ho terminato tutto il programma prima che lui partisse" ("I finished the whole program before he left").

Prima may also be followed by the preposition **di** plus the infinitive. "Ho terminato tutto il programma *prima di* pranzare" ("I finished the whole program before having lunch").

c) **Senza che** (without): "Ha fatto tutto da solo senza che nessuno l'aiutasse" ("He did everything by himself without anyone / anybody helping him").

Senza may also be followed by the infinitive. "Sono andata via senza salutare nessuno" ("I left without saying goodbye to anyone / anybody").

d) **Benché, sebbene, malgrado, nonostante, quantunque** (although, in spite of...): "Ieri è uscito benché fosse stanco morto" ("He went out yesterday, even though he was dead tired").

e) **Purché, a patto che, a condizione che,** (provided that, on the condition that): "Mi ha raccontato tutto a patto che non lo dicessi a nessuno" ("He/She told me everything on the condition that I not tell it to anyone").

Page 417 - Box 1

1) The sequence of tenses is very important in determining the relation between the principal clause and the subordinate clause. In Italian, <u>when the verb in the principal clause refers to the present</u> "*Ora penso che... , Adesso penso che...*" ("Now I think that"), it may be followed in the subordinate clause by:

   a) The **Present Subjunctive (Congiuntivo Presente)** if the actions in the principal clause and in the subordinate clause are simultaneous: "Penso (ora) che lui sia qui (ora)" ["I think (now) that he is here (now)"]; or if the action of the subordinate clause refers to the future: "Penso (ora) che parta (domani)" ["I think (now) that he'll leave / he is going to leave / may leave (tomorrow)"]. This last sentence may also be expressed by the future indicative. "Penso (ora) che partirà (domani)" ["I think (now) that he'll leave / he is going to leave (tomorrow)"].

   b) The preposition **di** plus the **Present Infinitive (Infinito Presente)** if the subjects of the principal clause and subordinate clause are the same and if the verb in the subordinate clause expresses a present or future action in relation to the verb in the principal clause. "Penso (ora) di andare (ora)" ["I think (now) I'll go (now)"]; "Penso (ora) di partire (domani)" ["I think (now) I'm going to leave (tomorrow)"]. This last type of sentence requires the future tense in English.

   c) The **Present Perfect Subjunctive (Congiuntivo Passato)** if the verb in the subordinate clause is past in relation to the verb in the principal clause. "Penso (ora) che *sia partito* (ieri)" ["I think (now) that he has left (yesterday)"].

   d) The preposition **di** plus the **Past Infinitive (Infinito Passato)** if the subjects of the principal clause and subordinate clause are the same and if the verb in the subordinate clause is past in relation to the verb in the principal clause. "Penso (ora) di avere finito (ieri)" ["I think (now) I finished (yesterday)"]. This last type of sentence requires the present perfect indicative in English.

Page 417 - Box 2

1) <u>When the verb in the principal clause is in a past tense,</u> it may be followed in the subordinate clause by:

   a) The **Imperfect Subjunctive (Congiuntivo Imperfetto)** if the actions in the principal clause and in the subordinate clause are simultaneous: (Ieri alle 9) "Pensavo che lui partisse" (Ieri alle 9). [(Yesterday at nine o'clock) "I thought he was leaving" (Yesterday at nine o'clock)]; or if the action of the subordinate

104

clause is future in relation to that in the principal clause. (Ieri alle 9) "Pensavo che lui partisse" (Ieri alle 10). [(Yesterday at nine o'clock) "I thought that he was going to leave". (At ten o'clock)].

b) **The Past Perfect Subjunctive (Congiuntivo Trapassato)** if the verb in the subordinate clause is past in relation to the verb in the principal clause: (Ieri alle 9) "Pensavo che lui fosse partito" (Ieri alle 8) [(Yesterday at nine o'clock) "I thought that he had left" (Yesterday at eight o'clock)].

c) The **Conditional Perfect (Condizionale Passato)** if the verb in the subordinate clause is future in relation to that in the principal clause: (ieri alle 9) "Pensavo che lui sarebbe partito" (Ieri alle 10). [(Yesterday at nine o'clock) "I thought that he would leave", (Yesterday at ten o'clock)]. In subordinate clauses which express a future action in the past, the conditional perfect is used in Italian instead of the simple conditional that is often used in English.

d) The preposition **di** plus the **Present Infinitive (Infinito Presente)** if the subjects of the principal clause and subordinate clause are the same and the verb in the subordinate clause expresses a present or future action in relation to the verb in the principal clause. (Ieri alle 9) "Pensavo di partire" (Ieri alle 9). [(Yesterday at nine o'clock) "I thought of leaving" (Yesterday at nine o'clock)]; (Ieri alle 9) "Pensavo di partire" (Ieri alle 10). [(Yesterday at nine o'clock) "I thought I was going to leave" (Yesterday at ten o'clock)].

e) The preposition **di** plus the **Past Infinitive (Infinito Passato)** if the subjects of the principal clause and subordinate clause are the same and the verb in the subordinate clause is past in relation to the verb in the principal clause. (Ieri alle 9) "Pensavo di averti chiamato" (Ieri alle 8). [(Yesterday at nine o'clock) "I thought that I *had called* you" (Yesterday at eight o'clock)]. This last type of sentence requires the past perfect indicative in English.

18 TAKE A LOOK AT THE EVERYDAY LANGUAGE

1. - <u>La sai *l'ultima* di mio fratello Antonio</u>?
   - No, non conosco *l'ultima novità* di tuo fratello, dimmela.
2. - *Che intenzioni ha*? Che cosa vuol fare? Vuol partire o vuol restare?
   - Non so *che cosa si sia messo in testa*.
3. - Tua madre *ha* sempre *avuto un debole* per tuo fratello.
4. - Tu pensi che Giovanni *abbia una simpatia, una preferenza* per me?
   - Sì, penso proprio che *abbia un debole* per te.
5. - Mia madre girava, girava, era *tutta emozionata*.
6. - Enrico, come mai sei *tutto sudato*?
   - Ho fatto una corsa, temevo di arrivare in ritardo.
7. - *Come è andata a finire* l'avven-
     tura in montagna di tuo zio?
   - *È andata a finire bene*, è riusci-
     to a raggiungere il rifugio. Si è
     conclusa bene.
8. - *Dove eri andato a finire*? Ti ab-
     biamo cercato dappertutto.
   - <u>Mi ero messo a</u> fare un pisolino
     in giardino.

- Enrico, come mai sei *tutto sudato*?
- Ho fatto una corsa, temevo di arrivare in ritardo.

A   WHAT'S DIFFERENT

1) The Italian idiomatic expression **"La sai l'ultima...?"** corresponds to the English **"Do you know the latest...?"** as in the sentence "*La sai l'ultima di mio fratello Antonio*?" ("*Do you know the latest about my brother Antonio*?").

2) The Italian expression **Che intenzioni ha?** corresponds to the English **What does he intend to do?** or **What is he going to do?** Consider the sentences "*Che intenzioni ha? Che cosa vuol fare? Vuol partire o vuol restare?*" which translate "*What does he intend to do? What does he want to do? Does he want lo leave, or does he want to stay?*".

3) The idiomatic expression **mettersi qualcosa in testa** translates the English **to**

have an idea about doing something, as in the sentence "Non so *che cosa si sia messo in testa*" ("I don't know *what idea he had in mind*").

4) The idiomatic expression **"avere un debole per qualcuno"** translates the English **"to have a weakness for someone"**, as in the sentence "Tua madre *ha* sempre *avuto un debole per tuo fratello*" ("Your mother *has* always *had a weakness for your brother*").

5) When the Italian adjective **tutto (all)** is used before another adjective, it can have the meaning of "completamente" ("*completely* "). Consider the following sentences. "Mia madre girava, girava, era *tutta emozionata*" ("My mother was pacing and pacing; she was *completely/totally upset* "); "Enrico come mai sei *tutto sudato*?" ("Enrico, how come you're *all sweaty*?").

6) The sentence **Come è andato/a a finire...?** translates the English **How did it end up?**, as in the sentence "*Come è andata a finire l'avventura* in montagna di tuo zio?" ("*How did* your uncle's *adventure* in the mountains *end up*?"). An answer to the abovementioned question could be **E' andata a finire bene/male (It ended well/badly)**, as in the example "*E' andata a finire bene*, è riuscito a raggiungere il rifugio" ("*It ended well*; he managed to reach the shelter").

7) Further, the subject of the idiomatic sentence **"Dove eri andato a finire?"** is "you"; and it may correspond to the English **"Where did you end up?"**.

8) The reflexive verb **mettersi**, followed by the preposition **a** plus an infinitive, means **to begin to do something**, as in the sentence "*Mi ero messo* a fare un pisolino" ("*I had begun* to take a nap").

Sorpresa	– Lui vuole diventare un pittore.	⟹	– Davvero?! – Possibile?! – Tu scherzi!
Chiedere di continuare a raccontare	– E poi? – E allora? E dopo? – Continua! – Dai! Continua!		
Chiedere di concludere	– E allora come è andata a finire? – Insomma, come è finita la cosa?		
Congratulazioni Approvazione	– Ecco il mio quadro.	⟹	– Complimenti! – Bravo! – Tutti i miei complimenti! – Che bravo! – Tu sì che sai dipingere! – Tu sì che sei un artista! – Questo sì che mi piace!
Disapprovazione			– Che schifo! – Ma questa è arte? – Non ci capisco niente! – Dovrebbe cambiare mestiere!

B   HOW TO SAY IT

1) In Italian, in order *to show surprise* (*Sorpresa*), the following expressions may be used.

"Davvero!"	"Really!"
"Possibile?!"	"Is it possible?!"
"Tu scherzi!"	"You're kidding!"

2) In order *to ask someone to go on telling you something* (*Continuare a raccontare*), the following expressions may be used.

"E poi?"	"And then?"
"E allora? E dopo?"	"And then? And after (that)?"
"Continua!"	"Continue!"
"Dai! Continua!"	"Come on! Continue!"

3) In order *to ask someone to conclude a story* (*Chiedere di concludere*), the following expressions may be used.

"E allora come è andata a finire?"   "And then how did it end up?"

"Insomma, come è finita la cosa?"   "Well/In short, how did the situation
                                                              end up?"

4) In order *to show congratulations or approval* (*Congratulazione, approvazione*), there are several phrases which you may use. The following examples are phrases used in the specific situation of admiring someone's work.

"Complimenti!"   "Congratulations!"

"Bravo!"   "Great!" "Well done!"

"Tutti i miei complimenti!"   "Congratulations!"

"Che bravo!"   "How great!"

"Tu sì che sai dipingere!"   "You really know how to paint!"

5) On the contrary, in order *to show disapproval* (*Disapprovazione*) *of someone's work*, the following expressions may be used.

"Che schifo!"   "How disgusting!"

"Ma questa è arte?"   "But this is art?"

"Non ci capisco niente!"   "I don't understand anything about it!"

"Dovrebbe cambiare mestiere!"   "You should change careers!"

19   GRAMMAR IN CONTRAST

1) In Italian, the possibility that an action might be subjected to a condition is generally expressed by a sentence introduced by **se** (if). This type of statement is called the **Periodo Ipotetico (Hypothetical Sentence).** There are three kinds of hypothetical sentences:

   a) **Periodo Ipotetico della Realtà (Hypothetical Sentence of Reality),** where the condition expressed in the subordinate clause is certain and real. "Se verrai, non ti pentirai" ("If you come, you'll not regret it"). In this kind of sentence, the future tense is used in Italian, as in English, to express actions which are probably going to happen at some time in the future. These sentences are generally introduced by **se** (if); but unlike English, the future tense is also used in Italian in the subordinate clause: "Se verrai..." ("If you come"). Sometimes an imperative tense is in the main clause and expresses the consequence. "Se vieni, avvertimi!" ("If you come, let me know!").

   b **Periodo Ipotetico della Possibilità (Hypothetical Sentence of Possibility),** where both the condition and the consequence are uncertain but possible. "Se venissi con te, avrei più fortuna" ("If I came with you, I would be luckier"). In this type of sentence, the verb in the subordinate clause (condition) is expressed by the *imperfect subjunctive*; and the verb in the main clause (consequence), by the *present conditional.*

   c) **Periodo Ipotetico della Impossibilità o Irrealtà (Hypothetical Sentence of Impossibility and Unreality),** where both the condition and the consequence are impossible and not true. "Se avessi le ali, volerei" ("If I had wings, I would fly"). In this type of sentence as well, the verb in the subordinate clause (condition) is expressed by the imperfect subjunctive; and the verb in the main clause (consequence), by the present conditional. There is also another type of "if" sentence of unreality used when the subordinate (conditional) clause is in the past. "Se tu gli avessi scritto, l'avresti fatto contento e ora saresti soddisfatto" ("If you had written to him, you would have made him happy and now you would be satisfied"). In this type of sentence the verb in the subordinate clause is expressed by the perfect conditional.

2) Sometimes a mixture of these tenses (imperfect subjunctive, past perfect subjunctive, present conditional, perfect conditional) may occur in the same sentence, as in the sentences above. Such usage is necessary when the subordinate clause refers to the past while the main clause refers to the present.

"Se tu gli avessi scritto, ora... saresti contento" ("If you had written to him, now... you would be happy").

Page 438 - Box 1/2

1) In Italian, sentences which have <u>present conditional verbs</u> in the main clause: **vorrei** ("I would like"); **desidererei** ("I wish"); **mi piacerebbe** ("I would like"); **bisognerebbe, occorrerebbe, sarebbe necessario** ("it would be necessary"); **sarebbe bello** ("it woul be nice") may be followed by:

   a) the conjunction **che** (that) plus *the* **imperfect subjunctive** when the actions expressed in the main clause and in the subordinate clause are simultaneous. "Vorrei che loro studiassero di più" ("I would like them to study more"). This type of sentence expresses a wish which is possible to realize.

   b) the **past perfect subjunctive** when the action in the subordinate clause is past in comparision with that in the main clause and, therefore, is impossible. "Vorrei che tu avessi studiato di più" ("I would like you to have studied more"). This last type of sentence expresses a strong wish that is now impossible to realize.

   c) an **Infinitive** "Sarebbe bello andarci di persona" ("It would be nice to go there in person").

2) The three structures seen in a), b) and c) above may also be introduced by a main verb in the <u>perfect conditional</u>.

   a) "Avrei voluto che mi telefonasse" ("I would have liked him/her to call me").

   b) "Avrei voluto che loro avessero invitato tutti" ("I would have liked them to have invited everyone").

   c) "Sarebbe stato bello ricevere di persona gli ospiti" ("It would have been nice to receive the guests in person").

   Each of these types of sentences relates a situation which is impossible to realize.

Page 438 - Box 3

1) In Italian, the adverb **Magari** followed by the imperfect subjunctive is used to express a strong hope or a wish perhaps impossible to realize. It corresponds to the English "*If only...*". "Ti piacerebbe fare il giro del mondo? - *Magari avessi* i soldi per farlo!" ("Would you like to go on a trip around the world? - *If only I had* the money to do it!").

2) **Magari** can also be followed by the past perfect subjunctive; in this case it is used to express a strong wish that is now impossible to realize. "Siete andati alla festa di Maria? - *Magari ci avesse invitati!*" ("Did you go to Mary's party? - *If only she had invited* us!").

19 TAKE A LOOK AT THE EVERYDAY LANGUAGE

1. - *Vi state preparando* per la montagna?
   - Sì, *facciamo i preparativi* per la partenza.
2. - Anche domani a pesca?
   - Sicuro. *Solita ora, solito posto*. E tu, Enzo, che cosa fai?
3. - Che facciamo domani? <u>Come al solito</u>?
   - Sì, ci vediamo alla *stessa ora* e allo *stesso posto*.
4. - *Quasi quasi...* mi fai venire la tentazione.
5. - Perché ti fermi sempre davanti alla pasticceria?
   - Dovrei essere forte, dovrei rispettare la dieta, ma *quasi quasi* entro e <u>mi compro</u> una fetta di quel dolce alla panna.
6. - Ho la sensazione che tu <u>mi *porti sfortuna*</u>.
7. - Lo sai che se un gatto nero <u>ti attraversa</u> la strada mentre tu passi, avrai certamente dei guai?
   - Ma <u>non dire sciocchezze</u>! Io non credo che un gatto nero che attraversa la strada *porti sfortuna*.
8. - Se tu avessi cambiato posto, non *saresti rimasto a bocca asciutta*.
   - Già, se ti avessi ascoltato, forse anch'io avrei preso dei pesci.

- Ho la sensazione che tu mi *porti sfortuna*.

A | WHAT'S DIFFERENT

1) The reflexive verb **prepararsi** has several meanings. In this case, it means **to get ready**. So, the sentence "*Vi state preparando* per la montagna?" can be translated "*Are you getting ready* for the mountains?".

2) The adjective **solito** translates the English **same**, **usual**; and often it has the same mening of **stesso**, **same**. Consider the sentences "Anche domani a pesca? -

Sicuro. *Solita ora, solito posto*" ("Are you going fishing tomorrow, too? - Sure. *Same time, same place*"); "Che facciamo domani? *Come al solito*? - Sì, ci vediamo alla *stessa ora* e allo *stesso posto*" ("What are we doing tomorrow? *The usual*? - Yes, we'll see each other at *the same time* and at *the same place*"). The idiomatic expression **"ci vediamo"** corresponds to the English **"We'll see each other"**, and it is very often used to make an appointment.

3) The idiomatic expression **"quasi, quasi"** is very often used to express the idea that perhaps you are going to do something, or that you would like to do something. So, a sentence such as "*Quasi, quasi mi fai venire la tentazione*" can be translated "*I'm almost tempted*".

4) The expression **portare sfortuna** corresponds to the English **to bring bad luck**. So, the sentence "Ho la sensazione che tu *mi porti sfortuna*" can be translated "I have the feeling that *you (may) bring me bad luck*".

5) The expression **Non dire sciocchezze!** may be translated **Don't talk nonsense** or **Don't be silly!**

6) The idiomatic expression **"rimanere a bocca asciutta"** may correspond to the English **"to be disappointed"**. So, the sentence "Se tu avessi cambiato posto, *non saresti rimasto a bocca asciutta*" can be translated "If you had changed places, *you would not have been disappointed*".

Enfasi sull'atto di asserire qualcosa	– Se venissi alla curva del del ponte avrei più fortuna? Dici sul serio?	– Non c'è dubbio. – Sul serio. – Non scherzo. – Davvero. – Ti assicuro.
Delusione, disinganno	– Hai preso molti pesci, sì o no?	– Macché nemmeno uno! – Purtroppo nemmeno uno! – Non dirmi niente!
Dispiacere	– Peccato! – Peccato che tu non abbia preso niente! – Come mi dispiace che non abbia preso niente! – Come mi dispiace!	

B   HOW TO SAY IT

1) In Italian, in order *to give emphasis to what someone asserts* (*Enfasi sull'atto di asserire qualcosa*), you may use the following expressions:

"Non c'è dubbio."   "There isn't any doubt."
"Sul serio."   "Seriously."
"Non scherzo."   "I'm not kidding."
"Davvero."   "Really."
"Ti assicuro."   "I assure you."

2) In order *to express disappointment or disillusion* (*Delusione, disinganno*), you may use expressions such as the following:

"Macché, nemmeno uno!"   "Forget it, not even one!"

"Purtroppo nemmeno uno!"   "Unfortunately, not even one!"

"Non dirmi niente!"   "Don't say anything to me about it!"

3) In order *to express displeasure* (*Dispiacere*), you may use the following expressions in general:

"Peccato!"   "It's a shame!"

"Come mi dispiace!"   "How sorry I am!"

Also, these expressions can be seen in those sentences specific to Unit 19:

"Peccato che tu non abbia preso niente!"   "It's a shame that you didn't catch
                                            anything!"

"Come mi dispiace che non abbia preso   "How sorry I am that you didn't catch
    niente!"   anything!"

20 GRAMMAR IN CONTRAST

Page 458 - Box 1/2/3

1) The Italian **Comparativo di Uguaglianza (Comparision of Equality)** is formed by **così... come** or **tanto... quanto** which translate the English "as... as". As in English the words **così... come** are placed around the adjective or adverb. "E' *tanto* intelligente quanto suo fratello" ("He/She is as intelligent/clever as his/her brother"). **Così** or **tanto** (as / so) are placed before the adjective and **quanto** or **come** (as) after the adjective. Contrary to English, the first term of the comparision "così" or "tanto" is frequently omitted in Italian. "E' gentile come sua sorella" ("He/She is as kind as his/her sister").

2) Unlike English which has two forms for the **Comparativo di Maggioranza (Comparision of Superiority)**, the Italian has only one way of expressing the comparativo di maggioranza. It is formed by placing **più** (more) before the adjective or adverb. "La mia casa è più grande della tua" ("My house is larger than yours"). The second term of the comparision **di** translates the English "than", and it is generally followed by a noun, a pronoun, or an ordinal number.

3) Il **Comparativo di minoranza (Comparision of inferiority)** is formed by placing **meno** (less) before the adjective or adverb and **di** (than) as the second term of the comparision. "Perugia è meno grande di Roma" ("Perugia is smaller than Roma").

Page 458 - Box 4/5

Page 459 - Box 1/2/3

1) In Italian, the conjunction **che** (than) is used when the comparision of superiority or inferiority is between:

   a) *Two adjectives or two qualities*: "Quella ragazza è più *simpatica* che *bella*" ("That girl is nicer than she is beautiful").

   b) *Two nouns or two quantities*: "Ho letto più *romanzi* che *novelle*" ("I have read more novels than short stories").

   c) *Two verbs or two actions*: "E' sicuramente più difficile *scrivere* che *parlare* una lingua" ("It is certainly more difficult to write than to speak a language").

   d) *Two prepositional phrases*: "Mi piace più mangiare *a casa* che *al ristorante*" ("I like eating at home better than in a restaurant").

   e) *Two adverbs*: "Meglio *tardi* che *mai*" ("Better late than never").

Note that when these adjectives, nouns, verbs, phrases and adverbs are subjectsor objects of the same verb, the second term of comparision becomes **che** (than), as in English, instead of *"di"*.

Page 459 - Box 4

1) Unlike the English **Relative Superlative,** the Italian **Superlativo Relativo** has just one form. The superlativo relativo is formed by placing the definite articles before **più** (the most; the... est) and **meno** (the least). "E' stato *il* giorno *più* bello della mia vita" ("It was the most beautiful day of my life"); "E' *la* persona *meno* simpatica che io conosca" ("He/She is the least pleasant person I know").

2) Note that in Italian, sometimes the adjectives may precede the noun as in English. "E' stato il più bel giorno della mia vita" ("It was the most beautiful day of my life").

Page 460 - Box 1/2

1) The Italian **Superlativo Assoluto (Absolute Superlative)** has many forms.

a) The charateristic forms **–issimo –issima –issimi –issime** imply no comparision and correspond to the English forms made by "very + adjective" or "extremely + adjective". "E' un signore gentilissimo" ("He is a very kind man"). This superlative is formed by adding the suffix **–issimo** to the adjective or adverb after dropping the final vowel: "gentil*issimo*" (very kind); "ricch*issimo*" (very rich); "bell*issima*" (very beautiful); "simpatic*issimo*" (very nice). The adjectives ending in **–cco** (like *ricco*) insert an **h** before adding **–issimo** to keep the same original hard sound of the "c". Those ending in **–co** (like *simpatico*) take the ordinary suffixes (*–issimo, –issima, –issimi, –issime*).

b) The absolute superlative is also formed by placing certain adverbs like *molto, tanto, assai* (very) before the adjective or adverb. "E' un signore molto ricco" ("He is a very rich man"); "Arriveremo molto tardi" ("We'll arrive very late").

c) In addition, the absolute superlative may be formed by means of prefixes like *arci–, stra–, ultra–, super–* (very). "Sono arcicontento" ("I'm very happy"); "E' straricco" ("He is super rich"); "E' un prodotto sopraffino" ("It is a first-rate product"). These are special forms used with only a few adjectives.

d) Another way of expressing the absolute superlative is by repeating the adjective. "Questo problema è facile facile" ("This is a very easy problem").

e) Finally, note these forms which are made by combining two adjectives: "Innamorato cotto" ("Head over heels in love"); "Pieno zeppo" ("Crammed full"); "Ricco sfondato" ("Rolling in money"); "Bagnato fradicio" ("Soaked to the skin").

1) Some very common Italian adjectives and adverbs have irregular comparative and superlative forms in addition to the regular forms. These irregular forms: *buono* (good); *più buono / migliore* (better); *il più buono / il migliore* (the best; the better); *buonissimo / ottimo* (very good), etc., have a more general meaning and are used more frequently than the regular ones.

20 TAKE A LOOK AT THE EVERYDAY LANGUAGE

1. - Era molto tempo che lui *le girava attorno*.
2. - Dove va lei, va lui: l'aspetta all'uscita dalla scuola, la ferma per la strada, vuole ballare solo con lei in discoteca, ...
   - Non continuare, ho capito; lui ha una simpatia per lei, *le gira intorno*, le fa la corte.
3. - *Cosa vuoi farci? Al cuore non si comanda*.
   - E' vero, non possiamo prendere nessun provvedimento, non possiamo cambiare niente, il cuore non ascolta consigli, non accetta ordini, l'amore arriva quando meno l'aspetti.
4. - Come si è decisa *a fare questo passo*?
   - Non so come abbia preso la decisione di sposarsi.
•5. - Non accetta le sue attenzioni, le sue gentilezze, le sue premure, insomma, *non vuole saperne di lui*.

A | WHAT'S DIFFERENT

1) The Italian idiomatic expression **"girare attorno"** or **"girare intorno a qualcuno/a"** corresponds in this specific situation to the English **"to court someone"**. So, the sentence "Era molto tempo che lui *le girava attorno*" can be translated "*He has been courting her for a long time*".

2) The idiomatic expression **"che cosa vuoi farci?"** corresponds to the English **"what do you want to do about it?"**. The other idiomatic sentence **"al cuore non si comanda"** may be translated **"you can't control your heart"**.

3) The expression **decidersi a fare questo/quel passo** corresponds to the English **to decide to take this/that step**. So, the sentence "Come si è decisa *a fare questo passo*" may be translated "How did she decide *to take this step*?".

4) The idiomatic sentence **"non vuole saperne di lui"** corresponds to the English **"she doesn't want to know anything about him"**, as in the sentence "Non accetta le sue attenzioni, le sue gentilezze, le sue premure, insomma *non vuole saperne di lui*" ("She doesn't accept his attentions, his favors, his kindnesses, in short *she doesn't want to know anything about him* ").

Sorpresa, incredulità	– Adalgisa si è fidanzata.		– No, non è vero! – È una bugia – È incredibile! – No, non ci credo! – No, non me lo dire!
Auguri	– Si sposeranno prestissimo.		– Auguri, allora! – Auguri di felicità! – Tanti auguri!
Correggersi	– Adesso non è più brutto	anzi al contrario invece	lo ha trovato bello.
Chiedere opinioni o giudizi	– Per me ha fatto una cattiva scelta.	– Tu che ne pensi? – Vorrei sapere cosa ne pensi. – Vorrei la tua opinione. – Che ne dici?	
Domandare accordo su un fatto	– Per me ha fatto una cattiva scelta. No? Non è vero? – Non credi?		
Credere	– Mi pare che abbia fatto bene. – Per me ha fatto bene. – Secondo me ha fatto bene.		
Dubbio	– Non so se ha fatto bene. – Non sono sicuro che abbia fatto bene.		

B HOW TO SAY IT

1) In Italian, in order *to show surprise* or *incredulity* (*Sorpresa, incredulità*), you may use the following expressions:

"No, non è vero!"	"No, it's not true!"
"E' una bugia!"	"It's a lie!"
"E' incredibile!"	"It's incredible!"
"No, non ci credo!"	"No, I don't believe it!"
"No, non me lo dire!"	"No, don't tell me that!" or "No, don't say that to me!"

119

2) In order *to wish something* or *to give someone your wishes* (*Auguri*), you may use the following expressions:

"Auguri, allora!"	"Best wishes!"
"Auguri di felicità!"	"Best wishes for your happiness!"
"Tanti auguri!"	"Best wishes!"

3) In order *to change* or *correct one's own opinion* (*Correggersi*), you may use the following expressions:

"Anzi"	"Rather"
"Al contrario"	"On the contrary"
"Invece"	"Instead"

So, the example "Adesso non è più brutto, anzi/al contrario/invece lo ha trovato bello" may be translated "He is not ugly any more, rather (etc.) she finds him handsome".

4) In order *to ask opinions* or *judgments* (*Chiedere opinioni* o *giudizi*), you may use the following expressions:

"Tu che ne pensi?"	"What do you think about it?"
"Vorrei sapere cosa ne pensi."	"I would like to know what you think about it."
"Vorrei la tua opinione."	"I would like your opinion."
"Che ne dici?"	"What do you have to say about it?"

5) In order *to look for agreement on a fact* (*Domandare accordo su un fatto*), you may use the following expressions:

"No?"	"Right?"
"Non è vero?"	"Isn't it true?"
"Non credi?"	"Don't you believe it?" or "Don't you think so?"

Consider the following example. "Per me ha fatto una cattiva scelta. No? Non è vero? Non credi?" ("To me he has made a bad choice. Right? Isn't it true? Don't you think so?").

6) In order *to say that something seems a certain way to you* (*Parere*), you may use the following sentences:

"Mi pare che abbia fatto bene."	"It seems to me that he has done well."
"Per me ha fatto bene."	"To me, he has done well."
"Secondo me, ha fatto bene."	"According to me, he did well."

7) On the contrary, in order *to express one's own doubt about something* (*Dubbio*), you may use the following expressions:

"Non so se ha fatto bene."	"I don't know whether he has done well."
"Non sono sicuro che abbia fatto bene."	"I'm not sure that he has done well."

21 GRAMMAR IN CONTRAST

Page 480 - Box 1/2/3/4

Page 481 - Box 1

1) The endings of the **Passato Remoto (Simple Past)** are identical in all three conjugations, and they maintain the characteristic vowel of the infinitive (a / e / i). The one exception is in the third person singular of first conjugation verbs (–are), which take **ò**: "andò" ("he/she went"). "Andò a casa dopo quello · spettacolo" ("He/She went home after that performance").

2) Many Italian verbs are irregular in the *passato remoto*: essere (to be); fare (to do, to make); dire (to say, to tell); bere (to drink); dare (to give); stare (to stay); etc. "Feci un'ottima figura all'esame" ("I cut a fine figure at the examination").

Page 481 - Box 2

1) The above-listed verbs are irregular in the first person singular, third person singular and third person plural of the *passato remoto*. However, they are regular in the other three persons. "Ebbi fortuna quel giorno" ("I was lucky that day").

Page 482 - Box 1

1) The **Trapassato Remoto (Past Perfect)** is formed by the simple past (passato remoto) of the helping verb and the past participle of the main verb. It is used only in subordinate clauses introduced by: *quando* ("when"); *appena* ("just..., as soon as..."); *dopo che* ("when, after..."). "Le telefonai appena ebbi ricevuto la sua lettera" ("I phoned her as soon as I had received her letter"). The trapassato remoto is also translated in English by the past perfect.

Page 482 - Box 2

1) The Italian *passato remoto* is generally used to describe actions which took place in the past and have no reference to the present. It is the characteristic historical or narrative tense.

Page 482 - Box 3

1) These adverbs are formed by adding **–mente** to the adjective. If the adjective ends

in –o, the adverb is formed by adding **–mente** to the feminine singular of the adjective: chiaro → **"chiara*mente*"** ("clearly"). If the adjective ends in –**ce**, the adverb is formed by adding **–mente** to the adjective: felice → "felice*mente*" ("happily"). "L'avventura si è risolta felicemente" ("The adventure ended happily"). If the adjective ends in **–le** or **–re**, the adverb is formed by dropping the final "e" and adding **–mente**: regolare → regolar*mente*. "L'autobus passa regolarmente alle 11" ("The bus passes by here regularly at 11 a.m.").

21 TAKE A LOOK AT THE EVERYDAY LANGUAGE

1. - Nonno, *che cosa mi racconti*?
   - Ti racconto una storia di tanti anni fa.
2. - Ciao, Giulio, *che cosa* mi racconti *di bello*?
   - Non ho niente di nuovo, di interessante da raccontarti.
3. - *È sufficiente* il vino per i tuoi amici?
   - Sì, è sufficiente, *basta*.
4. - Ti bastano i soldi per la gita?
   - Sì, sono sufficienti, mi *bastano*.
5. - Posso continuare la spiegazione?
   - No, hai parlato abbastanza, *basta* così.
6. - *Apri bene le orecchie*! Ascoltami con attenzione!
7. - Conosci questa storia? Sì? Va bene, (ciò) *vuol dire*, che te ne racconterò un'altra.
8. - Non trova mai il tempo per scrivermi: (ciò) *vuol dire* che non mi vuol bene!
9. - *Uffa*! Che caldo oggi!!
10. - E' un'ora che parla, *uffa* che noia!!

- E' un'ora che parla, *uffa* che noia!!

A | WHAT'S DIFFERENT

1) Italian sentences such as "*Ti racconto* una storia *di tanti anni fa*" and "*Che cosa mi racconti di bello*?" may be translated "*I am telling* you a story *about many years ago*" and "*What can you tell me that's nice*".

2) The word **basta** has many different meanings and uses in Italian.

   a) It can be a verb **bastare (to be enough/sufficient)**, as seen in the following sentence. "È sufficiente il vino per i tuoi amici? - Sì, è sufficiente, *basta*" ("Is the wine sufficient for your friends? - Yes, it's sufficient; *it's enough*"); "Ti bastano i soldi per la gita? - Sì, sono sufficienti, *mi bastano*" ("Do *you have enough money* for the trip? - Yes, it's sufficient; *I have enough*").

b) It can also be an interjection: **Basta! (Stop!)**. In this use, it expresses your wish to stop someone from continuing to do something, as in this example. "Posso continuare la spiegazione? - No, hai parlato abbastanza, *basta così*" ("Can/May I continue the explanation? - No, you have talked enough; *stop right there*").

c) The expression **Basta!** may also be used independently, apart from a specific sentence, in order to stop someone from continuing to do something.

3) The idiomatic expression **"Apri bene le orecchie"** is used to catch someone's attention; it may be translated **"Pay close attention"**.

4) The expression **(ciò) vuol dire** corresponds to the English **that means**, as in the sentence "Non trova mai il tempo per scrivermi: *(ciò) vuol dire* che non mi vuole bene!" ("He/She never finds the time to write to me: *that means* that he/she doesn't love me!").

5) The very idiomatic form **"Uffa!"** is used to express your intolerance of something very boring or something you cannot stand, as seen in the sentence "*Uffa che caldo oggi!*" ("*Ugh*! How hot it is today!").

Noia	– C'era una volta un re che aveva tre figlie.	– Uffa! – Che barba! – Basta!
Interrompere la comunicazione	– Basta! – Basta così! – Zitto! – Silenzio!	
Proseguire	– Cosa stavo dicendo? Ah, dicevo di quando... – Allora dicevo di quando... – Dunque dicevo...	

B   HOW TO SAY IT

1) In Italian, in order *to express boredom* (*Noia*) with something, you may use the following expressions:

"Uffa!"   "Ugh!"

"Che barba!"   "What a bore!"

"Basta!"   "Enough!" / "That's enough!"

2) In order *to interrupt communication* (*Interrompere la comunicazione*) with someone in an abrupt manner, you may use the following expressions:

"Basta!"	"Enough!"
"Basta così!"	"That's enough!"
"Zitto!"	"Be quiet!"/"Shut up!"
"Silenzio!"	"Silence!"

3) In order *to go on talking* (*Proseguire*), you may use expressions such as these:

"Cosa stavo dicendo? Ah, dicevo di quando..."	"What was I saying? Oh, I was telling about when..."
"Allora, dicevo di quando..."	"OK, I was telling about when..."
"Dunque dicevo..."	"Well then, I was saying...".

22 GRAMMAR IN CONTRAST

Page 502 - Box 1/2/3

1) The Italian **Forma Passiva (Passive Voice)** of transitive verbs is formed, as it is in English, by using the verb **essere** followed by the past participle of the main verb. "Il meccanico ripara la macchina → La macchina è riparata dal meccanico" ("The mechanic repairs the car. → The car is repaired by the mechanic"). The past participle agrees with the subject, and in the compound tenses both past participles agree with the subject. The tense of the auxiliary verb *"essere"* is the same as the time of the action which is being made passive. "Il professore ha spiegato una nuova lezione. → Una nuova lezione è stata spiegata dal professore" ("The teacher has explained a new lesson → A new lesson has been explained by the teacher"); "Il professore spiegò una nuova lezione → Una nuova lezione fu spiegata dal professore" ("The teacher explained a new lesson → A new lesson was explained by the teacher").

2) Unlike English, there are different ways to form the passive in Italian. The auxiliary **venire** (to come) is often used instead of the auxiliary *essere*. "Il professore spiega una nuova lezione → Una nuova lezione *viene* spiegata dal professore" ("The teacher explains a new lesson → A new lesson is explained by the teacher").

3) In forming a passive verb, we must remember that many intransitive English verbs are transitive in Italian such as: *ascoltare* (to listen to). Others are transitive in English and not in Italian such as: *domandare a qualcuno* (to ask someone).

Page 503 - Box 2

1) In the Italian passive form, the past participle of the main verb must always agree with the subject. "Chi mi ha invitato? → Da chi sono stato/a invitato/a?" ("Who invited me? → By whom have I been invited?").

Page 504 - Box 1

1) When the verb *dovere* (must; to have to) is followed by an infinitive, the past participle must agree with the subject in the passive. "Devi scrivere questa lettera → Questa lettera deve essere scritta / va scritta" ("You have to write this letter → This letter must be written").

127

1) In Italian another way to form the passive voice is by using the particle **si** called "particella passivante". **Si** followed by the third person singular or plural of the verb makes the verb itself passive. "Si comprano pochi giornali in Italia" ("Few newspapers are bought in Italy"); "Assegni circolari si accettano in questo negozio" ("Bank drafts are accepted in this store / shop").

22 TAKE A LOOK AT THE EVERYDAY LANGUAGE

1. - Roma fu fondata nel 753 a.C. (avanti Cristo).
2. - Quando conosceremo i risultati delle analisi?
   - Entro domani, ma *non è escluso* che si possano conoscere anche stasera.
3. - *Non si esclude* di trovare al centro del tumulo una grande camera sepolcrale.
4. - Che cosa pensano di trovare gli esperti?
   - *Ci si aspetta* di trovare una sepoltura centrale.
5. - Lui sarebbe capace di fare un'azione così riprovevole?
   - Da lui *ci si può aspettare* di tutto.
6. - Quando finiranno i lavori?
   - *Al momento*, i lavori sono stati sospesi.
7. - È tutto quello che si sa *per ora*?
   - Sì, *al momento* queste sono le sole notizie.

- Quando finiranno i lavori?
- *Al momento*, i lavori sono stati sospesi.

A WHAT'S DIFFERENT

1) The Italian phrase **Entro domani** corresponds to the English **By tomorrow**.

2) The Italian expression **Non è escluso che...** corresponds to the English idiom **It's not out of the question that...**

3) The impersonal Italian expression **Non si esclude di...** corresponds to the English **They can't exclude the possibility of...**

4) The Italian passive forms **ci si aspetta** and **ci si può aspettare** correspond to the English **they expect**, as in the sentences seen in Unit 22. "*Ci si aspetta di trovare* una sepoltura centrale*" ("*They expect to find* a central tomb"). Also, "Da lui *ci si può aspettare* di tutto" ("*You can expect* anything from [of] him").

5) The expressions **al momento** and **per ora** have the same meaning. So, the sentence "Quando finiranno i lavori? - *Al momento*, i lavori sono stati sospesi" may be translated "When will they finish work? - *For now*, work has been stopped". The question "E' tutto quello che si sa *per ora*?" may be translated "Is that all they know *for now*?".

Interesse		– Questo mi interessa molto! – Molto interessante!
Indifferenza	– Una grande necropoli è stata scoperta vicino a Roma.	– E con ciò? – Che m'importa? – Non m'importa affatto! – E allora? – Me ne frego. – Me ne infischio! – E a me...?

B   HOW TO SAY IT

1) In Italian, in order *to show one's own interest in something which happened* (*Interesse*), you may use the following expressions:

"Questo mi interessa molto!"	"This interests me a lot!"
"Molto interessante!"	"Very interesting!"

2) In order *to show one's own complete disinterest in something which happened* (*Indifferenza*), you may use the following expressions:

"E con ciò?"	"So what?"
"Che m'importa?"	"What do I care?"
"Non m'importa affatto!"	"It doesn't matter to me at all!"
"E allora?"	"So what?"
"Me ne frego."	"I don't give a damn."
"Me ne infischio!"	"I couldn't care less!"
"E a me...?"	"What difference does it make to me?"

23 GRAMMAR IN CONTRAST

Page 521 - Box 1/2/3/4/5/6

Page 522 - Box 1

1) When we transform **direct speech** introduced by a verb in the past tense to **indirect speech**, we have to make some changes in the structure of the sentence.

   a) If there is a simple present (*presente*) in *direct speech*, there is an imperfect (*imperfetto*) in *indirect speech*. "Egli disse: 'Non posso farci niente' → Egli disse che non poteva farci niente" ("He said, 'I can't do anything about it' → He said that he couldn't do anything about it").

   b) If there is a present perfect (*passato prossimo*) in *direct speech*, there is a past perfect (*trapassato prossimo*) in *indirect speech*. "Dichiarò: 'Ho fatto il possibile' → Dichiarò che aveva fatto il possibile" ("He declared, 'I have done my best' → He declared that he had done his best").

   c) If there is a simple past (*passato remoto*) in *direct speech*, there is a past perfect (*trapassato prossimo*) in indirect speech. "Gridò: 'Non fui io il responsabile' → Gridò che non era stato lui il responsabile" ("He shouted, 'I was not liable' →He shouted that he hadn't been liable").

   d) If there is a simple future (*futuro semplice*) in *direct speech*, there is a conditional perfect (*condizionale composto*) in *indirect speech*. "Comunicarono: 'Verremo prima possibile' → Comunicarono che sarebbero venuti prima possibile" ("They advised, 'We shall come as soon as possibile → They advised that they would come as soon as possibile"). Note that unlike Italian, the simple conditional tense is often used in the corresponding English sentence.

   e) If there is a simple future (*futuro semplice*) in *direct speech*, there is a simple future (*futuro semplice*) also in *indirect speech*, but only when the action has not yet occurred.

   "Stamattina mi ha promesso: 'Telefonerò domani → Stamattina mi ha promesso che telefonerà domani" ("This morning he promised me, 'I'll phone tomorrow' → This morning he promised me that he will phone tomorrow").

   f) If there is a present conditional (*condizionale semplice*) in *direct speech*, there is a conditional perfect (*condizionale composto*) in *indirect speech*. "Disse: 'Non farei mai una cosa simile' → Disse che non avrebbe mai fatto una cosa simile" ("He said , 'I would never do such a thing' → He said that he never would have done such a thing"). Note that in this sentence also the present conditional may be used in English instead of the conditional perfect.

g) If there is an imperative (*imperativo*) in *direct speech*, there is an imperfect subjunctive (*congiuntivo imperfetto*) or an infinitive (*infinito*) in *indirect speech*. "Lei implorò: 'Aspetta e aiutami!'. → Lei implorò che aspettassi e la aiutassi / di aspettare e di aiutarla" ("She implored, 'Wait and help me!' → She implored me to wait and help her"). Note that in this sentence, generally the infinitive is used in English.

Page 522 - Box 2

1) Other changes are necessary when changing from direct speech to indirect speech.

   a) *Personal pronouns* normally change from the first or second person to the third person. "Mi disse: 'L'ho fatto io' → Mi disse che l'aveva fatto lui" ("He said to me, 'I did it' → He told me that he had done it").

   b) *Possessive adjectives* also change from the first or second person to the third person. "Mi disse: 'Mio figlio studia a Torino' → Mi disse che suo figlio studiava a Torino" ("He said to me, 'My son studies in Torino' → He told me that his son studied in Torino").

   c) *Adverbs and adverbial phrases* of place and time change too. "Mi disse: 'Resta qui' → Mi disse di restare lì" ("He said to me, 'Stay here' → He told me to stay there"); "Mi disse: 'Verrò fra poco' → Mi disse che sarebbe venuto dopo poco" ("He said to me, 'I'll come shortly' → He told me that he would come shortly").

   d) When we change direct questions into indirect speech, some structural changes are necessary: the interrogative form of the verb changes to the declarative form; the question mark is omitted; and indirect speech is often introduced by **se** ("whether"). "Mi ha detto: 'Posso entrare?' → Mi ha chiesto se poteva entrare" ("He said to me, 'May I come in?' → He asked me whether he could / might come in").

   e) When we change commands or requests into indirect speech, the indirect commands or requests are generally expressed by the infinitive. "Mi disse: 'Vieni con me!' → Mi ordinò di andare con lui" ("He said to me, 'Come with me!' → He ordered me to go with him").

23 TAKE A LOOK AT THE EVERYDAY LANGUAGE

1. - *Che cosa c'è di strano*? C'è tanta gente che non ha l'automobile e perché dovrei averla io?
2. - Mario, ha messo un orecchino?
   - *Che cosa c'è di strano*? Oggi tanti ragazzi lo mettono.
3. - Perché mi guarda così? Le pare che *io abbia la faccia di uno* che dovrebbe avere l'automobile?
4. - Perché non compri quell'impermeabile unisex?
   - *Ho la faccia di uno* che porta l'unisex?
5. - L'aspettiamo davanti alla porta di casa sua?
   - Certo, se vuol tornare a casa *dovrà pur* passare per qui.
6. - È splendido questo panorama, *non ti pare*?
   - Sono d'accordo, è veramente incantevole.
7. - *Ti pare bello* avere rifiutato il prestito a Giovanni?
   - Hai ragione, ho fatto male a rifiutarglielo.
8. - E adesso dovrei comprare un'auto per far piacere a Lei? Ma sa che *Lei è un bel tipo*?
9. - Alzati e vai a vedere se è rimasta qualche luce accesa.
   - Secondo te dovrei alzarmi e fare il giro del castello? Ma sai che *sei un bel tipo*? Hai certe pretese!

- È splendido questo panorama, *non ti pare*?
- Sono d'accordo, è veramente incantevole.

A | WHAT'S DIFFERENT

1) The expression **Che cosa c'è di strano?** corresponds to the English **What's so strange?**, as in the sentence "*Che cosa c'è di strano*? C'è tanta gente che non ha l'automobile e perché dovrei averla io?" ("*What's so strange*? There are a lot of people who don't have a car, and why should I have one?").

2) Questions such as "*Le pare che io abbia la faccia di uno che* dovrebbe avere l'automobile?" and "*Ho la faccia di uno che* porta l'unisex?" may be translated "*Do I look like a person who* should have a car?" and "*Do I look like a person who* would wear unisex clothes?"

3) The expression **dovrà pur** corresponds to the English **He will have to... as well**. So, the sentence "Certo, se vuol tornare a casa *dovrà pur* passare per qui" may be translated "Sure, if he wants to return home, *he will have* to pass by here *as well*".

4) The idiomatic questions **"ti pare?"** and **"non ti pare?"** correspond to the English **"Do you think so?"** and **"Don't you think so?"**. So, the sentence "È splendido questo panorama, *non ti pare*?" can be translated "This panorama is splendid, *don't you think so?*".

5) The idiomatic question **"ti pare bello...?"** corresponds to the English **"Does it seem right to you?"**. So, the sentence "*Ti pare bello* avere rifiutato il prestito a Giovanni?" may be translated "*Does it seem right to you* to have refused Giovanni the loan?".

6) The idiomatic sentences **"Lei è un bel tipo!"** and **"Tu sei un bel tipo!"** correspond to the English "**You are really funny** (in the sarcastic sense)**!**" or "**You are a real piece of work!**". So, the sentence "E adesso dovrei comprare un'auto per far piacere a Lei? Ma sa che *Lei è un bel tipo*?" may be translated "And now I should buy a car to please you? But do you know that *you're a real piece of work*?".

7) The Italian preposition **secondo** corresponds to the English compound preposition **according to**, as in the phrase *secondo te* ("*according to you*").

Chiedere di esplicitare	– Non capisco perché quando uno dice 'Torino' dovrebbe, secondo Lei, andarci in automobile. – Va bene, ma allora Lei, cosa vuole da me? – Cosa vuole dire? – Scusi, non è chiaro. – Vuole essere più chiaro? – Mi faccia capire.

B HOW TO SAY IT

1) In Italian, in order *to ask someone to be more clear in expressing his/her ideas* (*Chiedere di esplicitare*), you may use sentences such as those seen in Unit 23.

"Non capisco perché quando uno dice 'Torino' dovrebbe, secondo Lei, andarci in automobile."

"I don't understand why when someone says 'Torino', he should, according to you, go there by car."

"Va bene, ma allora Lei, cosa vuole da me?"
"OK, granted, but what do you want from me?"

"Cosa vuole dire?"

"What are you trying to say?"

"Scusi, non è chiaro."

"Excuse me, you're/it's not clear."

"Vuole essere più chiaro?"

"Can you be clearer?"

"Mi faccia capire."

"Let me understand."

24 GRAMMAR IN CONTRAST

Page 542 - Box 1/2/3/4

Page 543 - Box 1/2/3/4

1) The **Infinito (Infinitive)** is used in Italian:

a) In the exclamatory and interrogative comments: "Non poter partire! Che sfortuna!" ("Not to be able to leave! How unlucky!"); "Che dire? Che fare in quella situazione?" ("What's there to say and what's there to do in that situation?").

b) *As an imperative:* "Non sporgersi dal finestrino" ("Don't lean out of the window").

c) *As a noun:* "Hai il dovere di parlare" ("It is your duty to talk").

d) *As an English gerund:* "Il viaggiare e il vedere altri paesi mi dà soddisfazione" ("Travelling and seeing other countries gives me satisfaction").

e) *As a subject:* "Fumare non fa bene alla salute" ("Smoking is not good for your health").

f) *As an object:* "Non amo viaggiare" ("I don't like travelling"). The infinitive as a subject or as an object can also be preceded by the definite article: il viaggiare ("travelling"). When the Italian present infinitive has the function of a subject or an object, it corresponds to the English gerund, which ends in **–ing**. This form is also called the verbal substantive (sostantivo verbale): il viaggiare ("travelling"); lo scrivere ("writing"). Unlike English, the present infinitive is used in Italian after forms such as: *prima di...* ("before"); senza ("without..."); prima di partire ("before leaving"). The same forms are generally followed by the gerund in English.

g) After prepositions: "Voglio imparare a giocare a tennis" ("I want to learn to play tennis").

h) After conjugated verbs: "Posso trovare la strada di casa" ("I can find my way home").

2) **The past infinitive (infinito passato)** is formed by the infinitive of the auxiliary verb plus the past participle of the main verb. "È finito sotto al tavolo dopo aver bevuto tre litri di birra" ("He ended up under the table after having drunk three litres of beer"). Note that in Italian when **dopo** (after) is followed by an infinitive, it is always in the perfect tense.

1) Unlike English the conjunction **dopo** (after) is always followed by a past infinitive in Italian. "Dopo aver pranzato prendo un caffè" ("After having dined / dining, I have a coffee"). This sentence is equivalent to: "Dopo che ho pranzato prendo un caffè" ("After I have dined, I have a coffee"). The first is called **forma implicita**; the second, **forma esplicita**. When changing the first sentence into the second, we have to pay attention to the verb in the main sentence.

1) The Italian **Participio Presente (Present Participle)** is formed by adding: **–ante / –ente / –ente** to the stem of first, second and third conjugation infinitives, respectively. It is used in Italian as:

   a) *An adjective:* "E' un film divertente" ("It is an amusing film").

   When the Italian present participle has an adjectival function, it also corresponds to the English adjectival form ending in **–ing**. "Sei sempre sorridente" ("You are always smiling").

   b) *A noun:* "E' una stupenda cantante" ("She is a wonderful singer").

   c) *A verbal adjective:* "Tutte le famiglie abitanti in questo palazzo devono lasciare lo stabile" ("All families living in this building must leave it").

2) The Italian **Past participle (Participio Passato)** is used as:

   a) *An adjective:* "Ho comprato una rivista illustrata" ("I have bought an illustrated magazine").

   b) *A noun:* "Gli ospiti non sono ancora arrivati" ("The guests have not arrived yet").

   c) *A verb:* "Maria è andata a ballare" ("Mary has gone dancing"); "Ho studiato l'Italiano per due anni" ("I studied Italian for two years").

1) In Italian, as in English, *the present participle* can be used when it is the equivalent of a relative clause. "Gli studenti frequentanti il corso medio, sono in aumento" → "Gli studenti che frequentano il corso medio sono in aumento" ("Students attending the intermediate course are increasing" → "Students who attend the intermediate course are increasing").

The abovementioned sentences are equivalent, but the first is called **forma implicita**; the second, **forma esplicita**. When changing from the first sentence to the second, we have to pay attention to the verb in the main sentence.

2) Generally, the past participle is used in the same way in English as in Italian. "Uscito di casa, non disse più una parola" ("Having left home, he didn't say a word").

In Italian, when the reference in the participial phrase is the same as the subject of the sentence, the past participle may be placed at the very beginning of the sentence. "Preoccupato per il ritardo del figlio, uscì per cercarlo" ("Worried about his son's being late, he went out to look for him"). Please note that in English as well, the past participle may be placed at the very beginning of the sentence. Furthermore, in Italian when the reference in the participial phrase is different from the subject of the sentence, the past participle may still by placed at the very beginning of the sentence. "Partita la zia, si mise a piangere" ("His aunt having left, he started to cry"). Please note that in English the past participle may not be placed at the beginning of the phrase in this type of sentence.

| Page 546 - Box 3 |

| Page 547 - Box 1/2/3/4 |

| Page 548 - Box 1 |

1) The Italian **Gerundio Presente (Gerund)** is formed by adding **–ando** / **–endo** / **–endo** to the stem of first, second and third conjugation infinitives, respectively. It is used in Italian as:

a) *A means:* "Imparai molto leggendo" ("I learned a lot by reading"). This use of the gerund corresponds to the English form ending in **–ing** when it is preceded by the preposition **by**.

b) *A way or manner:* "Mi ha raccontato le sue avventure piangendo" ("Crying, he told me his adventures").

c) *A coincidence:* "Lo incontrai uscendo di casa" ("I met him on leaving the house"). Please note that in this usage the Italian gerund can only refer to the subject.

d) A cause or reason: "Fumando e bevendo si è rovinato la salute" ("By smoking and drinking, he ruined his health").

e) *A condition:* "Facendo così, non risolverai niente" ("Acting like this / behaving like this, you will not resolve anything"). Unlike Italian, the English form corresponding to the Italian gerund is often introduced by prepositions such as: "on", "upon", "at", "in", "by", etc.

2) The Italian **Past Gerund (Gerundio Passato)** is formed by the gerund of the auxiliary verbs *essere* or *avere* followed by the past participle of the main verb. "Essendo arrivati in ritardo, non entrammo" ("Having arrived late, we didn't get in").

Page 548 - Box 2

1) In Italian, the *gerund* can also be used when it is equivalent to a clause of time, cause, or condition. "Fumando così, ti rovinerai la salute" → "Se fumerai così, ti rovinerai la salute" ("By smoking like this, you are going to ruin your health" → " If you smoke like this, you are going to ruin your health"); "Lo incontro uscendo di casa" → "Lo incontro quando esco di casa" ("I meet him on leaving the house" → "I meet him when I leave the house").

24 TAKE A LOOK AT THE EVERYDAY LANGUAGE

1. - Da dove comincia questa storia?
   - La storia *prende il via* da un episodio quasi insignificante.
2. - Il potente signore non vuole che il povero parroco celebri il matrimonio di Renzo e Lucia?
   - Sì, *per mezzo* dei "bravi" *lo ha diffidato dal* benedire il loro matrimonio.
3. - *Per amor del cielo*! Quando dico niente o è niente o è una cosa che non posso dire.
4. - Stasera riferirò a tuo padre che mi hai rubato dei soldi.
   - *Per amor del cielo*, non dirglielo!
5. - Ludovico, che fai con l'orecchio alla parete?
   - *Taci*, sta zitta, altrimenti non sento quello che dicono i nostri vicini.

- Ludovico, che fai con l'orecchio alla parete?
- *Taci*, sta zitta, altrimenti non sento quello che dicono i nostri vicini.

A   WHAT'S DIFFERENT

1) The Italian expression **Prendere il via** is often followed by the preposition **da** plus a noun and means **to start**. So, the sentence "La storia *prende il via da* un episodio quasi insignificante" may be translated "The story *starts with* an almost insignificant episode".

2) The expression **per mezzo di** corresponds to the English **by** or **through**; and the verb **diffidare**, to the verbs **to distrust** or **to warn**. So, the sentence "... *per mezzo dei 'bravi' lo ha diffidato dal benedire il loro matrimonio*" may be translated "... *by means of the 'bravi', he threatened him not to bless their marriage*" (This last sentence is a reference to *The Betrothed* by Alessandro Manzoni. The original Italian title is *I promessi sposi*).

3) The idiomatic exclamation **"Per amor del cielo!"** corresponds to the English **"For the love of heaven!"**. So, the sentence "*Per amor del cielo non dirglielo!*" may be translated "*For the love of heaven, don't tell him!*".

4) The verb **tacere** translates the English verbs **to be silent** or **to be quiet**. In this imperative form **taci! (be quiet!)**, it expresses a sharp order to be quiet. So, the sentence "*Taci, sta zitta*, altrimenti non sento quello che dicono i nostri vicini" may be translated "*Be quiet, shut up,* otherwise I won't hear what our neighbours are saying!".

Lamentarsi	– Povero me! – Dio mio!	
Domandare l'intenzione dell'interlocutore nel dire qualcosa	– Come niente?	Che cosa vorrebbe farmi credere? Che cosa vuole dire? Dove vuol arrivare?
Supplicare	– Per l'amor del cielo, tacete! – Per l'amor di Dio, tacete!	

B | HOW TO SAY IT

1) In Italian, in order *to complain* (*Lamentarsi*), such exclamations as the following may be used.

"Povero me!"   "Poor me!"

"Dio mio!"   "My God!"

2) In order *to ask someone in an abrupt way what someone really means and what his/her intentions are in saying something* (*Domandare l'intenzione dell'interlocutore nel dire qualcosa*), you may use the sentences such as the following:

"Che cosa vorrebbe farmi credere?"   "What would you have me believe?"

"Che cosa vuole dire?"   "What do you mean?"

"Dove vuole arrivare?"   "What are you getting at?"

3) In order *to beseech or to plead with someone* (*Supplicare*), you may use exclamations such as the following:

"Per l'amor del cielo!"   "For the love of heaven!"

"Per l'amor di Dio!"   "For the love of God!"

In the following examples, these expressions are used in a specific situation which pleads with people to be silent.

"Per l'amor del cielo, tacete!"   "For the love of heaven, be quiet!"

"Per l'amor di Dio, tacete!"   "For the love of God, be quiet!"

EXERCISES

Units 1-2

A) *Insert the correct forms of the "articolo determinativo", and change the nouns to the plural.*

Example: posto, **il** posto → i posti

1) . . . . . . Treno	→	10) . . . . . Parete	→ . . . . . .
2) . . . . . . Ragazza	→	11) . . . . . Banco	→ . . . . . .
3) . . . . . . Signore	→	12) . . . . . Borsa	→ . . . . . .
4) . . . . . . Lavoro	→	13) . . . . . Stazione	→ . . . . . .
5) . . . . . . Lingua	→	14) . . . . . Giornale	→ . . . . . .
6) . . . . . . Banca	→	15) . . . . . Matita	→ . . . . . .
7) . . . . . . Professore	→	16) . . . . . Chiave	→ . . . . . .
8) . . . . . . Foglio	→	17) . . . . . Passaporto	→ . . . . . .
9) . . . . . . Segretaria	→	18) . . . . . Signora	→ . . . . . .

B) *Insert the correct form of the adjective, and change the sentences to the plural.*

Example:

Americano   Il ragazzo è   americano . . . . → I ragazzi sono americani .

1) *Straniero*   La ragazza è . . . . → . . . .

2) *Italiano*   Il signore è . . . . → . . . .

3) *Libero*   La sedia è . . . . → . . . .

4) *Occupato*   Il posto è . . . . → . . . .

5) *Aperto*   La banca è . . . . → . . . .

6) *Chiuso*   La segreteria è . . . . → . . . .

7) *Bravo*   Il professore è . . . . → . . . .

8) *Bello*   La cosa è . . . . → . . . .

9) *Moderno*   La stazione è . . . . → . . . .

10) Scomodo   Il banco è . . . .   → . . . .

11) Gentile   Il ragazzo è . . . .   → . . . .

12) Grande   La macchina è . . . .   → . . . .

13) Piccolo   La scuola è . . . .   → . . . .

14) Comodo   Il treno è . . . .   → . . . .

C) *Complete the following sentence with the correct forms of the verb ESSERE,and insert the prepositions* **Di, A, AL, ALLA, IN** *when they are necessary.*

Example: Paul . . . . . . un ragazzo americano . . . . . Boston.

            Paul   è   un ragazzo americano   di   Boston.

1) Paul e Marianne . . . . . stranieri, lui . . . . Boston, lei . . . . Zurigo.

2) Lei . . . . . italiana? Sì, ... Roma.

3) . . . . . dove . . . . . il professore? . . . . Firenze.

4) Le signorine non . . . . . . straniere, ... Perugia.

5) Maria non . . . . casa oggi.

6) I ragazzi . . . . Perugia, ... Italia per la prima volta.

7) Dove . . . . . . i ragazzi? . . . . treno.

8) Dove . . . . . . Anna? . . . . banca.

D) *Complete the following questions with the "Pronomi interrogativi"* **chi, che cosa,** *and insert the correct form of the verbs AVERE and ESSERE.*

Example: . . . . . è? . . . . . ragazzo straniero.

            Chi   è?   È un   ragazzo straniero.

1) . . . . Maria? È una ragazza italiana.

2) . . . . Paul? Ha una macchina nuova.

3) . . . . Paul e Marianne? Sono due ragazzi stranieri.

4) . . . . Una penna.

5) . . . . È il professore.

6) . . . . Sono i libri di Anna.

7) . . . . È la borsa della signora.

8) . . . . Sono delle chiavi.

9) . . . . un foglio? Paul ha un foglio.

10) . . . . ? È il passaporto di Paul.

E) *Insert the correct forms of* **c'è, ci sono** *and the "articoli indeterminativi" in the following sentences.*

Example: Sul tavolo . . . . libro.

            Sul tavolo   c'è   un   libro.

1) Sulla sedia . . . . giornale.

2) Nella borsa . . . . penne.

3) Sul banco . . . . quaderno.

4) Nella macchina . . . . chiave.

5) Sulla scrivania . . . . fotografia.

6) Nella valigia . . . . vestiti.

7) Nel bicchiere non . . . . niente.

8) Nella stanza . . . . oggetti.

F) *Translate the following sentences into Italian.*

Example: My name is Anna; I am an Italian girl.

            Mi chiamo Anna; sono una ragazza italiana.

1) What is your name? My name is Paul.

. . . .

2) Who is Marianne? Marianne is a Swiss girl.

. . . .

3) I am a foreign student.

. . . .

4) Paul and Marianne are foreigners; Paul is from Boston; Marianne, from Zurigo.

. . . .

5) We are in Italy, in Perugia for the first time.

. . . .

6) Where are the students? The students are in the classroom.

. . . .

7) I am in Italy to learn Italian.

. . . .

8) Do you have a pen?

. . . .

9) There are twelve students in the classroom.

. . . .

10) What do you have on your desk?

. . . .

EXERCISES

Units 3-4

A) *Complete the following sentences adding the endings of each verb, and read the sentences aloud without repeating the subjects.*

Example: (Io) aspett . . . . il treno che arriv . . . . da Roma.

           Aspetto   il treno che arriva   da Roma.

1) (Loro) part . . . . alle dieci per andare a Firenze.

2) Che cosa (tu) stud . . . . in classe?

3) Generalmente (io) prend . . . . un succo di frutta al bar.

4) (Lei) studi . . . . a Perugia? No, (io) studi. . . . a Roma.

5) (Noi) cap . . . . quando il professore parla.

6) (Tu) cap . . . . l'italiano? Sì, (io) cap . . . . bene l'italiano.

7) Che cosa (voi) mangi . . . . a colazione? (Noi) mang . . . . della frutta.

8) (Loro) fin . . . . di studiare e poi ved . . . . la TV.

9) (Io) aspett . . . . Maria alla stazione, (Lei) arriv . . . . alle due.

10) (Lui) cap . . . . e parl . . . . bene l'inglese.

11) Dove (tu) abit . . . . ? (Io) abit . . . . in campagna.

12) (Lei) prefer . . . . vivere in città o in campagna?

B) *Insert the correct forms of the verbs: ANDARE, FARE, STARE, and read the sentences aloud without repeating the subjects.*

Example (Io) . . . . sempre al cinema.

           Vado   sempre al cinema.

1) Che cosa (tu) . . . . ? (Io) . . . . a casa a studiare.

2) Come (Lei) . . . . ? (Io) . . . . abbastanza bene.

3) Che cosa (noi) . . . . stasera? (Noi) . . . . a teatro.

4) (Tu) . . . . all'università o (tu) . . . . a casa?

5) (Lei) non . . . . mai in discoteca.

6) (Tu) . . . . spesso al ristorante?

7) Che cosa . . . . (Lei) il fine settimana?

C) *Insert the correct forms of the "articoli (determinativi e indeterminativi)" ,and change the sentences to the plural).*

Example: . . . . amico è straniero. Ho . . . . amico straniero.

        a) L'amico è straniero. Ho un amico straniero

        b) Gli amici sono stranieri. Ho (degli) amici stranieri.

1) . . . . amica è italiana. Ho . . . . amica italiana.

. . . .

2) . . . . ufficio è piccolo. Abbiamo . . . . ufficio piccolo.

. . . .

3) . . . . università è antica. Abbiamo . . . . università antica.

. . . .

4) . . . . escursione è lunga. Facciamo . . . . escursione lunga.

. . . .

5) . . . . autobus è lento. C'è . . . . autobus lento.

. . . . Ci sono . . . .

6) . . . . esercizio è lungo. Faccio . . . . esercizio lungo.

. . . .

7) . . . . insegnante è bravo. Ho . . . . insegnante bravo.

. . . .

D) *Answer the following questions using the correct form of the "aggettivi possessivi".*

Example: a) È l'appartamento di Paolo?

        b) Sì, è il suo appartamento.

1) È la macchina di Anna? No, ...

2) Sono le chiavi di tua sorella? Sì, ...

3) Maria è l'amica di Aldo e Patrizia? Sì, ...

4) È il tuo libro? No, ...

5) È il cane di Gervasio? Sì, ...

6) Sono i professori di Paul? No, ...

7) È tuo padre? No, ...

8) È la borsa di Francesca? Sì, ...

9) Sono le cugine di Mario e Giovanni? Sì, ...

10) È la penna di John? Sì, ...

11) Sono le riviste di Carla? No, ...

12) È lo zio di Sara e Giuseppe? Sì, ...

E) *Insert the correct forms of the verbs ANDARE and VENIRE and the right preposition in each sentence.*

Example: (Io) . . . . mangiare . . . . casa.

           Vado   a   mangiare   a   casa.

1) (Noi) . . . . scuola . . . . piedi.

2) (Loro) . . . . banca . . . . cambiare i soldi.

3) (Io) . . . . vacanza . . . . mare.

4) (Noi) . . . . classe . . . . studiare.

5) Domani Carla . . . . teatro con Maria.

6) (Noi) . . . . drogheria . . . . comprare il pane.

7) (Tu) . . . . mangiare . . . . mensa?

8) (Tu) . . . . cinema . . . . noi?

9) . . . . festa . . . . Paolo.

10) Anche tu . . . . Paolo?

11) (Loro) . . . . lezione in bicicletta.

12) Paul . . . . Boston . . . . Stati Uniti.

F) *Translate the following sentences into Italian.*

Example: I go to Laura's to study Italian.

Vado da Laura a studiare l'italiano.

1) We go to Italy to see its beautiful towns; we want to go to Rome, to Venice, and to Florence.

2)) I can learn Italian very well if I go to school everyday.

3) Luisa is a friend of mine.

4) Paul opens his book.

5) Maria opens her bag.

6) I love my mother, my father, my brothers and my grandparents.

7) You must go to the doctor's right now.

8) We want to learn this language very well.

9) When are you going to school? I am going there right now.

EXERCISES

Units 5-6

A) *Give the "participio passato" of each of the following infinitives, and complete the "passato prossimo" with the correct form of the auxiliary verbs ESSERE or AVERE.*

Example: Visitare → Visitato → ho visitato

1) Andare ....

2) Rimanere ....

3) Comprare ....

4) Partire ....

5) Salire ....

6) Incontrare ....

7) Preferire ....

8) Fare ....

9) Dire ....

10) Leggere ....

11) Stare ....

12) Bere ....

B) *Change the following sentences to the "passato prossimo".*

Example: Oggi studio in biblioteca.

Ieri ho studiato in biblioteca.

1) Maria ed Anna vanno ad Assisi per una gita.

2) Lavoro tutto il giorno, e dopo cena esco.

3) Faccio gli esercizi in classe.

4) Franco e Maria partono per Firenze oggi.

5) Dove va a studiare Patrizia? Va a Venezia.

6) Non studio; preferisco guardare la TV.

C) *Insert the correct form of the indefinite articles, and complete the sentences with a suitable adjective.*

Example: È . . . . sbaglio . . . .

         È   uno   sbaglio grave.

1) È . . . . scolaro . . . .

2) È . . . . spettacolo . . . .

3) È . . . . zio . . . .

4) È . . . . studente . . . .

5) Sono . . . . spettacoli . . . .

D) *Form a sentence with each of the following nouns and change the sentences to the plural.*

Example: Università → È un'università antica.

                     Sono delle università antiche

1) Caffè

2) Città

3) Analisi

4) Ipotesi

5) Tesi

6) Bar

7) Sport

8) Film

9) Radio

10) Cinema

11) Tè

E) *Complete the following sentences with the correct form of the "Futuro".*

Example: Domani (io) (dovere). . . . fare molte cose.

        Domani dovrò fare molte cose.

1) Io (dovere) . . . . studiare molto se (volere) imparare bene l'italiano.

2) Anna e Paolo (fare) . . . . un lungo viaggio l'anno prossimo.

3) Quanto tempo (tu) (stare) . . . . a Perugia?

4) Quanti anni (avere) . . . . Carla?

5) Fra tre mesi (io) (sapere) . . . . parlare bene italiano.

F) *Translate the following sentences into Italian.*

Example: When Paul arrives, I shall be at home.

Quando Paul arriverà, sarò a casa.

1) If I am late for the theatre, I shall take a taxi.

2) When the students arrive, we shall start the lesson.

3) When are you going to go to Rome?

4) Do you know Paul and Marianne? I don't know them, but they are probably foreign students.

5) What time is it? It is probably one o'clock.

6) These magazines may be interesting, but Paul prefers to read Italian books.

7) Anna says (that) she has a very good teacher; it may be true.

8) When I have finished my lesson, I shall go to the library.

9) The teacher will be here in few minutes.

G) *Form a sentence with each of the following nouns and adjectives, and change the sentences to the plural.*

Example: amica → Ho un'amica italiana.

Ho delle amiche italiane.

1) amico →

2) antico →

3) greco →

4) medico →

5) ciclista →

6) grigio →

7) pronuncia →

8) pioggia →

9) farmacia →

10) bugia. →

EXERCISES

Units 7-8

A) Insert the correct forms of the "verbi riflessivi" ,and change the sentences to the "passato prossimo".

    Example: Maria . . . . divert . . . . in discoteca.

           - Maria   si   diverte   in   discoteca

           Anche ieri Maria si è divertita in discoteca.

1) (Noi) . . . . svegl . . . . sempre presto la mattina.

. . . .

2) Paolo . . . . ripos . . . . il sabato e la domenica.

. . . .

3) Marta e Carla . . . . ferm . . . . sempre a Firenze quando viaggiano.

. . . .

4) Giuseppe . . . . organizz . . . . sempre da solo in casa.

. . . .

5) (Loro) . . . . divert . . . . quando vanno alle feste.

. . . .

6) Gli studenti . . . . trov . . . . bene quest'anno.

. . . .

7) I signori Rossi generalmente . . . . sistem . . . . in buoni alberghi.

. . . .

8) Claudio e Sara vogliono sempre fermar . . . . in questa città.

. . . .

9) La signora . . . . deve svegliar . . . . sempre alle 7.

. . . .

10) Generalmente posso preparar . . . . in fretta.

. . . .

11) Marianne . . . . vuole ripos . . . . sempre la domenica.

. . . .

B) *Complete the following sentences inserting the correct form of each verb plus the right preposition and a temporal reference.*

Example: (Io) studiare . . . . l'italiano . . . .

Studio l'italiano da due anni.

1) Paul e Marianne (essere) . . . . . a Perugia . . . .
2) (Io) (abitare) . . . . a Perugia . . . .
3) (Noi) (conoscere) . . . . il professore . . . .
4) Gli studenti (aspettare) . . . . il treno . . . .
5) (Io) non (vedere) . . . . Maria . . . .
6) (Voi) (essere) . . . . in Italia . . . .
7) (Lei) . . . . quanto (tempo) (vivere) . . . . a Roma?
8) (Io) (stare) . . . . a Firenze . . . .

C) *Form a sentence with each of the following nouns and adjectives, and change the sentences to the plural.*

Example: foglio → Lo studente ha un foglio a righe.

Gli studenti hanno dei fogli a righe.

1) orologio ....
2) figlio ....
3) esercizio ....
4) vecchio ....
5) universitario ....
6) paio ....
7) centinaio ....
8) zio ....
9) addio ....
10) rumorio ....

D) *Translate the following sentences into Italian.*

Example: I have been studying Italian for one month.

Studio l'italiano da un mese.

1) Paul and Marianne never read Italian newspapers.
2) Peter doesn't know anybody in this city.

3) I won't buy anything.

4) I shall not invite anybody.

5) Maria and John didn't read any books.

6) I have known him for a long time.

7) They have been living there for two months.

8) How long have those students been studying Italian?

9) Paul has been studying German for three years.

E) *Answer the following questions using the correct forms of the "pronomi diretti deboli".*

Example: Carla, mi ascolti? Sì, ...

Sì, ti ascolto.

1) Conosci bene gli studenti? Sì, ...

2) Giovanna aspetta Mario davanti al cinema? Sì, ...

3) Marianne capisce la lezione? No, ...

4) La professoressa ti saluta sempre? Sì,. . . . .

5) (Loro) incontrano sempre Carla? No,. . . . .

6) Mario aiuta sempre i suoi amici? Sì,. . . . .

7) Capisci il professore quando parla? Sì,. . . . .

F) *Complete the following sentences inserting the correct forms of the "pronomi diretti forti".*

Example: Quel signore cerca te? Sì, cerca . . . .

Quel signore cerca te? Sì, cerca me.

1) Paolo invita proprio quella ragazza? Sì, invita . . . .

2) Maria? Vado sempre da . . . .

3) Gli studenti studiano sempre con te? Sì, studiano con . . . .

4) Chi ha salutato il professore? Ha salutato Carla? Sì, ha salutato . . . .

G) *Answer the following questions using the correct form of* **ci** *plus the third persons of the "pronomi diretti deboli".*

Example: Quando accompagni tua figlia al parco?

Ce la accompagno oggi pomeriggio.

1) Porti il cane a passeggiare? Sì, ... subito.

2) Accompagni Paolo e Sara al treno? Sì, ... stasera.

3) Potete spedire la lettera al professore? Sì, possiamo . . . . domattina.

4) Quanti studenti puoi portare alla gita? . . . . posso portare dieci.

5) Puoi mandare il pacco a casa di Anna? No, non . . . . posso
mandare.

H) *Translate the following sentences into Italian.*

Example: How many cigarettes do you smoke? I smoke a lot.

Quante sigarette fumi? Ne fumo molte.

1) Do you have any books? Yes, I have four.

2) Did you see Venice? Yes, I hope to return there.

3) Are you going back to the class? Yes, I shall go back there this afternoon.

4) How many pencils do you have? I don't have any.

5) How many magazines are on the table? There are three.

6) How many students are there? There aren't any.

EXERCISES

Units 9-10

A) *Change the following sentences to the past using the correct forms of the "Passato Prossimo", "Imperfetto" or "Trapassato Prossimo".*

Example: Quando Mario arriva a casa, io dormo.

Quando Mario è arrivato a casa, io dormivo.

1) Mentre ascolti la musica, Luisa studia . . . .

. . . .

2) Sono a casa, quando telefonano i miei genitori . . . .

. . . .

3) Paolo accende il televisore quando i programmi sono già cominciati . . . . .

. . . .

4) Mentre traduco la lettera di Mary, tu leggi un giornale . . . .

. . . .

5) Franco telefona sempre quando siamo fuori casa . . . .

. . . .

B) *Insert the correct forms of TROPPO, MOLTO, PARECCHIO, TANTO, POCO as either adverbs or adjectives.*

Example: Paul è uno studente . . . . bravo.

Paul è uno studente molto bravo

1) Il professore ha . . . . tempo libero per correggere gli esercizi, lui lavora . . . .

2) Giuseppe e Sara hanno mangiato . . . . dolci alla festa ed ora stanno . . . male.

3) Ho . . . . sete, voglio bere . . . . acqua.

4) Il treno è arrivato . . . . tardi e c'erano . . . . persone straniere.

5) Carla ha . . . . amiche straniere, e conosce . . . . lingue.

6) Questo caffè è . . . . caldo, preferisco una Coca Cola . . . . fredda.

158

C) *Insert the correct forms of the verbs SAPERE or CONOSCERE according to the meaning of the sentence.*

Example: Paul . . . . suonare il piano?

Paul   sa   suonare il piano?

1) Gli amici di Luigi . . . . molte lingue ma non . . . . parlare l'arabo.

2) (Tu) . . . . Luisa? No, (io) . . . . i suoi genitori.

3) Anna e Giulia . . . . bene l'Umbria.

4) (Tu) . . . . cucinare? Sì, (io) . . . . fare gli spaghetti e altri piatti italiani.

5) (Voi) . . . . a che ora comincia il film? No, non lo . . . .

6) Pietro . . . . tutti gli amici di John e . . . . parlare l'inglese abbastanza bene.

7) (Tu) . . . . perché Claudia non è venuta al mare? No, non lo . . . . . , forse perché non . . . . nuotare.

D) *Translate the following sentences into Italian.*

1) Paul eats a lot of spaghetti.

2) The students in our class study a lot.

3) Paul and Marianne have many Italian friends.

4) We know that teacher; he knows English and German, too.

5) Can you play guitar?

6) In Italy we know many good restaurants.

7) I felt bad last night, so I didn't go to the theatre.

8) I used to go to the beach in my country.

9) Paul was writing when Marianne arrived at home.

10) I had known Maria and Laura for a long time.

E) *Answer the following questions using the "pronomi diretti" and the correct forms of the "passato prossimo".*

Example: Hai visto Mary al cinema? Sì, l'ho vista

1) Quanti studenti sono venuti a scuola? . . . . 15.

2) Hai salutato Paul? No, non . . . . perché non . . . .

(Riconoscere) . . . .

3) Quanti amici hai invitato alla festa? . . . . 10.

4) Quante sigarette hai fumato? Non . . . . nessuna.

F) *Translate the following sentences using the verb FARE.*

Example: Foreign students play a lot of sports.

Gli studenti stranieri fanno molto sport.

1) We shall take a trip to Venice.

2) What does your father do? My father is a doctor.

3) We make many mistakes when we do the exercises.

4) Marianne is going to give a party for her birthday.

5) Students have breakfast at the bar.

6) What are you doing? I'm making coffee.

7) Get the students to write this exercise.

8) I am making Marco write that sentence again.

9) Let my friends in!

EXERCISES

Units 11-12

A) *Complete the following sentences with the correct forms of the "Condizionale (presente o passato)".*

1) Luigi non studia molto, forse (dovere) . . . . imparare un mestiere.

2) Anna (volere) . . . . diventare medico ma ha dovuto interrompere gli studi.

3) Studio ingegneria e (piacere) . . . . diventare uno specialista in elettronica.

4) (Essere necessario) . . . . una attenta analisi dei problemi dell'ambiente e dell'ecologia.

5) (Volere) . . . . fare il giro del mondo ma (volerci) . . . . troppo tempo e troppo denaro.

6) (Essere opportuno) . . . . usare meno la macchina e camminare di più.

7) Secondo i giornalisti la notizia (essere) . . . . esatta.

B) *Translate the following sentences into Italian:*

1) You ought to learn the pronouns.

2) They should have phoned last night.

3) I should write that letter.

4) She could help her friend.

5) I would have liked to come earlier.

6) He ought never to have gone there.

7) It would have been more suitable to discuss the problem.

C) *Complete the following sentences with the correct forms of the "articoli" and "aggettivi".*

1) In quel locale c'è . . . . pianista molto . . . .

2) Ada è . . . . giornalista molto preparat . . . .

3) Manet è . . . . grand . . . . artista, ... pittore impressionist . . . .

4) Devi far visitare il bambino da . . . . specialista.

5) . . . . cinema italian . . . . è molto interessant . . . .

6) Montale è . . . . grand . . . . poeta italian . . . . contemporane . . . .

7) Non riesco a risolvere quest . . . . difficil . . . . problema.

8) . . . . panorama delle colline umbre è meraviglios. . . . . .

D) *Answer the following questions using the "Pronomi combinati".*

1) Puoi scrivere una lettera a tua madre? . . . .

2) Potete dirci dov'è la biblioteca? . . . .

3) Signor Rossi, vuole consegnarci le chiavi? . . . .

4) Paolo, vuoi raccontarci quello che hai visto? . . . .

5) Carla, puoi comprarmi il giornale? . . . .

6) Professore, può rispiegarci i pronomi? . . . .

7) Paolo, vuoi dirci la verità? . . . .

8) Signori, possono spedirci il pacco? . . . .

9) Ragazzi, quanti libri potete prestarci? . . . .

10) Giovanni, porterai i fiori a Maria? . . . .

E) *Translate the following sentences into Italian.*

1) She writes to him and to her.

2) We showed it to him, not to them.

3) He himself explained it to me.

4) They greeted you and me.

5) We prefer to write to them.

6) I wish to send it to her.

7) I hope to talk to them.

F) *Insert the correct form of the verb PIACERE/NON PIACERE; DISPIACERE.*

1) Mi . . . . passare un anno in Italia per imparare bene la lingua.

2) Quel regalo non le è . . . . molto.

3) Mi . . . . partire così presto, avrei voluto restare di più.

4) Carlo ama lo sport; gli . . . . nuotare e sciare.

5) Ti . . . . darmi un'informazione?

G) *Translate the following sentences into Italian.*

1) Did you like that film?

2) Foreigners like Italian artistic masterpieces.

3) They don't like swimming.

4) I would like to learn Italian very well.

5) She dislikes onions.

6) We like Italian food.

7) She doesn't like to do the exercises.

8) I'm very sorry about these problems.

9) Do you mind my smoking?

EXERCISES

Units 13-14

A) *Answer the following questions inserting the correct forms of the "pronomi", "participi passati" and "aggettivi".*

1) Chi ti ha dato quelle informazioni? . . . . ha . . . . il signor Rossi.

2) Dove hai spedito il pacco? . . . . a Roma.

3) C'è stata una gita; sai quanti studenti ci sono andati? . . . . sono . . . . circa quindici.

4) Manderai dei fiori a Laura per il suo compleanno? Sì, ... ho già . . . .

5) Mi presti gli sci? Mi dispiace. . . . . ho già . . . . a Paolo.

6) Quanti regali ci ha mandato il nonno? . . . . ha . . . . molt . . .

7) Quante lettere ti ha scritto Mary? . . . . ha . . . . divers . . . .

8) Quante sigarette ha fumato Mario? Non . . . . ha . . . . nessun . . . .

B) *Insert the correct forms of "preposizioni" and "pronomi".*

1) Carla ti aspettiamo, domani vieni a cena . . . . ?

2) Tuo padre ti ammira e crede molto . . . .

3) Spesso penso . . . . anche se sei molto lontano.

4) Conto . . . .

5) Tutta la responsabilità della famiglia e . . . . che è il padre.

6) Maria è molto gentile non sono mai arrabbiato . . . .

C) *Substitute the "Numeri Cardinali" with the correct forms of the "Numeri Ordinali".*

1) È la (1) . . . . volta che sono in Italia.

2) Lui è il (2) . . . . studente della (4) . . . . fila.

3) Domenica è il (7) . . . . giorno della settimana.

4) Mary e Paul abitano al (10) . . . . piano del palazzo.

5) Siamo nel (20) . . . . secolo.

6) Questo è il (3) . . . . corso che frequento.

D) *Complete the following sentences with the correct forms of the "Imperativo Formale".*

1) Professore, (parlare) . . . . un po' più forte, per favore.

2) Signora, (fare) . . . . in fretta, c'è poco tempo.

3) Sig. Bianchi, (andare) . . . . in segreteria prima possibile.

4) Signori, (entrare) . . . . uno alla volta, per favore.

5) Dottore, mi raccomando (venire) . . . . subito in ospedale.

6) Signora, (portare) . . . . questo libro a casa e lo (leggere) . . . .

7) Signore, non (andare) . . . . via subito.

E) *Translate the following sentences into Italian.*

1) Please, don't smoke in the classroom, Sir!

2) Those cakes are not good, do not eat them, Madam!

3) Mrs. Rossi, here is the book; give it to the students!

4) Do me this favour, Sir!

5) Miss. Bianchi, write to your mother, write to her soon!

EXERCISES

Units 15-16

A) *Change the following formal sentences to informal sentences.*

Example: Professore, parli più lentamente.

Mario, parla più lentamente.

1) Signori, scrivano questa lettera.

Studenti, ... questa lettera.

2) Signorine, finiscano di mangiare.

Bambini, ... di mangiare.

3) Sig. Rossi, mi faccia questo piacere.

Carla, ... questo piacere.

4) Professore, ci spieghi l'Imperativo.

Maria, ... l'Imperativo.

5) Cameriere, mi porti un bicchiere d'acqua, per favore.

Anna, ... un bicchiere d'acqua per favore.

6) Signore, si alzi presto domattina.

Chiara, ...

7) Se è stanco, non vada a scuola a piedi, ci vada con l'autobus.

Se . . . . stanco, ... a scuola a piedi, ... con l'autobus.

8) Inviti i suoi amici alla festa; li inviti tutti.

Giulia, ... i . . . . amici alla festa; . . . . tutti.

9) Signore, non vada a quella mostra, non è interessante.

John, ... a quella mostra, non è interessante.

10) Professoressa, abbia pazienza con lui.

Luigi, ... con lui.

11) Signore, dica pure ciò che desidera.

Paola, ... pure ciò che . . . .

12) Signori, per favore stiano in fila.

Ragazzi, per favore . . . . in fila.

13) Signorina, per favore mi presti i suoi libri, me ne presti almeno uno.

Luisa, per favore . . . . i . . . . libri, ... almeno uno.

14) Signora, faccia una vacanza, ma la faccia subito.

Sara, ... una vacanza, ma . . . . subito.

15) Non se ne vada, deve ancora vedere molte cose interessanti.

. . . . , ... ancora vedere molte cose interessanti.

B) *Change the "Pronomi relativi" che and chi to the corresponding forms of the "Pronomi relativi" il quale / la quale / i quali / le quali.*

1) Non conosco i ragazzi che sono in classe.

. . . .

2) Mi piacciono le persone che sono sincere.

. . . .

3) Ecco gli studenti di cui ti ho parlato.

. . . .

4) La famiglia con cui vivo è molto simpatica.

. . . .

5) I fogli che sono sul banco sono di Paolo.

. . . .

6) Ti dico subito le ragioni per cui sono qui.

. . . .

7) I regali che ho comprato per i miei genitori sono veramente belli.

. . . .

8) La città in cui abito è molto calma.

. . . .

9) Non conosco quella ragazza a cui hai dato i dischi.

. . . .

10) La gente con cui sono andata a cena è proprio simpatica.

. . . .

C) *Translate the following sentences into Italian.*

1) Where is the book about which you are speaking?
2) He who likes a foreign country wants to go there.
3) The girl to whom I am reading the book is my sister.
4) There are students who learn quickly.
5) We don't know what they want, exactly.
6) I don't understand what he is saying.
7) The house in which I live is very comfortable.
8) Forgive those who offend you.
9) He who goes slowly goes well and far.
10) This is the writer whose books are famous.

EXERCISES

Units 17-18

A) *Complete the following sentences with the correct forms of the "Congiuntivo presente/passato".*

1) Credo che Paul e Mary (partire) . . . . ieri sera.

2) Penso che tu (avere) . . . . ragione.

3) Speriamo che gli studenti (superare) . . . . l'esame.

4) Si dice che gli italiani (amare) . . . . mangiare molto.

5) Desidero che lui (restare) . . . . a casa.

6) Può darsi che domani (esserci) . . . . il sole.

7) Suppongo che Anna e Stefano (andare) . . . . a casa prima della fine della festa.

8) Spero che voi (capire) . . . . la lezione di ieri.

9) È necessario che Maria (spedire) . . . . quella lettera subito.

10) Bisogna che loro (parlare) . . . . con il professore.

B) *Transform the following sentences as in the example:*

È necessario studiare. (Io) → È necessario che io studi.

1) Bisogna andare subito in segreteria. (Noi) → . . . .

. . . .

2) Occorre avere pazienza con la gente. (Voi) → . . . .

. . . .

3) È necessario rispiegare la lezione. (Il professore) → . . . .

. . . .

4) Occorre parlare lentamente. (Io) → . . . .

. . . .

5) Bisogna ascoltare la radio, guardare la TV, parlare con la gente per imparare una lingua straniera. (Gli studenti) → . . . .

. . . .

6) È necessario risolvere il problema presto. (Voi) → . . . .

. . . .

C) *Insert the correct "Congiunzioni", "Locuzioni" and "Espressioni" which introduce the subjunctive or the infinitive.*

1) Andrò alla conferenza . . . . sia stanco morto.

2) Farò questo esame . . . . sia utile alla mia professione.

3) Verrà alla festa . . . . non si senta bene.

4) . . . . tu parta, ti darò le informazioni.

5) Posso andare a casa da sola . . . . tu ti disturbi.

6) Andrò da loro . . . . mi possano dare una mano a risolvere questo problema.

7) . . . . che tu stia a casa per finire il lavoro.

8) . . . . difendere l'ambiente.

9) . . . . che tu parta così presto.

10) . . . . che loro siano già andati via.

D) *Translate the following sentences using the "Congiuntivo presente/passato" or the "Infinito".*

1) I hope she will write.

2) He thinks they are intelligent.

3) I believe I am late.

4) I think they left yesterday.

5) It is necessary that you study this lesson very well.

6) They want the teacher to speak slowly.

7) I am glad they have arrived.

8) His father wants him to return to school.

9) It is likely that I shall leave.

10) It is necessary to clean the room.

11) I believe I am right.

12) You think you are the best student.

E) *Change the following question to the past using the "Congiuntivo", as in the example:*

È necessario che tu studi → <u>Era</u> necessario che tu <u>studiassi.</u>

1) Penso che tu abbia capito il congiuntivo → . . . .
. . . .

2) Voglio che restiate a casa → . . . .

3) Desidero che partiamo → . . . .

4) Mi sembra che sia straniera → . . . .

5) Suppongo che siano partiti → . . . .

6) Bisogna che loro vadano alla posta → . . . .
. . . .

7) È giusto che gli studenti abbiano buoni insegnanti → . . . .
. . . .

8) Si racconta che sia uno strano tipo → . . . .
. . . .

9) Affinché mi aiutino, vado da loro → . . . .
. . . .

10) Prima che parta, gli telefonerò → . . . .
. . . .

11) Nonostante sia molto stanco, andrò a lezione → . . . .
. . . .

12) Credo che sia sincero → . . . .

F) *Insert the correct forms of the "Congiuntivo", "Infinito" or "Condizionale" in the following sentences.*

1) Penso . . . . Giovanni (arrivare) . . . . ieri sera.

2) Suppongo . . . . tu (essere) . . . . molto studioso.

3) Ho creduto . . . . (loro) (essere) . . . . sinceri.

4) Ho paura . . . . (Paola) (partire) . . . . domani.

5) Penso . . . . Paolo (studiare). . . . . molto.

6) Mi pare . . . . quello studente (arrivare) . . . . ieri mattina.

7) Ieri sera, verso le 9 ho telefonato perché pensavo . . . . i miei amici (arrivare) . . . . già a casa.

8) Prima di fare l'esame pensavo . . . . (essere) . . . . più difficile.

9) Mario pensava . . . . (io) (conoscere) . . . . molta gente.

10) Temo . . . . (essere) un po' testarda.

G) *Translate the following sentences into Italian.*

1) I thought that she had been here already.

2) I believed that she was leaving.

3) They feared that we were not coming.

4) They called him in order that he might help them with the work.

5) I believed that I knew this language very well.

6) We all doubted that there would be no smog.

7) I didn't know that they knew Italian well.

8) She was hoping that the children had eaten already.

9) Mary said that she would give the book to Paul.

EXERCISES

Units 19-20

A) *Complete the following sentences with the correct tenses of the "Indicativo" or "Condizionale".*

1) Se verrai a cena da noi, (divertirsi) . . . .

2) Se parlassi bene l'italiano, (trovare) . . . . un lavoro qui.

3) Se fai così, (sbagliare) . . . . proprio tutto.

4) Se mi avesse ascoltato, ora (stare) . . . . meglio.

5) Se gli studenti avessero studiato costantemente, (superare) . . . . l'esame

6) Se fossi più costante, (imparare) . . . . di più.

B) *Translate the following sentences into Italian.*

1) If you come, we'll go to the movie together.

2) If they had read the paper, they would have told you the news.

3) If we knew how to do the exercises, we would tell you.

4) If one month is not enough, we'll stay longer.

5) If I were in Italy, I would visit Capri.

6) If I had been in Italy, I would have visited Capri.

7) If I go to Rome, I'll visit the Pantheon.

8) If he were hungry, he would eat.

C) *Complete the following sentences with the correct forms of the "Congiuntivo".*

1) Magari (parlare) . . . . italiano perfettamente.

2) Sarebbe necessario che voi (andare) . . . . a Roma a comprare i libri.

3) Ieri mi sarebbe piaciuto che le mie amiche (arrivare) . . . . un po' prima per stare un po' insieme a loro.

4) Sabato scorso Carla ha dato una festa molto bella per il suo compleanno; magari ci (invitare) . . . .

5) Vorrei che tu mi (ascoltare) . . . . di più.

6) Avrei voluto che gli studenti (arrivare) . . . . in orario alla lezione.

D) *Complete the following sentences with the correct forms of the "Comparativi" and "Superlativi".*

1) Paolo è simpatico . . . . sua sorella.

2) Mi piace . . . . nuotare . . . . sciare.

3) Quel film è . . . . bello di questo anno.

4) Leggo . . . . romanzi . . . . giornali.

5) Assisi è . . . . grande . . . . Perugia.

6) Roma è . . . . piccola . . . . New York.

7) Questo studente è molto bravo. È brav . . . .

8) La gente è assai simpatica qui. È simpatic . . . .

9) È . . . . studiare un po' al giorno.

10) Questo vino è . . . . buono dell'Umbria.

E) *Complete the following sentences with the preposition di or the conjunction che.*

1) Non mangiare tanto; sei più largo . . . . lungo.

2) Scrivere è più difficile . . . . parlare.

3) Maria è più gentile . . . . Luisa.

4) Gianni è più noioso . . . . spiritoso.

5) Vivo più volentieri in campagna . . . . in città.

6) Quel ragazzo ragiona più istintivamente . . . . razionalmente.

7) Mi piace più il mare . . . . montagna.

F) *Translate the following sentences into Italian.*

1) Anna is less diligent than Paolo.

2) This city is older than that one.

3) This is the most beautiful church in the town.

4) Paola is as studious as she is intelligent.

5) It is less easy to write than to speak.

174

6) This is the newest museum in town.

7) People are extremely amusing here.

8) He is not so nice as his sister.

9) I'm less tired than you.

10) This is the least interesting book.

11) She is a very beautiful woman.

12) He is the youngest boy in the class.

EXERCISES

Units 21-22

A) *Translate the following sentences into Italian.*

   1) John received a letter from his Italian friends six years ago.

   2) Michelangelo worked in Rome for many years.

   3) He spoke to them on the phone a long time ago.

   4) Dante was the greatest Italian poet.

   5) My grandfather had a very interesting life.

   6) Caesar was a famous general.

   7) Perugia was an Etruscan town.

   8) In the Second World War many famous monuments were destroyed in Italy.

   9) Perugino was one of the great artists who worked in Perugia.

  10) Giacomo Leopardi was a great famous Italian poet.

B) *Complete the following sentences inserting the "avverbi" instead of the "aggettivi".*

   1) Il professore parla (veloce) . . . .

   2) Lui si comporta (naturale) . . . .

   3) Ragazzi siete arrivati (finale) . . . . !

   4) Il treno passa (regolare) . . . .

   5) Questo esercizio è (particolare) . . . . .difficile.

C) *Change the following sentence to the "Forma passiva" using the verb <u>venire</u> instead of the verb <u>essere</u>.*

   Example: Maria fa un dolce → Un dolce viene fatto da Maria.

   1) Gli studenti scrivono gli esercizi → . . . .

      . . . .

   2) Penso che Paolo inviti Carla → . . . .

      . . . .

3) Pensavo che loro completassero il lavoro → . . . .

. . . .

4) Luisa ammira molto quel quadro → . . . .

. . . .

5) La gente amava quella città → . . . .

. . . .

6) John amerebbe questa musica → . . . .

. . . .

7) Pensavo che il professore avesse spiegato la lezione in italiano → . . . .

. . . .

8) I turisti ammireranno questa mostra → . . . .

. . . .

9) È necessario scrivere questo esercizio → . . . .

. . . .

10) Dovresti imparare la lezione → . . . .

. . . .

D) *Translate the following sentences into Italian.*
   1) Italian is spoken here.
   2) The house was bought by Mr. and Mrs. Bianchi.
   3) The names of Raffaello, Giotto and Michelangelo are known to all.
   4) The invitations have been sent by post.
   5) The work was not finished.
   6) One learns better when one has time.
   7) All courses must be preregistered in this university.
   8) One is happy when one is well.
   9) Many stories were told about him.
   10) The story of Perugia can be followed in the work of many famous artists.

EXERCISES

Units 23-24

A) *Change the following direct sentences to indirect sentences.*

Example: Maria disse: "Non posso fare questo lavoro".
          Maria disse che non poteva fare quel lavoro.

1) Paolo ha detto: "Non sono uscito ieri". . . . .

2) Gli studenti dissero: "Verremo a lezione domani". . . . .

3) Stamattina il professore ha detto: "Spiegherò il Congiuntivo ancora". . . . .

4) Il bambino ha rotto il vaso eppure aveva promesso, "Non giocherò più
   a pallone in casa". . . . .

5) Lui pregò l'amico, "Dammi una mano!". . . . .

6) Mario disse a Luisa, "Ho fatto io quel lavoro". . . . .

7) Giovanni disse: "I miei figli studiano molto". . . . .

8) Anna ha detto a Sara, "Vieni con me in vacanza". . . . .

B) *Translate the following sentences into Italian.*

1) He said that he had lost his umbrella.

2) She said she had been waiting for ages.

3) Paul said that Mary would be in Paris on Monday.

4) She said she had taken the house with him.

5) Ann said that she wanted to go alone.

6) He told his mother that he was starting the work the next day.

7) She told him she had seen Mary two days before.

8) He told Tom to get his coat.

9) She asked whether she could use my phone.

10) They said that they would be there.

C) *Complete the following sentences with the suitable forms of the "Infinito" (Presente/passato); "Participio" (Presente/passato); or "Gerundio" (Presente/passato).*

1) . . . . troppo fa male alla salute.

2) . . . . si possono conoscere molti paesi.

3) È un libro molto . . . .

4) Mi piace . . . . sport.

5) Credo di . . . . gentile con loro.

6) Arriva sempre a lezione . . . .

7) . . . . così, se ne andò di casa.

8) . . . . tardi, non sono entrata in classe.

9) Vado in cucina a . . . . da . . . .

10) . . . . le lingue è . . . .

D) *Change the following sentences to the "Forma implicita".*

Example: Dopo che ho studiato, esco.

Dopo aver studiato, esco.

1) Penso che partirò domani.

. . . .

2) Dopo che aveva bevuto il caffè, cominciava a lavorare.

. . . .

3) Dopo che avrò imparato l'italiano, troverò lavoro.

. . . .

4) Dopo che fu uscito di casa, si sentì meglio.

. . . .

5) Se lavorerai tanto, ti ammalerai.

. . . .

6) Mentre parlava, uscì.

. . . .

E) *Translate the following sentences into Italian.*

1) Before going to Rome, I visited Venice.

2) By studying hard, they learned the language.

3) In reading the exercises, he found a mistake.
4) Her friend having left, Mary started to cry.
5) Having finished their homework, they went out for a walk.
6) After having finished the lessons, the students have to do this exercise.
7) We love swimming and playing tennis.
8) We spent our time admiring the great artistic masterpieces in Rome and Florence.
9) It was an amusing film.
10) Students attending this course love talking in Italian.
11) I meet Paul everyday on going home.

ANSWER KEY

Units 1-2

A
1. il; i treni
2. la; le ragazze
3. il; i signori
4. il; i lavori
5. la; le lingue
6. la; le banche
7. il; i professori
8. il; i fogli
9. la; le segretarie
10. la; le pareti
11. il; i banchi
12. la; le borse
13. la; le stazioni
14. il; i giornali
15. la; le matite
16. la; le chiavi
17. il; i passaporti
18. la; le signore

B
1. straniera; Le ragazze sono straniere.
2. italiano; I signori sono italiani.
3. libera; Le sedie sono libere.
4. occupato; I posti sono occupati.
5. aperta; Le banche sono aperte.
6. chiusa; Le segreterie sono chiuse.
7. bravo; I professori sono bravi.
8. bella; Le case sono belle.
9. moderna; Le stazioni sono moderne.
10. scomodo; I banchi sono scomodi.
11. gentile; I ragazzi sono gentili.
12. grande; Le macchine sono grandi.
13. piccola; Le scuole sono piccole.
14. comodo; I treni sono comodi.

C
1. sono; è, di; è, di
2. è; sono, di
3. di, è; è, di
4. sono; sono, di
5. è, a / in
6. sono, a; in
7. sono; sono, in
8. è; è, in

D
1. chi, è
2. che cosa, ha
3. chi, sono
4. chi, ha
5. chi, è
6. che cosa, sono
7. che cosa, è
8. che cosa, sono
9. che cosa, è
10. che cosa, è

E
1. c'è, un
2. ci sono, delle
3. c'è, un
4. c'è, una
5. c'è, una
6. ci sono, dei
7. c'è
8. ci sono, degli

F
1. Come ti chiami? Mi chiamo Paul. / Come si chiama? Mi chiamo Paul.
2. Chi è Marianne? E' una ragazza svizzera.
3. Sono uno studente straniero.
4. Paul e Marianne sono stranieri; Paul è di Boston; Marianne, di Zurigo.
5. Siamo in Italia, a Perugia per la prima volta.
6. Dove sono gli studenti? Gli studenti sono in classe.
7. Sono in Italia per imparare l'italiano.
8. Hai una penna? / Ha una penna?
9. Ci sono dodici studenti in classe.
10. Che cosa c'è sul tuo banco? / Che cosa c'è sul suo banco?

ANSWER KEY

Units 3-4

A
1. ono
2. i
3. o
4. a; o
5. iamo
6. isci; isco
7. ate; iamo
8. iscono, ono
9. o; a
10. isce; a
11. i; o
12. isce

B
1. fai; sto
2. sta; sto
3. facciamo; andiamo
4. vai, stai
5. va
6. vai
7. fa

C
1. L'; un'; Le amiche sono italiane. Ho delle amiche italiane.
2. L'; un; Gli uffici sono piccoli. Abbiamo degli uffici piccoli.
3. L'; un'; Le università sono antiche. Abbiamo delle università antiche.
4. L'; un'; Le escursioni sono lunghe. Facciamo delle escursioni lunghe.
5. L'; un; Gli autobus sono lenti. Ci sono degli autobus lenti.
6. L'; un; Gli esercizi sono lunghi. Faccio degli esercizi lunghi.
7. L'; un; Gli insegnanti sono bravi. Ho degli insegnanti bravi.

D
1. Non è la sua macchina.
2. Sono le sue chiavi.

3. È la loro amica.
4. Non è il mio libro.
5. È il suo cane.
6. Non sono i suoi professori.
7. Non è mio padre.
8. È la sua borsa.
9. Sono le sue cugine.
10. È la sua penna.
11. Non sono le sue riviste.
12. È suo zio.

E
1. andiamo, a, a
2. vanno, in, a
3. vado, in, a
4. andiamo, in, a
5. va, a
6. andiamo, in, a / per
7. vai, a, alla
8. vai, al, con
9. andiamo, alla, di
10. vai, da
11. vanno, a / alla
12. va, a, negli

F
1. Andiamo in Italia per/a vedere le sue belle città; vogliamo andare a Roma, a Venezia e a Firenze.
2. Posso imparare molto bene l'italiano se vado a scuola ogni giorno.
3. Luisa è una mia amica.
4. Paul apre il suo libro.
5. Maria apre la sua borsa.
6. Amo mia madre, mio padre, i miei fratelli e i miei nonni.
7. Devi andare dal dottore subito.
8. Vogliamo imparare molto bene questa lingua.
9. Quando vai a scuola? Ci vado subito.

ANSWER KEY

Units 5-6

A
1. andato; sono andato/a
2. rimasto; sono rimasto/a
3. comprato; ho comprato
4. partito; sono partito/a
5. salito; sono salito/a
6. incontrato; ho incontrato
7. preferito; ho preferito
8. fatto; ho fatto
9. detto; ho detto
10. letto; ho letto
11. stato; sono stato/a
12. bevuto; ho bevuto

B
1. sono andate
2. ho lavorato, sono uscito
3. ho fatto
4. sono partiti
5. è andata, è andata
6. ho studiato, ho preferito

C
1. uno; studioso
2. uno; interessante
3. uno; simpatico
4. uno; bravo
5. degli; noiosi

D Since each of the sentences in this section is original, there is no set answer.

E
1. dovrò, vorrò
2. faranno

3. starai
4. avrà
5. saprò

F
1. Se sarò in ritardo per andare a teatro, prenderò un taxi.
2. Quando gli studenti arriveranno, cominceremo la lezione.
3. Quando andrai a Roma?
4. Conosci Paul e Marianne? Non li conosco ma saranno studenti stranieri.
5. Che ora è? Sarà l'una.
6. Queste riviste saranno interessanti, ma Paul preferisce leggere libri italiani.
7. Anna dice che ha un buon insegnante; sarà vero.
8. Quando avrò finito la lezione, andrò in biblioteca.
9. L'insegnante sarà qui tra pochi minuti.

G Since each of the sentences in this section is original, there is no set answer.

ANSWER KEY

Units 7-8

A 1. ci, iamo; ci siamo svegliati
    2. si, a; si è riposato
    3. si, ano; si sono fermati
    4. si, a; si è organizzato
    5. si, ono; si sono divertiti
    6. si, ano; si sono trovati
    7. si, ano; si sono sistemati
    8. si sono voluti fermare / hanno voluto fermarsi
    9. si, are; si è dovuta svegliare / ha dovuto svegliarsi
  10. mi, mi sono potuto/a preparare / ho potuto prepararmi
  11. si, are; si è voluta riposare / ha voluto riposarsi

B 1. sono, da, ...
    2. abito, da, ...
    3. conosco, da, ...
    4. aspettano, da, ...
    5. vedo, da, ...
    6. siete, da, ...
    7. da, vive
    8. sto, da, ...

C Since each of the sentences in this section is original, there is no set answer. However, the correct plural forms of the nouns to be used are listed below.
    1. orologi
    2. figli
    3. esercizi
    4. vecchi
    5. universitari
    6. paia
    7. centinaia
    8. zii
    9. addii
  10. rumorii

D
1. Paul e Marianne non leggono mai giornali italiani.
2. Peter non conosce nessuno in questa città.
3. Non comprerò niente.
4. Non inviterò nessuno.
5. Maria e John non hanno letto nessun libro.
6. Lo conosco da molto tempo.
7. Vivono là da due mesi.
8. Da quanto tempo quegli studenti studiano l'italiano?
9. Paul studia il tedesco da tre anni.

E
1. li conosco
2. lo aspetta
3. la capisce
4. mi saluta
5. la incontrano
6. li saluta
7. lo capisco

F
1. lei
2. lei
3. me
4. lei

G
1. ce, lo, porto
2. ce, li, accompagno
3. ce, la, possiamo portare / possiamo portarcela
4. ce, ne, posso portare / posso portarcene
5. ce, lo, posso mandare / posso mandarcelo

H
1. Hai qualche libro? Sì, ne ho quattro.
2. Hai visto Venezia? Sì, e spero di ritornarci.
3. Ritornerai a lezione? Sì, ci ritornerò questo pomeriggio.
4. Quante matite hai? Non ne ho nessuna.
5. Quante riviste sono sul tavolo? Ce ne sono tre.
6. Quanti studenti ci sono? Non ce n'è nessuno.

ANSWER KEY

Units 9-10

A   1. ascoltavi; studiava
2. ero; hanno telefonato
3. ha acceso; erano cominciati
4. traducevo; leggevi
5. telefonava; eravamo

B This exercise gives you free choice among the correct forms. Remember that the adverb forms are invariable.

C   1. sanno / conoscono, sanno
2. conosci, conosco
3. conoscono
4. sai, so
5. sapete, sappiamo
6. conosce, sa
7. sai, so, sa

D   1. Paul mangia molti spaghetti.
2. Gli studenti nella nostra classe studiano molto.
3. Paul e Marianne hanno molti amici italiani.
4. Conosciamo quel professore; lui sa l'inglese ed anche tedesco.
5. Sai suonare la chitarra?
6. In Italia conosciamo molti buoni ristoranti.
7. Mi sentivo male ieri sera, così non sono andato/a a teatro.
8. Andavo di continuo alla spiaggia nel mio paese.
9. Paul stava scrivendo quando Marianne è arrivata a casa.
10. Conoscevo Maria e Laura da molto tempo.

E   1. Ce, ne, sono venuti
2. L'ho, salutato; l'ho, riconosciuto

3. Ne, ho, invitati
4. Ne, ho, fumata

F 1. Faremo un viaggio a Venezia.
   2. Che cosa fa tuo padre? Mio padre fa il medico / Mio padre è medico.
   3. Facciamo molti sbagli quando facciamo gli esercizi.
   4. Marianne farà/darà una festa per il suo compleanno.
   5. Gli studenti fanno colazione al bar.
   6. Che (cosa) fai? Faccio (sto facendo) il caffè.
   7. Fai scrivere questo esercizio agli studenti.
   8. Faccio riscrivere quella frase a Marco.
   9. Fai entrare i miei amici!

ANSWER KEY

Units 11-12

A 1. dovrebbe
2. avrebbe voluto
3. mi piacerebbe
4. sarebbe necessaria
5. vorrei; ci vorrebbe
6. sarebbe opportuno
7. sarebbe

B 1. Dovresti imparare i pronomi.
2. Dovrebbero aver telefonato ieri sera.
3. Dovrei scrivere quella lettera.
4. Potrebbe aiutare la sua amica.
5. Mi sarebbe piaciuto venire prima.
6. Non avrebbe mai dovuto esserci andato.
7. Sarebbe stato più opportuno discutere il problema.

C 1. un, bravo
2. una, preparata
3. uno, grande, un, impressionista
4. uno
5. Il, italiano, interessante
6. un, grande, italiano, contemporaneo
7. questo, difficile
8. Il, meraviglioso

D 1. posso scrivergliela / gliela posso scrivere.
2. possiamo dirvelo / ve lo possiamo dire.
3. voglio consegnarvele / ve le voglio consegnare.
4. voglio raccontarvelo / ve lo voglio raccontare.
5. posso comprartelo / te lo posso comprare.
6. posso rispiegarveli / ve li posso rispiegare.

7. posso dirvela / ve la posso dire.
8. possiamo spedirvelo / ve lo possiamo spedire.
9. possiamo prestarvene / ve ne possiamo prestare.
10. glieli porterò.

E 1. Lei scrive a lui e a lei.
2. Lo abbiamo mostrato a lui non a loro.
3. Lui stesso me lo ha spiegato.
4. Loro hanno salutato te e me.
5. Preferiamo scrivergli. / Preferiamo scrivere loro.
6. Desidero mandarglielo.
7. Spero di parlargli / parlare loro.

F 1. piacerebbe
2. piaciuto
3. dispiace
4. piace
5. dispiacerebbe

G 1. Ti è piaciuto quel film?
2. Gli stranieri amano i capolavori artistici italiani.
3. Non amano nuotare / A loro non piace nuotare.
4. Vorrei imparare l'italiano molto bene.
5. A lei non piacciono le cipolle. / Non le piacciono le cipolle.
6. Ci piace il cibo italiano!
7. A lei non piace fare gli esercizi. / Non le piace fare gli esercizi.
8. Sono molto dispiaciuto/a per questi problemi.
9. Ti dispiace se fumo?

ANSWER KEY

Units 13-14

A
1. Me, le, date
2. Lo, spedito
3. Ce, ne, andati
4. glieli, mandati
5. li, prestati
6. Ce, ne, mandati, molti
7. Me, ne, scritte, diverse
8. ne, fumata, nessuna

B
1. con, noi
2. in, te
3. a, te
4. su, di, te
5. su, di, lui
6. con, lei

C
1. prima
2. secondo
3. settimo
4. decimo
5. ventesimo
6. terzo

D
1. parli
2. faccia
3. vada
4. entrino
5. venga
6. porti
7. vada

E
1. Per favore signore, non fumi in classe!
2. Questi dolci non sono buoni; non li mangi, signora!
3. Signora Rossi, ecco il libro; lo dia agli studenti!
4. Signore, mi faccia questo piacere!
5. Signorina Bianchi, scriva a sua madre; le scriva subito!

ANSWER KEY

Units 15-16

A
1. scrivete
2. finite
3. fammi
4. spiegami
5. portami
6. alzati
7. sei, non andare; vacci
8. invita, tuoi; invitali
9. non, andare
10. abbi
11. dimmi, desideri
12. state
13. prestami, tuoi; prestamene
14. fa / fai; falla
15. non andartene, devi

B
1. i quali
2. le quali
3. dei quali
4. con la quale
5. i quali
6. per le quali
7. i quali
8. nella quale
9. alla quale
10. con la quale

C
1. Dov'è il libro di cui / del quale parlate?
2. Colui che ama un paese straniero ci vuole andare.
3. La ragazza a cui / alla quale leggo il libro è mia sorella.
4. Ci sono studenti che / i quali imparano molto velocemente.
5. Non sappiamo ciò che vogliono esattamente.

6. Non capisco ciò che dice.
7. La casa in cui / nella quale vivo è molto comoda.
8. Dimentica coloro che ti offendono / chi ti offende.
9. Chi va piano va sano e va lontano.
10. Questo è lo scrittore i cui libri sono molto famosi.

ANSWER KEY

Units 17-18

A   1. siano partiti
2. abbia
3. superino
4. amino
5. resti
6. ci sia
7. vadano
8. abbiate capito
9. spedisca
10. parlino

B   1. che andiamo in segreteria.
2. che abbiate pazienza con la gente.
3. che il professore rispieghi la lezione.
4. che parli più lentamente.
5. che gli studenti ascoltino la radio, guardino la TV, parlino con la gente,
   per imparare bene una lingua straniera.
6. che risolviate il problema presto.

C   1. benché / nonostante che / sebbene
2. purché
3. benché / nonostante che / sebbene
4. prima che
5. senza che
6. affinché
7. È necessario che / Bisogna che
8. Bisogna / E' necessario
9. È necessario
10. Penso che

D   1. Spero che lei scriva.
2. Pensa che loro siano intelligenti.

3. Credo di essere in ritardo.
4. Penso che siano partiti ieri.
5. E' necessario che tu studi questa lezione molto bene / che voi studiate questa lezione molto bene.
6. Vogliono che il professore parli lentamente.
7. Sono felice che siano arrivati.
8. Suo padre vuole che lui ritorni a scuola.
9. Sembra che io debba partire.
10. E' necessario pulire la stanza.
11. Credo di aver(e) ragione.
12. Pensi di essere il miglior studente.

E
1. Pensavo / ho pensato che tu avessi capito il congiuntivo.
2. Volevo / ho voluto che voi restaste a casa.
3. Desideravano / hanno desiderato che partissimo.
4. Mi sembrava / mi è sembrato che fosse straniera.
5. Supponevo / ho supposto che fossero partiti.
6. Bisognava che andassero alla posta.
7. Era giusto che gli studenti avessero buoni insegnanti.
8. Si raccontava che fosse uno strano tipo.
9. Affinché mi aiutassero, andavo / sono andato da loro.
10. Prima che partisse, gli ho telefonato.
11. Nonostante fossi molto stanco, sono andato a lezione.
12. Credevo / ho creduto che fosse sincero.

F
1. sia arrivato
2. sia
3. fossero
4. parta
5. studi
6. sia arrivato
7. fossero arrivati
8. sarebbe stato
9. conoscessi
10. di

G
1. Pensavo / ho pensato che lei fosse già stata qui.
2. Credevo che lei partisse.

3. Avevano paura / temevano che non venissimo.
4. Lo hanno chiamato affinché li aiutasse nel lavoro.
5. Credevo / ho creduto di conoscere molto bene questa lingua.
6. Noi tutti dubitavamo che non ci sarebbe stato smog.
7. Non sapevo che conoscessero l'italiano bene.
8. Sperava che i bambini avessero già mangiato.
9. Maria diceva / ha detto che avrebbe dato il libro a Paolo.

ANSWER KEY

Units 19-20

A 1. ti divertirai
2. troveresti
3. sbagli
4. sarebbe stato
5. avrebbero superato
6. impareresti

B 1. Se verrai, andremo al cinema insieme.
2. Se avessero letto il giornale, ti avrebbero detto le notizie.
3. Se sapessimo come fare gli esercizi, te lo diremmo.
4. Se un mese non sarà abbastanza, resteremo più a lungo.
5. Se fossi in Italia, visiterei Capri.
6. Se fossi stato in Italia, avrei visitato Capri.
7. Se andrò a Roma, visiterò il Pantheon.
8. Se avessi fame, mangerei.

C 1. parlassi
2. andaste
3. fossero arrivate
4. avesse invitati
5. ascoltassi
6. fossero arrivati

D 1. come
2. più, che
3. il più
4. più, che
5. meno, di
6. più, di
7. bravissimo
8. simpaticissima
9. più, che
10. il più

E 1. che
2. che
3. di
4. che
5. che
6. che
7. della

F 1. Anna è meno diligente di Paolo.
2. Questa città è più antica di quella.
3. Questa è la chiesa più bella della città / nella città.
4. Paola è tanto studiosa quanto intelligente.
5. E' meno facile scrivere che parlare.
6. Questo è il museo più nuovo in città / nella città.
7. La gente è molto divertente qui.
8. Non è così simpatico/a come / quanto sua sorella.
9. Sono meno stanco di te.
10. Questo è il libro meno interessante.
11. E' una donna bellissima / molto bella.
12. E' il ragazzo più giovane in classe / della classe.

ANSWER KEY

Units 21-22

A 1. John ricevette (ha ricevuto) una lettera dai suoi amici italiani sei anni fa.
     2. Michelangelo lavorò (ha lavorato) a Roma per molti anni.
     3. Lui parlò (ha parlato) a loro al telefono molto tempo fa.
     4. Dante fu (è stato) il più grande poeta italiano.
     5. Mio nonno ebbe (ha avuto) una vita molto interessante.
     6. Cesare fu (è stato) un generale famoso.
     7. Perugia fu (è stata) una città etrusca.
     8. Durante la seconda guerra mondiale molti monumenti famosi furono distrutti (sono stati distrutti) in Italia.
     9. Il Perugino fu (è stato) uno dei grandi artisti che lavorarono (hanno lavorato) a Perugia.
   10. Giacomo Leopardi fu (è stato) un grande poeta italiano.

B 1. velocemente
     2. naturalmente
     3. finalmente
     4. regolarmente
     5. particolarmente

C 1. Gli esercizi vengono fatti dagli studenti.
     2. Penso che Carla venga invitata da Paolo.
     3. Pensavo che il lavoro venisse completato da loro.
     4. Quel quadro viene molto ammirato da Luisa.
     5. Quella città veniva molto amata dalla gente.
     6. Questa musica verrebbe molto ammirata da John.
     7. Pensavo che la lezione venisse spiegata dal professore in italiano.
     8. Questa mostra verrebbe molto ammirata dai turisti.
     9. E' necessario che questo esercizio venga scritto.
   10. La lezione dovrebbe venire imparata da te.

D 1. Qui si parla l'italiano.
     2. La casa fu / venne acquistata dai signori Bianchi.

3. I nomi di Raffaello, Giotto e Michelangelo sono noti a tutti.
4. Gli inviti sono stati inviati per posta.
5. Il lavoro non fu / venne finito.
6. Si impara meglio quando si ha tempo.
7. In questa università tutti i corsi devono essere / venire prenotati.
8. Si è felici quando si sta bene.
9. Si raccontavano (furono / vennero raccontate) molte storie su di lui.
10. La storia di Perugia può essere / venire seguita nei lavori di molti artisti famosi.

ANSWER KEY

Units 23-24

A
1. Paolo ha detto che non era uscito il giorno prima.
2. Gli studenti dissero che sarebbero venuti a lezione il giorno dopo.
3. Stamattina il professore ha detto che avrebbe spiegato il congiuntivo ancora.
4. Il bambino ha rotto il vaso eppure aveva promesso che non avrebbe giocato più a pallone in casa.
5. Lui pregò l'amico che gli desse una mano (di dargli una mano).
6. Mario disse a Luisa che aveva già fatto lui quel lavoro (di aver già fatto lui quel lavoro).
7. Giovanni disse che i suoi figli studiavano molto.
8. Anna ha detto a Sara di andare con lei in vacanza (che andasse con lei in vacanza).

B
1. Lui ha detto / disse che aveva perso il suo ombrello (di aver perso il suo ombrello).
2. Lei disse / ha detto che aspettava da tanto.
3. Paul disse / ha detto che Mary sarebbe stata a Parigi lunedì.
4. Lei disse / ha detto di avere preso la casa con lui.
5. Ann disse / ha detto di voler andare sola.
6. Lui disse / ha detto a sua madre che cominciava il lavoro il giorno dopo.
7. Lei gli disse che aveva visto Mary due giorni prima.
8. Lui disse / ha detto a Tom di mettere il cappotto.
9. Lei chiese se poteva usare il mio telefono.
10. Dissero che sarebbero stati là.

C
1. Mangiare
2. Viaggiando
3. affascinante / interessante
4. fare
5. essere stato/a
6. correndo
7. Dicendo

8. Essendo
9. fare, mangiare
10. Studiare, interessante

D
1. Penso di partire domani.
2. Dopo aver bevuto il caffè, cominciava a lavorare.
3. Dopo aver imparato l'italiano, troverò un lavoro.
4. Dopo essere uscito di casa, si sentì meglio.
5. Lavorando tanto, ti ammalerai.
6. Parlando, uscì.

E
1. Prima di andare a Roma, ho visitato Venezia.
2. Studiando intensamente, hanno imparato la lingua.
3. Nel leggere gli esercizi, lui ha trovato uno sbaglio.
4. Essendo partiti i suoi amici, Mary ha cominciato a piangere.
5. Avendo finito i compiti, sono usciti per una passeggiata.
6. Dopo aver finito le lezioni, gli studenti devono fare questo esercizio.
7. Ci piace nuotare e giocare a tennis.
8. Abbiamo passato il tempo ammirando i grandi capolavori artistici a Roma ed a Firenze.
9. E' stato un film divertente.
10. Gli studenti che frequentano (frequentanti) questo corso amano parlare in italiano.
11. Incontro Paul ogni giorno nell'andare a casa.

VOCABULARY

CGIL	Confederazione Generale Italiana del Lavoro; Federation of Italian Trade Unions
CISL	Confederazione Italiana Sindacati Lavoratori; Federation of Italian Trade Unions
DC	Democrazia Cristiana; Christian Democrat Party
DP	Democrazia Proletaria; Proletarian Democracy
DSE	Dipartimento Scuola e Educazione; Department of Schools and Education
ENI	Ente Nazionale Idrocarburi; National Hydrocarbon Corporation
FIAT	Fabbrica Italiana Automobili Torino; Italian Automobile Factory of Turin
IRI	Istituto per la Ricostruzione Industriale; Istitute for the Reconstruction of Industry
MSI-DN	Movimento Sociale Italiano - Destra Nazionale; Italian Social Movement, National Right Wing
PCI	Partito Comunista Italiano; Italian Communist Party
PLI	Partito Liberale Italiano; Italian Liberal Party
PR	Partito Radicale Radical Party
PRI	Partito Repubblicano Italiano; Italian Republican Party
PSDI	Partito Socialista Democratico Italiano; Italian Socialist Democratic Party
PSI	Partito Socialista Italiano; Italian Socialist Party
Raidue	Channel Two
Raitre	Channel Three
Raiuno	Channel One
Tv	Television, Tv
UIL	Unione Italiana Lavoratori; Italian Labor Office
WWF	World Wildlife Federation

a	to, at, in
abbandonare	to abandon, to leave, to desert
abbandonarsi	to let oneself go, to give oneself up to something
abbastanza	enough
abbellire	to embellish, to adorn, to beautify
abbraccio	hug, embrace
abilità	ability
abitante	inhabitant
abitare	to live, to dwell
abitato	lived, inhabited
abitazione	habitation, dwelling, residence
abituarsi	to be used to...
abitudine	habit
abusare	to abuse
accademico	academic
accadere	to happen
accanto	near
accendere	to light
accendino	lighter
acceso	lit, lighted
accettare	to accept
accettazione	acceptance
acciaio	steel
accidenti	damn!
accogliere	to receive, to grant, to consent to
accomodarsi	to make oneself comfortable
accompagnare	to accompany
acconsentire	to consent, to agree
accontentare	to satisfy, to content
accordo	agreement, consent
accorto	shrewd, sagacious, cunning
accostarsi	to come near, to go near
aceto	vinegar
acqua	water
acquatico	aquatic
acquistare	to acquire
acquisto	acquired
acustica	acoustic
adatto	correct, suitable
addio	farewell, good-bye
addizione	addition
addormentare	to put to sleep, to send to sleep
addormentarsi	to fall asleep
adesso	now
adozione	adoption
adulto	adult, grown-up
aereo	airplane
affare	business, affair, matter
affascinante	fascinating, glamorous
affatto	at all
affermare	to affirm
affermazione	affirmation
affettato	affected
affezionato	affectionate, fond, loving
affidare	to entrust
affinché	so that, in order to
affitto	rent
affollato	crowded
affresco	fresco
africano	African
agenzia	agency
aggiornato	up-to-date
aggiungere	to add
agire	to act
agitare	to agitate, to shake, to stir
agosto	August
agricolo	agricultural
agricoltura	agriculture
aguzzo	sharp, pointed
aiutare	to help, to aid
aiuto	help, aid
albergo	hotel
albero	tree
alcolico	alcoholic
alcuno	any, some; anybody, anyone
aldilà	beyond
alimentare	to feed; adj. alimentary, food
alimentazione	feeding
alimento	food
allacciare	to fasten
allacciarsi	to fasten
alleanza	alliance
alleato	allied
allegorico	allegoric/al
allegro	happy, cheerful
allestire	to prepare
allievo	student, pupil
allontanare	to move, to send out, to send away
allontanarsi	to go away, to leave
allora	then, well ... then, so, therefore
almeno	at least
alpino	alpine
altezza	height
alto	high, tall
altresì	also, as well, too
altrimenti	otherwise
altro	other
alunno	student, pupil
alzarsi	to get up
amabile	lovable, likeable
amante	lover, adj. fond (of)
amare	to love
amaro	bitter
amatore	lover, amateur
ambiente	environment
americano	American
amica	friend
amicizia	friendship
amico	friend, friendly
ammalato	ill
amministrativo	administrative
ammirare	to admire, to wonder at

ammirazione	admiration	armare	to arm
ammodernamento	modernization	armato	armed
amore	love	armonia	harmony
analisi	analysis	arrabbiarsi	to become angry / to get angry
analizzare	to analyze		
anche	also, too	arrabbiato	angry, mad
ancora	still, yet	arredamento	interior decoration, furnishing
andare	to go		
andarsene	to go away, to leave	arrestarsi	to stop
anello	ring	arrivare	to arrive
anestesia	anaesthesia	arrivederci	good-bye
angelo	angel	arrivederla	good-bye (formal)
animale	animal	arte	art
animato	animated	artefice	artificer, author, creator
annegato	drowned person	articolo	article
anno	year	artificiale	artificial
annoiarsi	to be bored	artifizio	artifice, affectation
ansante	panting	artigianato	craftsmanship
antico	ancient	artigiano	artisan, craftsman
antifascista	anti-Fascist	artista	artist
antipartito	anti-party	artisticamente	artistically
antipasto	antipasto / hors d'oeuvre	artistico	artistic
antipatico	disagreeable, unpleasant	asciutto	dry
antisistema	anti-establishment	ascoltare	to listen (to)
anzi	rather, on the contrary	ascolto	listening
anziché	rather than, instead of	aspettare	to await / to wait for
aperitivo	apéritif	aspetto	aspect, look, appearance
aperto	open	aspirazione	aspiration
apice	apex, top, summit	assai	very
appannare	to blur, to dim	assassino	assassin, killer, murderer
apparecchiare	to prepare, to set (to lay) the table	assegno	check
		assente	absent
apparire	to appear	assemblea	meeting, assembly
appartamento	apartment	assicurare	to assure, to insure
appartenere	to belong	assieme	together
appassionante	fascinating	assistente	assistant
appassionato	passionate, n. fan	assistenziale	ente = welfare center, organization
appena	just		
appiattimento	n. flattening (out)	assolato	sunny
applicare	to apply	assolutamente	absolutely
apprendere	to learn	assoluto	absolute
apprezzabile	appreciable, valuable	assumere	to take on, to assume
apprezzare	to appreciate	assurgere	to rise
approfittare	to gain, to profit	atlantico	Atlantic
approssimativo	approximate	atletica	athletic
approvazione	approval	atmosfera	atmosphere
appuntamento	appointment	atteggiamento	attitude
appunto	exactly	attempato	elderly, aged
aprile	April	attendere	to wait, to await
aprire	to open	attentamente	attentivelly, carefully
aprirsi	to open, to bust open, to confide	attento	attentive, careful
		attenzione	attention
arbitrario	arbitrary	atterrire	to terrify, to frighten
archeologico	archaeological	attesa	waiting, wait
architetto	architect	attimo	moment
archivio	archives	attivamente	actively
arco	arch	attivare	to activate
area	area, surface	attività	activity
argomento	subject, topic	attivo	active
aria	air	atto	action, act, deed

attore	actor	banco	bench, counter, bank
attorno	around, about	barba	beard
attraversare	to cross, to pass through	barca	boat
attraverso	through, across	basarsi	to base
attuale	present, current	base	base
attualità	news, topicality	basilica	basilica
attualmente	at present, currently	basilico	basil
augurare	to wish	bastare	to be enough, to be sufficient
augurio	wish	bastimento	ship, vessel, cargo boat
aula	lecture hall, classroom	battere	to beat, to strike, to hit
aumentare	to increase	beato	blessed, lucky, blissful
aumento	increase, rise	beh!	well!
australiano	Australian	bellezza	beauty, handsomeness
autarchico	autarchic	bello	fine, beautiful, handsome,
auto	car		lovely
autobiografia	autobriography	bene	well
autobus	bus (in town)	benedire	to bless
automobile	automobile, car	benino	pretty well, not bad
automobilismo	motoring	bere	to drink
automobilistico	adj. car, motor, driving	bevanda	drink
autonomia	autonomy, self-government	bianco	white
autonomo	autonomous	bibita	drink
autore	author	biblico	biblical
autoritario	authoritarian, authoritative	biblioteca	library
autorità	authority	bicchiere	glass
autostop	hitch-hiking	bicicletta	bicycle
autostrada	speedway, motorway	biennio	a period of two years
autoveicolo	motor vehicle	bigiotteria	trinkets shop
autunno	autumn	bigliettaio	ticket clerk, ticket collector,
avanti	ahead, in front, forward;		box-office attendant
	enter!	biglietto	ticket, note, card, note (bill)
avere	to have	bilancio	budget, balance sheet
avvelenare	to poison	biodegradabile	biodegradable
avvenimento	event, occurrence	biondo	fair, blond
avvenire	to happen, to occur	bipede	biped
avvento	coming, accession, advent	birra	beer, ale
avventura	adventure	bisognare	must, to have to, to need to
avversario	contrary, opposing; opponent	bisogno	need, necessity, want
avvertire	to warn, to inform, to caution	bisognoso	poor, needy
avviarsi	to set out	bistecca	steak
avvicinare	to approach, to draw	bloccare	to block, to stop
	near(er), to bring near(er)	bocca	mouth
avvicinarsi	to get closer, to get nearer	boccia	bowl
avvincere	to grip, to enthrall	boom	boom
avvisare	to inform	borghese	middle-class, bourgeois
avviso	notice	borsa	hand bag, purse, pocketbook
azienda	firm, business, board	bosco	woods, wood
aziendale	adj. firm, company	bottega	shop
azione	action	botteghino	box-office
azzurro	blue, azure	bottiglia	bottle
bacio	kiss	braccio	arm
bagaglio	luggage, baggage	brasiliano	Brasilian
baia	bay	bravo	good (at), good, skilled, nice
balbettare	to stammer, to stutter	breccia	breach
ballare	to dance	breve	brief, short
ballerino	dancer, ballet-dancer	brillante	brilliant
ballo	dance	briscola	"briscola", trump
bambina	baby, child	brivido	shiver, creeps
bambino	baby, child	brodo	broth
banca	bank	brontolare	to grumble, to mumble

bruno	brown, dark, (hair, eyes)	cappella	chapel
brutto	ugly	cappotto	coat
buca	pit, hole, hollow	cappuccino	cappuccino (coffee with milk)
buco	hole	carattere	character, nature, disposition
bugia	lie	caratteristica	characteristic
bugiardo	liar	caratterizzare	to characterize, to distinguish
buio	dark, darkness	carbone	coal, carbon
buonasera	good evening	cardiaco	cardiac
buongiorno	good morning	carica	office, appointment
buono	good	caricare	to load, to take on, to charge, to wind up
burocratico	bureaucratic		
burocrazia	bureaucracy	carico	load, cargo, burden
bussare	to knock	carie	decay, cavity
buttare	to throw	carino	nice, charming, cute
caccia	hunting, shooting	carismatico	charismatic
cacciata	hunting party	carne	flesh, meat
cacciatore	hunter, huntsman	carnevale	carnival
cadavere	corpse	caro	dear, expensive
cadere	to fall	carriera	career
caduta	fall, drop	carro	cart, wagon
caffè	coffee, café	carta	paper
calcio	kick, football (Brit.), soccer (Am.)	cartolina	postcard
		casa	house, home
caldo	adj. warm; n. heat	casello	toll house
calma	calm	caso	chance, case, event
calza	sock, stocking	cassaforte	safe
calzatura	footwear	cassetta	small case, box
calzoni	trousers, pants, slacks	castano	chestnut-colored, brown
cambiare	to change	castello	castle
cambio	change, exchange	categoria	category, class
camera	bedroom, room	cattedrale	cathedral
cameriera	maid, waitress	cattivo	bad, evil, wicked, naughty
cameriere	waiter	cattolico	catholic
camicia	shirt, blouse	catturare	to capture, to catch, to seize
caminetto	fireplace	causa	cause, reason
camminare	to walk	causare	to cause
campagna	country, countryside	cavaliere	rider, horseman, knight
campeggio	camp, camping ground	cavalletto	horse, trestle, tripod, easel
campione	champion	cavallo	horse
campo	field	cavare	to pull out, to draw out
canale	canal, channel	ce	there; to us, us
candidato	candidate	celebrare	to celebrate
cane	dog	celebrazione	celebration
canoa	canoe	celebre	famous, celebrated
canottaggio	rowing, boating	celebrità	fame, celebrity
cantante	singer	cena	dinner, supper
cantare	to sing	cenare	to have dinner, to have supper
cantina	cellar		
canto	singing, song, lyric, canto	cenere	ash
capace	able, capable	censo	wealth, substance; census
capacità	ability, capability	centinaio	hundred
capanna	hut, cabin	cento	hundred
capire	to understand	centrale	central
capitale	capital	centralità	central position
capitano	captain	centrare	to center, to adjust
capitare	to happen, to chance	centrismo	center party policy
capitolo	chapter	centrista	center party supporter
capo	head	centro	centre (Brit.), center (Am.)
capolavoro	masterpiece	cerca	search, quest
capotavola	head of the table	cercare	to look for, to search, to seek

cercatore	seeker, inquirer
cerimonia	ceremony
cero	large candle
certamente	certainly, surely
certo	certain, sure
cespuglio	bush, thicket
cesta	basket
cestino	basket, wastepaper basket
cesto	basket, goal
ceto	class (social)
che	who, whom, which, that, what
chi	who? whom? which? whose? he who, whoever
chiacchierare	to chat, to chatter
chiacchierata	chat
chiamare	to call
chiamarsi	to be called
chiarire	to make clear, to explain
chiaro	clear, bright, light
chiave	key
chiedere	to ask, to ask for, to demand, to beg
chiedersi	to ask, to inquire
chiesa	church
chilometro	kilometer (Am.), kilometre (Brit.)
chimico	adj. chemical; n. chemical, chemist
chirurgo	surgeon
chissà	goodness knows! who knows!
chitarra	guitar
chiudere	to shut, to close
chiudersi	to close, to withdraw
chiuso	closed, shut
ci	us, to us; there; ourselves, each other
ciao	hello! hi! bye! so long!
cibo	food
ciclismo	cycling
ciclista	cyclist
ciclo	cycle
cielo	sky, heaven
ciliegia	cherry
cima	top, summit, peak
cimitero	cemetery
cinema	cinema, movies
cinematografo	cinema, movies
cinese	Chinese
cinquanta	fifty
cinque	five
cintura	belt
ciò	that, this
cioccolata	chocolate
cioccolatino	chocolate
cioccolato	chocolate
cioè	that is, namely
circa	about, approximately
circolare	circular
circondare	to surround, to encircle
circostante	surrounding, neighboring
citare	to summon, to cite, to quote
cittadina	citizen (f), small town, country town
cittadino	citizen (m)
città	city, town
civile	civil
civiltà	civilization
classe	class, form (Brit.), grade (Am.)
classico	classic, classical
clima	climate
club	club
coalizione	coalition
coalizzare	to unite
coda	tail
coinvolgere	to involve
colazione	breakfast, lunch
colei	she, her
collaborare	to collaborate
collaborazione	collaboration
collana	necklace
collettività	collectivity, community
collettivo	collective
collezione	collection
collina	hill
collo	neck
colonna	column, pillar
colonnato	colonnade
colore	color, hue
coloro	they, them
colossale	colossal, gigantic
colpire	to hit, to strike
colpo	blow, stroke, shot, scoop
colto	cultivated, cultured
colui	he, him
comandamento	commandment
comandante	commander
comandare	to be in command, to command
combattere	to fight
combinazione	combination
come	as, like, how
cominciare	to begin, to start
comitato	committee
comizio	meeting, assembly
commedia	play, comedy
commento	comment, remark
commerciale	commercial, business, trade
commercio	commerce, trade, business
commesso	clerk
commettere	to commit
commissariato	commissionership
commissario	commissary, commissioner
commuovere	to move, to touch, to affect
comodo	useful, convenient, comfortable
compagnia	company
compagno	companion, buddy, mate, fellow, chum
compendiare	to abridge, to summarize

competenza	competence
competizione	competition, contest
compiere	to complete, to perform, to finish
compito	duty, task, exercise, homework
compleanno	birthday
complemento	complement
complesso	complex, complicated
completamente	completely, entirely
completare	to complete, to finish
completo	complete
complicato	complicated, complex
complice	accomplice, accessory
complimento	compliment
comporre	to compose
comportarsi	to behave
compositore	composer, typesetter
comprare	to buy, to purchase
comprendere	to include, to comprehend, to understand
comprensibile	intelligible, comprehensible
comprensione	understanding, comprehension
comprensivo	understanding, sympathetic
compressa	tablet
computer	computer
comunale	municipal, city, town
comune	adj. common; n. municipality
comunicare	to communicate, to transmit
comunicazione	communication
comunista	communist
comunque	in any case, anyhow; however, no matter how
con	with
concerto	concert
concetto	concept, idea
conchiglia	shell, conch
concludersi	to conclude
concorrere	to go together, to concur
concretezza	concreteness
condannare	to sentence, to condemn, to convict
condizione	condition
conducente	driver
confederazione	confederation, confederacy, league
conferenza	lecture, conference
confermare	to confirm
confezione	manufacturing
confidenza	confidence, trust
confine	border, frontier
conflittuale	conflicting
confondersi	to get mixed up, to become confused
confortevole	comforting, comfortable
confronto	comparision
confuso	confused, muddled, vague
conoscenza	knowledge
conoscere	to know
conoscitore	expert, connoisseur
conquista	conquest
conquistatore	to conquer, to subdue
consegnare	to deliver, to hand over
conseguente	consequent
conseguenza	consequence
conseguire	to attain, to reach
consenso	consent
consentire	to consent, to assent
conservare	to preserve, to keep
considerare	to consider, to think of, to regard
considerazione	consideration
consigliabile	advisable, expedient
consigliare	to advise
consiglio	advice
consumo	consumption
contadino	farmer, peasant
contanti	cash, ready money
contare	to count
contatto	contact
contemporanea-mente	simultaneously contemporaneously
contemporaneo	contemporary, simultaneous
contendersi	to contend, to compete
contento	content, happy
contestazione	contest, dispute
continuare	to continue
continuo	continuous
conto	account, bill
contorno	contour, outline; pl. vegetables
contrada	(town) district
contrarietà	set back, misfortune
contrario	contrary, opposite
contrastante	contrasting, clashing
contrasto	contrast, opposition, difference
contratto	contract
contro	against
controllabile	controllable
controllare	to check, to examine, to control
controllo	control, check, examination
convegno	meeting
convenire	to meet, to gather
convergere	to converge
conversazione	conversation, talk
convincere	to convince, to persuade
convinto	convinced, persuaded
coppa	cup
coppia	couple, pair
coprire	to cover
coraggio	courage, bravery
corale	choral, unanimous
cordiale	hearty, cordial
coro	chorus, choir
corporativo	corporative, relating to guilds
corposo	adj. having body (ref. to wine)

214

correre	to run	cuore	heart
corsa	run, race, course, track	cupola	dome
corso	course; main street of a town	cura	cure, treatment
corte	court	curabile	curable
corteggiare	to court, to woo, to pay court	curare	to take care of, to look after, to cure
corteggiato	courted		
cortese	kind, polite, courteous	curiosità	curiosity
cortesia	kindness, politeness, courtesy	curioso	curious
		curriculum	curriculum vitae, academic curriculum
corto	short (measurement)		
cosa	thing, matter, affair	curva	curve, bend
così	so, thus; like this, this way; like that, that way	da	from, to, at, by, like, as
		dai	go on!
costante	constant	danno	damage, loss, injury, harm
costanza	constancy, steadfastness	danza	dance
costare	to cost	dappertutto	everywhere
costiero	coastal	dare	to give
costituente	constituent	darsi	to devote oneself
costituire	to constitute, to found, to establish	datore	giver
		davanti	in front
costituirsi	to set oneself up; to give oneself up	davvero	really, indeed
		debito	debt, duty
costituzionale	constitutional	debole	weak, feeble
costituzione	establishment, constitution	debolezza	weakness, feebleness
costoso	costly, expensive, dear	decidere	to decide, to determine
costringere	to compel, to force, to oblige	decidersi	to make up one's mind
costruire	to build, to construct	decimo	tenth
costruirsi	to establish, to build	decisamente	decidedly
costruzione	construction	decisione	decision
costume	custom, use, usage, habit; pl. morals; costume	decisivo	decisive
		deciso	decided
creare	to create	décolleté	décolleté
creatività	creativity	decorare	to decorate, to adorn
creazione	creation	decorazione	decoration, ornament
credere	to believe, to trust; to think	dedicare	to dedicate
credito	credit	definire	to define
crema	cream	definitivamente	once and for all, definitively
crepapelle	a--: to an extreme	definitivo	definitive, final
crescere	to grow, to increase, to rise	delicatezza	delicacy
crisi	crisis	delicato	delicate
cristianità	Christendom, Christianity	deltaplano	glider, hang-glider
cristiano	Christian	democratico	adj. democratic; n. democrat
criterio	criterion	democrazia	democracy
critico	adj. critical; n. critic, reviewer	denaro	money
cronaca	chronicle, news	dente	tooth
crostaceo	crustacean	dentista	dentist
crudele	cruel	dentro	in, inside, within
cucchiaino	teaspoon	denuncia	change, indictment, denunciation
cucciolo	puppy		
cucina	kitchen, cuisine, cooking	deputato	deputy; M.P. (Brit.); Rep. in Congress (Am.)
cucinare	to cook		
cucire	to sew, to stitch	derubare	to rob
cugina	cousin (f.)	descrivere	to describe, to relate
cugino	cousin (m.)	deserto	desert, wilderness
cui	that, whom, which	desiderare	to wish, to want, to long for, to yearn for, to desire
culla	cradle		
cultura	culture, learning	desiderio	wish, desire, longing
culturale	cultural	designer	designer
cumulo	heap, pile, lot	dessert	dessert
cuocere	to cook	destinare	to destine, to assign, to allot

destra	right hand, right, the right	dirigersi	to turn one's steps
destro	right, right-hand	diritto	straight
determinare	to determine	disavventura	mishap, misadventure
detestare	to detest	discendente	adj. descending; n. descendant
dettagliatamente	in detail		
di	of, some, any, from, in, by	disciplina	subject of study, discipline
diagnosi	diagnosis	disco	record, disk
dialetto	dialect	discorso	speech; conversation, talk
dialogo	dialogue	discoteca	disco, discoteque
diametro	diameter	discutere	to discuss
diario	diary, journal	discutibile	debatable
diaspora	diaspora	disegnare	to draw, to sketch, to design
diavolo	devil	disgrazia	misfortune, disgrace
dicembre	December	disoccupato	unemployed
dichiarare	to declare	dispersivo	wasteful
diciannove	nineteen	dispiacere	to be sorry, to regret; n. regret
diciannovesimo	nineteenth	disponibile	available
diciassette	seventeen	disposizione	disposition
diciassettesimo	seventeenth	disposto	ready, disposed
diciottesimo	eighteenth	disputa	discussion, debate, dispute
diciotto	eighteen	distaccare	to detach, to separate
dieci	ten	distacco	detachment
dieta	diet	distinto	distinct
dietetico	dietetic	distinzione	distinction
dietro	behind	distratto	absent-minded, inattentive
difendere	to defend	distruggere	to destroy
difesa	defense	distruzione	destruction
difettoso	defective, faulty	disturbare	to disturb, to bother
diffamare	to defame	disturbarsi	to trouble oneself
differente	different, unlike	disturbo	trouble, nuisance, disturbance
differenza	difference		
difficile	difficult, hard	disumano	inhuman
difficoltà	difficulty	dito	finger
diffidare	to distrust, to mistrust	ditta	firm, business
diffondere	to diffuse, to spread	divenire	to become, to grow, to turn
diffusamente	diffusely	diventare	to become, to grow, to turn
diffusione	diffusion	diversificato	diversified
diga	dam, dike	diverso	different
dignità	dignity	divertente	amusing, entertaining
dilettantistico	amateurish	divertimento	amusement, entertainment
dimensione	dimension, size	divertire	to amuse, to entertain
dimenticare	to forget	divertirsi	to enjoy oneself, to have a good time
dimenticarsi	to forget		
dimora	residence, abode, home	dividere	to divide
dimostrare	to show, to demonstrate	diviso	divided
dinamico	dynamic, energetic	divino	divine, godlike
dinanzi	in front, in front of, before	divulgazione	popularization
dinosauro	dinosaur	dizionario	dictionary
dio	god	doccia	shower
dipartimento	department	documento	document, paper
dipendente	dependent	dodici	twelve
dipendere	to derive, to depend, to proceed	dolce	sweet, dessert
		dolcezza	sweetness
dipingere	to paint	dolore	sorrow, grief, pain, ache
dipinto	adj. painted; n. painting	doloroso	painful, sorrowful
dire	to say, to tell	domanda	question
direttamente	directly	domandare	to ask (for), to demand, to beg
diretto	direct		
direttore	manager, director	domandarsi	to ask oneself, to wonder
direzione	direction, way	domani	tomorrow

domattina	tomorrow morning	emarginare	to margin; to exclude
domenica	Sunday	emigrante	emigrant
domestica	maid, domestic	emigrare	to emigrate
dominare	to dominate, to control	emigrazione	emigration
donna	woman	emozionante	exciting
dopo	after, afterwards, then, later	emozionato	excited
dopoguerra	postwar period	enorme	enormous, huge
doppio	double	en plein air	in the open air
dormire	to sleep	entrambi	both
dorsale	dorsal	entrare	to enter, to go in, to come in
dottore	doctor, physician; graduate	entro	in, within
dove	where	entusiasmo	enthusiasm
dovere	must, to have to; to owe	episodio	episode
dovunque	everywhere, anywhere, wherever	epoca	epoch, age, era
		eppure	and yet, but
dramma	drama, play	equilibrio	balance
drammatico	dramatic	erba	grass, herb
drammaturgo	dramatist, playwright	erede	heir, heiress
drappo	cloth	eroe	hero
drogato	drugged	eroico	heroic
dubbio	doubt	eroismo	heroism
due	two	esalazione	exhalation
duello	duel	esaltante	exalting
dunque	so, therefore, then, well then	esaltazione	exaltation
duomo	cathedral	esame	examination, exam
durante	during	esaminare	to examine
durare	to last	esattamente	exactly
durata	duration, length	escludere	to exclude
duro	hard	esclusione	exclusion
e	and	esclusivamente	exclusively
eccellenza	excellence	esclusivo	exclusive
eccetera	et cetera	escursione	excursion, trip
eccezione	exception	esecutivo	executive
ecco	here, there, here is, here are, there is, there are	esempio	example
		esemplare	exemplary
ecologia	ecology	esercitare	to exercise, to practice, to train
economia	economy		
economicamente	economically	esercito	army
economico	economic, economical	esercizio	exercize
edificio	building, edifice	esibizione	exhibition
educativo	educational, instructive	esigere	to require, to demand, to exact
educazione	upbringing, breeding, good manners		
		esilio	exile, banishment
efficace	efficacious, effectual, effective	esistenza	existence
		esistere	to exist
efficiente	efficient	esodo	exodus
egli	he	esperienza	experience
eh	hey!	esperto	expert, skilled, skilful, expert
elaborazione	elaboration		
elegante	elegant	esporre	to show, to exhibit, to display
eleganza	elegance	esportare	to export
eleggere	to elect	esportazione	export
elementare	elementary	espressione	expression
elemento	element	espressivo	expressive
elettorale	electoral	esprimere	to express
elettrico	electric, electrical	esprimersi	to express oneself, to speak
elettrodomestico	household appliance	essa	she, it, her
elettronica	electronics	esse	they, them
elettronico	electronic	essenziale	essential
elezione	election	esserci	to be there

essere	to be	favorevole	favorable, propitious
essi	they, them	favorire	to favor, to favour
esso	he, him, it	fazenderos	farmers (Span.)
est	east	febbraio	February
estate	summer	febbre	fever, temperature
esterno	external	fedele	faithful
estero	foreign; n. foreign countries	felice	happy, lucky
esteso	large, wide, extensive	felicemente	happily
esteticamente	aesthetically	felicità	happiness
estinzione	extinction	femminile	female, feminine
estivo	adj. summer	femminilità	womanliness, femininity
estremamente	extremely	fenomeno	phenomenon
estro	inspiration, whim	ferie	holidays, vacation
eternità	eternity	ferita	wound, injury .
etrusco	Etruscan	fermamente	firmly
ettaro	hectare	fermare	to stop
età	age	fermarsi	to stop
europeistico	Europeanistic	fermata	stop
europeo	European	fermo	still, steady, firm
evidente	evident, obvious	ferragosto	mid - August holidays
evitare	to avoid	ferro	iron
evoluzione	evolution	ferrovia	n. railway, railroad
export	export	ferroviario	adj. railway, railroad
fa	ago	fertile	fertile
fabbrica	factory, works	fervore	fervour, fervor
fabbricazione	manufacture	festa	holiday, feast
faccia	face	fetta	slice
facciata	façade	fiaba	fable
facile	easy	fiancheggiare	to flank
facilmente	easily	fianco	side, flank
facoltà	school (within a university)	fidanzamento	engagement
fallire	to fail, to go bankrupt	fidanzarsi	to get engaged
fama	fame, renown	fidanzata	fiancée
fame	hunger	fidanzato	fiancé
famiglia	family	fidarsi	to trust, to rely
familiare	adj. domestic, family	fiducia	trust, confidence
famoso	famous, renowned	fiero	proud
fanatismo	fanaticism	figlia	daughter
fantasia	imagination, fantasy	figlio	son
fantasioso	fanciful	figura	figure
fantasma	ghost, phantom	figurarsi	to imagine
fantastico	imaginary, fantastic	fila	row, line, file
fantoccio	puppet	film	film, motion picture, movie
fare	to do, to make	filo	thread, wire
farmacia	pharmacy, chemist's shop, drugstore	filosofico	philosophic (al)
		filosofo	philosopher
farsi	to grow, to get	finale	last, final
fascino	charm, fascination	finalmente	finally, at last
fascismo	fascism	finanziario	financial
fascista	fascist	finchè	till, until
fase	stage, period, phase	fine	f. end; m. purpose, end, aim
fastidioso	troublesome, tiresome	finestra	window
fasto	pomp, splendor	finestrino	window (car, train)
fatica	weariness, fatigue	finire	to finish
faticosamente	laboriously	finito	finished
faticoso	fatiguing, tiring; laborious	fino a	till, untill, up to
fatto	fact, action, deed	finora	till now, up to now
fattoria	farm	finzione	pretence, sham
favoloso	fabulous	fiore	flower
favore	favour, favor	fiorente	blooming, flowering

fiorentino	Florentine		function
fiorire	to flower	fuoco	fire
firma	signature	fuori	out, outside
firmare	to sign	furto	theft, larceny
fisica	physics	fusilli	a type of long, curly pasta
fisico	physical	futuro	future (adj. and n.)
fisionomia	physiognomy	galera	prison, jail
fisso	fixed	galleria	tunnel
fiume	river	gamba	leg
flora	flora	gangster	gangster
focaccia	cake	gara	competition, contest, race
focolare	hearth, fireplace	garage	garage
foglio	sheet	garantire	to guarantee
folclore	folklore	garbo	politeness, courtesy
folkloristico	folkloristic	gareggiare	to compete, to vie
folle	mad, insane	gas	gas
fondare	to found, to establish	gatto	cat
fondo	bottom	gelateria	ice cream shop
fontana	fountain	gelato	n. ice cream; adj. frozen, icy
fonte	spring, source	generale	general
foresta	forest, woods	generalmente	generally
forma	form, shape	generazione	generation
formaggio	cheese	genere	kind, race, gender
formare	to form	generoso	generous
formarsi	to form, to develop	geniale	ingenious, clever
formazione	formation	genio	genius
fornire	to supply, to provide, to furnish	genitore	parent
		gennaio	January
forse	perhaps, maybe	gente	people
forte	strong	gentildonna	gentlewoman, lady
fortilizio	fort	gentile	kind, polite
fortuna	fortune, luck	gentilezza	kindness, politeness
fortunato	lucky, fortunate	genuino	genuine
forza	strength, force	geografia	geography
foto	photo, snapshot	gergo	slang, jargon
fotografia	photograph	gettare	to throw
fra	between, among	ghiaccio	ice
fragola	strawberry	già	already, formerly, of course, yes
frammento	fragment		
francescano	Franciscan	giallo	yellow; n. mystery story, thriller
fratello	brother		
freccia	arrow	giardino	garden
freddezza	coldness	ginnastica	gymnastics
freddo	cold (adj. and n.)	ginocchio	knee
fregare	to take in, to pinch, to steal	giocare	to play
frequentare	to frequent, to attend, to patronize	gioco	play, game
		gioia	joy, delight
fresco	fresh, cool	gioiello	jewel
fretta	haste	giornale	newspaper
frigorifero	refrigerator	giornalista	journalist, reporter
fronte	f. forehead, m. front	giornata	day
frutta	fruit (in general)	giorno	day
frutto	fruit(s), result(s)	giostra	joust, tournament
fuggire	to run away, to flee	giovane	adj. young; n.m. young man, n.f. young woman
fulmine	lightning, thunderbolt		
fumare	to smoke	giovanile	juvenile, youthful
fumo	smoke	giovedì	Thursday
funebre	funeral, funereal	gioventù	youth
funzionale	functional	girare	to turn, to travel, to tour
funzionare	to work, to operate, to	giro	short walk, tour

gita	trip, excursion	idolo	idol
giudice	judge	idoneo	fit, suitable
giudiziario	judicial	ieri	yesterday
giudizio	judgment, sentence	iettatore	bird of ill omen
giugno	June	il	the
giungla	jungle	illuminazione	illumination
giustacausa	just cause	illusione	illusion
giustizia	justice	illustrare	to illustrate, to explain
giusto	just, right	illustrato	illustrated
gli	the, to him, to it, to them	illustrazione	illustration
gliela	it (f.) to him, her, them	illustre	illustrious
gliele	them (f.) to him, her, them	imitare	to imitate
globale	total, inclusive	immaginario	imaginary
glorioso	glorious	immagine	image
godere	to enjoy	immediatamente	immediately, at once
goloso	greedy	immediato	immediate
gomito	elbow	immenso	immense
gomma	rubber, gum, tire, eraser	immettere	to admit, to let in
gonna	skirt	immigrato	immigrant
gotico	gothic	imparare	to learn
governare	to govern	impartire	to impart
governo	government	impazzata	all'-----: madly
gradazione	gradation	impegnarsi	to commit oneself
gradevole	agreable, pleasant	impegnato	engaged, bound, committed
gradito	pleasant, welcome	impegno	engagement, obligation
grado	degree, rank	imperatore	emperor
grande	great, big, large	impermeabile	raincoat
grandezza	greatness	impero	empire
grandioso	grand, majestic, grandiose	impeto	impetus
granduca	grand duke	impianto	plant, installation
grasso	fat, stout	impiegare	to employ, to use
gratuito	free, gratuitous	impiegato	employee
grave	heavy, grave, serious	impiego	use, employment
grazie	thanks	implorare	to implore, to beg
grazioso	pretty, graceful	imponente	stately, imposing
greco	Greek	imporre	to impose
gridare	to shout	impostare	to start, to set up; to post, to
grigio	grey, gray		mail
grosso	big, large	importanza	importance
gruppo	group	importare	to import
guaio	trouble, difficulty	impossibile	impossible
guadagnare	to gain, to earn	imprecisato	undetermined
guadagnarsi	to earn	impresa	undertaking, enterprise
guado	ford	improbabile	improbable
guardare	to look (at), to gaze (at), to	improvvisato	improvised
	watch	improvviso	sudden, unexpected
guardarsi	to mind, to beware	imprudente	imprudent, rash, unwise
guarire	to recover, to heal	in	in, at, on, inside, by
guasto	adj. damaged, n. damage	inaugurare	to inaugurate
guerra	war	incalzare	to follow closely
guida	guide	incantare	to enchant
guidare	to guide, to lead, to drive	incantevole	charming
gustare	to taste	incanto	enchantment, charm, spell
gusto	taste	includere	to include
idea	idea	incominciare	to begin, to start
ideale	ideal	incompleto	incomplete
idealizzare	to idealize	incondizionato	unconditional
identificare	to identify	incontrare	to meet
identificarsi	to identify oneself	incontrarsi	to meet
idioma	idiom	incontro	meeting, encounter

incredibile	incredible, unbelievable	integrarsi	to integrate
incredulo	incredulous	integrazione	integration
incrociarsi	to cross, to intersect, to meet	intelligente	intelligent
incrocio	crossing	intelligenza	intelligence
indicare	to indicate	iintendere	to hear, to understand,
indice	forefinger; index		to mean
indipendente	independent	intendersi	to be expert
indipendenza	independence	intensamente	intensely
indirizzo	address	intenzione	intention
indispensabile	essential	interessante	interesting
indisturbato	undisturbed	interesse	interest
individualismo	individualism	interessarsi	to take an interest
individuo	individual	interlocutore	interlocutor
indomani	the next day	internazionale	iinternational
indossare	to wear, to put on	interno	internal, interior
industria	industry	intero	whole, all, entire
industriale	adj. industrial, n. industrialist	interpretare	to interpret
industrializzare	to industrialize	interpretazione	interpretation
industrializzazione	industrialization	interrogare	to question, to ask
infatti	in fact, as a matter of fact	interrompere	to interrupt
inferiore	inferior, lower	intervenire	to intervene, to interfere
inferiorità	inferiority	intervento	intervention, interference,
infermiera	nurse		operation
inferno	hell	intervista	interview
infiggere	to drive, to fix	intervistare	to interview
infine	at last, finally	intervistato	interviewed
informare	to inform	intorno	around, about
informatica	computer science	invadere	to invade
informato	informed	invecchiato	aged
informazione	information	invece	instead
ingegnere	engineer	inverno	winter
ingegneria	engineering	inviare	to send, to forward
ingiustamente	unjustly, unfairly	inviolabile	inviolable
ingiusto	unjust, unfair	invitare	to invite
inglese	English	invitato	guest
ingrassare	to fatten	invito	invitation
ingresso	entry, entrance	io	I
iniziare	to begin, to start	ipotesi	hypothesis
iniziativa	initiative	ippica	horse racing
inizio	beginning	ironico	ironic
innalzare	to raise, to elevate	iscriversi	to enrol
innalzarsi	to rise	iscrizione	enrolment, matriculation,
innamorarsi	to fall in love		registration
innamorato	in love, fond; n. lover	isola	island
innervosire	to get on someone's nerves	ispirare	to inspire
innovatore	adj. innovating, n. innovator	ispiratore	adj. inspiring, n.m. inspirer
inoltre	besides	ispiratrice	n.f. inspirer
insalata	salad	ispirazione	inspiration
insegnamento	teaching	istante	instant
insegnante	teacher	istintivamente	instinctively
insegnare	to teach	istituire	to instituite, to set up, to
insieme	together		establish
insignificante	insignificant	istituzionale	institutional
insistere	to insist	istituzione	institution
insomma	in short, in a word	istruzione	education
instabile	unsteady, unstable	italiano	Italian
insuccesso	failure	italo-americano	Italo-American
insuperabile	insuperable	italo-argentino	Italo-Argentinian
intanto	meanwhile, in the meantime	italo-brasiliano	Italo-Brazilian
intatto	intact	italo-canadese	Italo-Canadian

italo-uruguayano	Italo-Uruguayan	liberare	to free, to liberate
jazz	jazz	libero	free
la	the, her, it	libertino	adj. loose, n. libertine
là	there	libertà	liberty, freedom
lacrima	tear	libreria	bookstore, bookshop
ladino	Ladin	libro	book
ladro	thief	licenziamento	dismissal, discharge
lago	lake	liceo	high school, secondary
laguna	lagoon		school
lamentarsi	to lament	lieto	happy, glad
lancia	lance	lieve	light, slight
lanciare	to throw, to fling, to hurl	limitare	to limit
largo	adj. wide, broad; n. breadth, width	limitarsi	to limit oneself
		limitazione	limitation
lasagna	lasagna	limite	limit
lasciare	to leave, to bequeath	linea	line
lasciarsi	to let oneself, to allow oneself	lingua	tongue, language
		linguaggio	language
lassù	up there	linguistico	linguistic
laterale	lateral, side	liquoroso	strong (said of liquor)
latifondista	rich landowner	lira	lira, Italian monetary unit
latino	Latin	lirico	lyric
lato	side	litigare	to quarrel, to argue
latte	milk	litro	liter, litre
laurea	university degree	livello	n. level
laureato	graduate	lo	the, him, it
lavanderia	laundry	locale	local
lavarsi	to wash oneself	località	locality
lavastoviglie	dishwashing machine	logicamente	logically
lavatrice	washer, washing machine	logico	logical
lavorare	to work, to labour, to toil	lombardo	Lombard
lavorato	wrought, worked	lontananza	distance
lavoratore	worker	lontano	far, far off, far away
lavorazione	processing, working	loricato	adj. loricate
lavoro	work, labour	loro	their, their own, theirs, they, them, to them, you (formal pl.), to you (formal pl.)
le	the, to her, to it, them (f.)		
legare	to tie, to bind		
legarsi	to tie oneself, to bind oneself	lotta	struggle, fight
legato	tied, bound	lotteria	lottery
legge	law	lotto	state lottery
leggendario	legendary	luce	light
leggere	to read	luglio	July
leggero	adj. light	lui	he, him
leggio	reading desk	lumaca	snail
legislativo	legislative	lume	light
lei	she, her, you (formal)	lunedì	Monday
lentamente	slowly	lungo	adj. long, prep. along
lessico	lexicon	luogo	place
lettera	letter	lupacchiotto	wolf-cub
letterario	literary	lupo	wolf
letteratura	literature	ma	but
letto	bed	macchè	of course not! go on! come off it!
lettore	reader		
lettorato	modern language assistantship	maccherone	maccherone
		macchia	spot, stain, blot
lettura	reading	macchina	machine, car
lezione	lesson, class	macchinario	machinery
li	them (m.)	madonna	lady, madonna
lì	there	madre	mother
liberale	liberal	maestro	master, teacher

magari	if only
maggio	May
maggioranza	majority
maggiordomo	butler
maggiore	greater, larger, bigger, older
magico	magic, magical
magistrato	official, authority
magistratura	magistrature, magistracy
maglia	stitch, jersey
maglione	pullover, sweater
magnifico	magnificent
magro	thin, lean
mah	who knows!
mai	never, ever
maiolica	majolica
malato	adj. sick, ill; n. patient
malattia	sickness, illness, disease
male	n. evil, ill, pain, ache; adv. badly
malgrado	in spite of, despite
malinconia	melancholy, gloom, notwithstanding
maltrattamento	ill treatment
mamma	mama, mummy
mancanza	lack, want, absence
mancare	to lack, to be lacking, to miss
mandare	to send
mangiare	to eat
manifestazione	display, manifestation
mano	hand
mantenere	to keep, to maintain
maratona	marathon
marchesa	marquise
marcia	march, gear
marcialonga	crosscountry skiing
mare	sea, seaside
marinaro	seafaring
marino	adj. marine, sea
marito	husband
marmellata	jam, marmalade
marmo	marble
martedì	Tuesday
marzo	March
mascherato	masked, disguised
maschio	adj. male, n. male, boy,
massa	mass, heap
massimo	greatest, maximum
massmedia	mass media
masticare	to chew
matematica	mathematics
matematico	adj. mathematical, n. mathematician
materia	matter, substance; subject
materiale	material
materialmente	materially
materno	motherly, maternal
matita	pencil
matrimonio	marriage, matrimony, wedding
mattina	morning
mattino	morning
maturato	matured
maturità	ripeness, maturity
me	me, to me
meccanico	adj. mechanical, n. mechanic
medesimo	same
mediare	to mediate
medicare	to medicate
medicina	medicine
medico	adj. medical, n. doctor
medievale	medieval
medio	middle
mediocre	mediocre
medioevale	medieval
medioevo	Middle Ages
mediterraneo	Mediterranean
meglio	better, best
mela	apple
melodramma	opera, melodrama
meno	less, fewer
mensa	table, university restaurant
mensile	monthly
mentale	mental
mentre	while, as, when, whereas
menzione	mention
mercante	merchant, trader, dealer
mercato	market
merce	goods, wares
mercoledì	Wednesday
merenda	snack
meritare	to deserve, to merit
meritevole	deserving, worthy
mescolare	to mix, to blend
mescolarsi	to mix, to blend, to mingle
mese	month
mestiere	trade, craft
metà	half
metallo	metal
metalmeccanico	metallurgical and mechanical
metano	methane
meteorologico	meteorological, weather
metodo	method
metro	meter, metre
metropoli	metropolis
metropolitana	underground, tube, subway
mettere	to put, to place, to set
mettersi	to begin, to wear
mezzanotte	midnight
mezzo	adj. half, n. half, middle, means
mezzogiorno	midday, noon
mi	me, to me, myself
migliaio	about a thousand
miglio	mile
migliore	better, best
mila	thousand (pl.)
milanese	Milanese
miliardo	billion
milionario	millionaire

223

milione	million
militare	military
milizia	troops
mille	thousand (s.)
millennio	millennium
minacciare	to threaten
minestra	soup
miniappartamento	mini-apartment
minimo	least, smallest, minimum
ministro	minister
minoranza	minority
minore	smaller, younger
minuto	adj. small, minute, n. minute
mio	my, mine
miracolo	miracle
miseria	misery
misericordia	mercy
mistero	mystery
misto	mixed
misura	measure, measurement, amount
misurare	to measure
mobile	adj. mobile, movable; n. piece of furniture
mobilitare	to mobilize
mobilitazione	mobilization
mocassino	mocassin
moda	fashion, style
modello	model, pattern
moderato	moderate, temperate
moderazione	moderation
moderno	modern
modesto	modest
modo	way
moglie	wife
molare	molar
molino	mill
moltiplicazione	multiplication
molto	much, a lot of; pl. many; adv. very
momento	moment
monarchia	monarchy
mondi	worlds
mondiale	adj. world
mondo	world
moneta	coin
monotono	monotonous
montagna	mountain
monumentale	monumental
monumento	monument
morale	moral
moralmente	morally
morbido	soft
morire	to die
mortadella	mortadella
morte	death
morto	dead
mostra	exhibition, show, exhibit
mostrare	to show
mostrarsi	to show oneself, to appear

motivo	reason, grounds
moto	motorbike, motorcycle
motocicletta	motorcycle
motore	motor
movimentista	one who participates in a political movement
movimento	movement, traffic, bustle
mozzarella	mozzarella (a type of cheese)
mucchio	heap, pile, stack
muovere	to move
muoversi	to move, to stir
muro	wall
museo	museum
musica	music
musicale	musical
muso	muzzle, face
muto	dumb, mute
napoletano	Neapolitan
narrare	to narrate, to tell, to relate
nascere	to be born
nascita	birth
naso	nose
nato	born
natura	nature
naturale	natural
naturalistico	naturalistic
naturalmente	naturally
nautica	navigation
nazifascismo	nazifascism
nazionale	national
nazionalista	nationalist
nazione	nation
ne	of or about him, her, it, them; some
nè	neither, nor
neanche	not even, even
necessario	necessary
necessità	necessity
necropoli	necropolis
negare	to deny
negozio	shop, store
nemmeno	not even
neofascismo	neo-fascism
neofascista	neo-fascist
neolatino	Neo-Latin
neorealismo	neoralism
neppure	not even
nerbo	nerve
nero	black
nervosamente	nervously
nervoso	nervous
nessuno	pron. no one, nobody; adj. no, none
nettamente	spotlessy
nevicare	to snow
nevralgia	neuralgia
niente	nothing
nipote	m. nephew, grandson; f. niece, granddaughter

no	no	offerta	offer
noi	we, us	officina	workshop
noia	boredom	offrire	to offer
noioso	boring	offrirsi	to offer oneself
nome	name	oggetto	object
nominare	to name	oggi	today
non	not	ogni	each, every, any
nonché	let alone	ognuno	everybody, everyone, each
nonna	grandmother		one
nonno	grandfather	oh	oh
nono	ninth	ohimé	alas
nonostante	prep. notwithstanding; conj.	olio	oil
	although	oliva	olive
nord	north	oltre	adv. further, longer; prep.
norma	rule, norm, standard		beyond, besides
normalità	normality	ombra	shade, shadow
nostalgia	homesickness, nostalgia	ombrello	umbrella
nostro	our, ours, our own	ombrellone	beach umbrella
nota	note	omicidio	homicide, murder
notare	to note	omogeneo	homogeneous
notevole	noteworthy	onda	wave
notevolmente	remarkably	onore	honor, honour
notizia	news	opera	opera, work
noto	well-known	operaio	worker, workman
notte	night	operare	to operate, to work
notturno	adj. night, nocturnal, n.	operatore	operator
	nocturne	opinione	opinion
nove	nine	opportuno	opportune
novella	short story, tale	opposizione	opposition
novità	novelty, newness, news	oppure	or, or else, otherwise
nozze	wedding, marriage, nuptials	ora	n. hour, time; adv. now
nucleo	nucleus	orario	hours, timetable, schedule
nulla	nothing	orchestrale	adj. orchestral, n. orchestra
numero	number		member
numeroso	numerous	ordinamento	arrangement, order
nuoto	swimming	ordinare	to order, to arrange
nuovo	new	ordine	order
nutrire	to feed, to nourish	orecchino	earring
nutritivo	nutritious	orecchio	ear
o	either, or	oreficeria	goldsmith's shop, jeweller's
oasi	oasis		shop
obbediente	obedient	organismo	organism
obbedire	to obey	organizzare	to organize
obbligatorio	compulsory, obligatory	organizzarsi	to get organized
obbligo	obligation, duty	organizzazione	organization
obelisco	obelisk	organo	organ
obiettivo	objective	orgoglioso	proud
occasione	opportunity, occasion,	orientamento	orientation, bearings
	chance	orientarsi	to get one's bearings
occhiali	eyeglasses	originale	original
occhio	eye	origine	origin
occidentale	western	ormai	by now, by this time
occorrente	necessary, required	oro	gold
occorrere	to want, to need	orologio	clock, watch
occupare	to occupy	orrore	horror
occuparsi	to occupy oneself, to attend	orso	bear
	to	oscar	Oscar
occupazione	occupation, job	ospedale	hospital
odore	smell, odor, scent, odour	ospitare	to extend hospitality, to
offendere	to offend		shelter, to host

ospite	host, hostess, guest	partecipazione	sharing
osservare	adj. observing; n. observer	partenza	departure
osservazione	observation	particolare	adj. particular, n. detail
ossessione	obsession	particolarmente	particularly
ossia	or rather, that is	partire	to depart, to leave
osteria	tavern, inn	partita	game, match
ottanta	eighty	partito	political party
ottenere	to obtain, to get	parziale	partial
ottimamente	very well, extremely well	passaggio	passing, passage
ottimo	very good, excellent, best	passaporto	passport
otto	eight	passare	to pass, to elapse, to speand
ottobre	October	passato	past (adj. and n.)
otturazione	stopping, filling	passeggiata	walk, stroll
ove	where, when	passionale	passionate
ovest	west	passione	passion, suffering
pacco	parcel	passo	step, pace
pace	peace	pasta	dough, pasta, pastry
padre	father	pasticceria	pastry shop
padrone	master, owner, landlord	pasto	meal
paesaggio	landscape, scenery	pastore	shepherd
paesano	adj. country, rural; n. countryman, peasant	patata	potato
		patente	license
paese	town, village, country	paternalista	paternalist
pagare	to pay	patria	country, fatherland, native land
pagina	page		
paio	pair, couple	patriottico	patriotic
palazzo	palace	pattinaggio	skating
palco	stand, platform, stage	patto	pact, agreement
palio	horserace in Siena; also the banner given as a prize for the winning district	paura	fear, dread
		pausa	pause, interval, break
		paziente	patient (adj. and n.)
pallacanestro	basketball	pazienza	patience
pallanuoto	waterpolo	pazzia	madness, insanity
pallavolo	volleyball	pazzo	mad, crazy, insane
palo	pole, post	peccato	sin
pane	bread	peggio	worse, the worst
panino	roll, sandwich	peggiore	worse, the worst
panna	cream	pena	punishment
panorama	view, panorama	penisola	peninsula
pantaloni	trousers, slacks	penna	pen
Papa	Pope	pennello	brush, paintbrush
papà	daddy, dad	pensare	to think
papale	papal	pensiero	thought
paradiso	paradise, heaven	pensione	pension, boarding house
parco	park	pentirsi	to repent, to regret
parecchio	quite a lot of, several	penultimo	penultimate, next to the last
parere	to seem, to look, to appear	per	through, for, in
parete	wall	percentuale	percentage
pare	equal, even	perché	why, because
paritario	on equal terms	perciò	so, therefore
parlamentare	parliamentary	percorso	run, distance, course, route
parlamento	Parliament	perdere	to lose, to miss, to waste
parlare	to talk, to speak, to address	perdersi	to get lost
parlato	spoken	perdita	loss
parmigiano	Parmesan, from Parma	perdono	forgiveness, pardon
parola	word	perfettamente	perfectly
parroco	parish priest, parson	perfetto	perfect
parte	part	perfezione	perfection
partecipante	participant	pericolo	danger, peril, risk
partecipare	to take part, to share	pericoloso	dangerous, perilous, risky

226

periodico	adj. periodic; n. periodical	plastico	plastic
periodo	period, sentence	pluralità	plurality
permesso	permission, leave	poco	little, few
permettere	to permit, to allow, to let	poema	poem
persona	person	poesia	poetry, poem
personaggio	character	poeta	poet
personale	personal	poi	then, afterwards
personalità	personality	poiché	since, as
personalizzato	personalized	poker	poker
pertanto	therefore	politecnico	polytechnic
però	however, but, nevertheless	politica	politics
pesante	heavy	politicamente	politically
pesare	to weigh	politico	adj. political, n. politician
pesca	peach; fishing	polizia	police
pescare	to fish	poliziesco	adj. police
pescatore	fisherman	poltrona	easy-chair, arm-chair
pesce	fish	pomeriggio	afternoon
peso	weight	pomodoro	tomato
pessimamente	very badly	ponte	bridge
pessimo	very bad	popolano	adj. of the common people; n. man pf the people
petrolio	oil, petroleum		
pettegolezzo	gossip	popolare	popular
pezzo	piece	popolarità	popularity
piacere	to like, to be fond of	popolazione	population
piacevole	pleasant	popolo	people, nation, race
piangere	to cry, to weep	porcheria	dirt, filth, disgusting stuff, trash
pianista	pianist		
piano	adj. flat, level; adv. slowly; n. piano	porgere	to offer, to give
pianta	plant, plan, map	porre	to put, to place, to set
piantagione	plantation	porta	door, gate, goal
piantare	to plant	portare	to carry, to bring, to take, to wear
pianura	plain		
piatto	n. plate, dish; adj. flat	portata	course, range, flow, capacity
piazza	square	porto	harbor, harbour, port
piazzale	square	portoghese	Portuguese
piccolo	small, little	posata	a piece of silverware
picnic	picnic	posizione	position
piede	foot	possedere	to possess
piccola	small, little	possibile	possible
piegare	to fold, to bend	posta	post, mail
piegarsi	to bend	postbellico	postwar
piemontese	Piedmontese	postnapoleonico	post-Napoleonic
pienamente	fully, completely, entirely	posto	place, job, post, position, spot
pieno	full		
pietra	stone	potatura	pruning, trimming
pilota	pilot	potente	powerful, potent
pinacoteca	picture gallery	potenza	power
pino	pine, pinetree	potere	to be able, can may
pioggia	rain	poverino	poor guy, poor fellow
piovere	to rain	povero	poor
pipe	pipes	povertà	poverty
piscina	swimming pool	pranzare	to dine, to have dinner
pisolino	nap, snooze, doze	pranzo	dinner
pittore	painter	pratica	practice
pittorico	pictorial	praticante	practising
pittura	painting, picture	praticare	to practise
piuttosto	rather, pretty, somewhat	praticato	practised
pizza	pizza	pratico	practical
pizzeria	pizza shop	prato	meadow, lawn
più	more, ...er	precedente	preceding, previous

precedenza	precedence, priority	primavera	spring
precedere	to precede	primo	first
precisare	to specify, to state exactly	principale	principal, main
precisione	precision, accuracy	principe	prince
preciso	precise, exact	principio	beginning, principle
precorrere	to forerun, to anticipate	privare	to deprive
preesistere	to preexist	privato	private
preferenza	preference	privo	devoid, destitute
preferibilmente	preferably	probabile	probable
preferire	to prefer	probabilmente	probably
pregare	to pray, to ask, to beg, to request	problema	problem
		proclamare	to proclaim
prego	not at all! don't mention it! please!	procurare	to procure, to get
		prodotto	product
preistorico	prehistoric	produrre	to produce, to yield
premiare	to award a prize, to reward	produttore	adj. productive, n. producer
preminenza	preeminence	produzione	production, manufacture
premio	prize, reward	profano	secular, profane
premura	hurry, haste	professionale	adj. professional
prendere	to take, to catch, to get, to have	professione	profession, trade
		professionismo	professionalism
prendersi	to grab	professionista	n. professional
prenotare	to book, to make a reservation	professionistico	professionalist
		professore	professor (m.)
preoccuparsi	to worry, to be worried	professoressa	professor (f.)
preoccupato	worried	profitto	profit
preparare	to prepare	profondamente	deeply, profoundly
prepararsi	to get ready	profondo	adj. deep; depth
preparativo	preparation	profumo	perfume, scent
preparazione	preparation	progettista	planner, designer
prepotente	overbearing	programma	program, plan
prepotenza	overbearing manner	proibire	to prohibit
presentare	to present, to introduce	proibitivo	prohibitive
presentarsi	to present oneself	proletario	proletarian, (adj. and n.)
presentazione	presentation, introduction	promettere	to promise
presente	present (adj. and n.)	promontorio	promontory, headland
presenza	presence	promozione	promotion
presidente	president	promuovere	to promote
presso	adv. nearby, close; prep. near, close to, in care of	pronto	ready, hello!
		pronunzia	pronunciation
prestare	to lend	proporre	to propose
prestigio	prestige	proporzionale	proportional
prestito	loan	proposito	purpose
presto	soon, early; inter. hurry up! quick!	proposta	proposal
		proprietà	property
pret-à-porter	ready-to-wear	proprietario	owner, proprietor
prete	priest	proprio	adj. typical, real; poss. adj. one's own; adv. just, exactly
pretesa	pretension, pretense		
prevalente	prevalent	prosciutto	ham
prevalenza	prevalence	proseguire	to continue, to carry on
prevalere	to prevail	prossimo	near, close, next
prevedere	to foresee, to forecast, to provide for	protagonista	protagonist
		proteggere	to protect, to shield
previsione	forecast	protesta	protest
prezioso	precious	protestare	to protest
prezzo	price	provare	to prove, to try
prigione	prison, jail	proverbio	proverb, saying
prima	before	provincia	province
primato	preeminence, supremacy, record	provocare	to provoke
		provvedimento	measure, precaution

prudente	prudent
psicologico	psychological
pubblicare	to publish
pubblicazione	publication
pubblicità	advertising
pubblico	public (adj. and n.)
pugilato	boxing
pulito	clean
puntare	to push, to point
punto	point, degree
purchè	provided, as long as, if only
pure	also, too, as well, ever
purgatorio	purgatory
puro	pure
purtroppo	unfortunately
po'	a little
qua	here
quadrato	square (adj. and n.)
quadro	picture, painting
qualche	some, any
qualcosa	something, anything
qualcuno	someone, somebody, anyone, anybody
quale	which, what
qualità	quality
quando	when
quantità	quantity
quanto	adv. how; adj. how much, how many
quantunque	although
quaranta	forty
quarantaquattro	forty-four
quarto	fourth
quasi	almost, nearly
quattordicesimo	fourteenth
quattordici	fourteen
quattro	four
quello	that, those, that one
questione	question, matter
questo	this, these, this one
qui	here
quindi	so, therefore
quindicesimo	fifteenth
quindici	fifteen
quindicinale	fortnightly, every two weeks
quinquennale	quinquennial
quinte	(thet.) wings
quinto	fifth
quotidiano	daily (adj. and n.)
rabbia	rage, anger
racchetta	racket
raccogliere	to pick up, to gather, to receive
raccomandare	to recommend
raccomandarsi	to ask
raccomandazione	recommendation
raccontare	to tell, to narrate
racconto	story, tale
radicale	radical
radio	radio
radiografia	radiography
ragazza	girl, girlfriend
ragazzo	boy, boyfriend, guy
raggiungere	to reach, to arrive at
ragione	reason, right
ragionevole	reasonable
rallentare	to slow down
rancore	grudge
rapidamente	swiftly, rapidly
rapido	swift, rapid, quick
rapporto	report, statement
rappresentante	n. representative
rappresentare	to represent
rappresentativo	adj. representative
raramente	rarely
raro	rare
razionalmente	rationally
razza	race, breed, kind
re	king
realizzare	to carry out, to achieve, to realize
realizzazione	realization, achievement
realtà	reality
reazione	reaction
recarsi	to go
recente	recent
recitare	to recite
recitazione	recitation
recuperare	to recover, to salvage
recupero	recovery
referendum	referendum
regalare	to present, to give
regalato	presented, given
regalo	gift, present
regata	regatta
regime	regime; regimen, diet
regionalista	regionalist
regione	region
regista	director
registrare	to register, to record, to tape
registro	register
regno	kingdom, realm, reign
regola	rule
regolare	regular
regolarmente	regularly
relativo	relative
religione	religion
religioso	religious
rendere	to give back, to return, to render
replica	reply, retort
reprimere	to repress, to check
repubblica	republic
repubblicano	republican
residenza	residence
resistenza	resistance
respingere	to repel, to drive back
responsabile	responsible
responsabilità	responsibility
restare	to stay, to remain

resti	remains, remnants
restituire	to return, to give back, to restore
resto	remainder, rest, change
rete	net, network
retta	with *dare* - to pay attention to; n. fee
rettile	reptile
riassumere	to summarize, to sum up
riassuntivo	summarizing
ricambio	replacement, exchange, return
ricchezza	wealth, riches
ricco	rich, wealthy
ricerca	search, research
ricevere	to receive, to get
richiamare	to call again, to recall, to call back
richiedere	to ask, to require
ricominciare	to begin again
ricomporsi	to reform, to reassemble
riconoscere	to recognize
ricordare	to remember
ricordarsi	to remember
ricordo	recollection, memory, souvenir
ricorrere	to have recourse, to appeal, to recur
ricostruire	to rebuild
ricostruzione	reconstruction
ridere	to laugh
riemergere	to reemerge
riempire	to fill (up), to stuff
rientrare	to reenter, to return
rientro	reentry, return
rievocazione	recalling
riferimento	reference
riferire	to refer, to report
riferirsi	to refer, to concern
rifiutare	to refuse
rifiuto	refusal, waste
riflettere	to reflect
riflusso	reflux, flow
riforma	reform
riformare	to reform
rifugio	shelter, refuge
riga	line, row, rule
rigatone	rigatone (a type of pasta)
rigore	rigor
rigoroso	rigorous
riguardare	to go over, to regard, to concern
rilevare	to notice
rilievo	relief
rimandare	to send back
rimanere	to remain, to stay
rimborso	refund
rimettersi	to start again, to recover
rimproverare	to reproach, to rebuke
rinascimento	Renaissance
rincrescere	to regret, to mind, to be sorry
ringraziare	to thank
rinuncia	renunciation
rinunciare	to renounce
rinvenire	to recover one's senses, to come to
rione	ward, district, quarter
riparare	to shelter, to repair, to remedy
ripetere	to repeat
ripetersi	to repeat oneself
riportare	to bring back, to take back, to return
riposarsi	to rest, to have a rest
riprendere	to retake, to recover, to resume
riprovare	to try again
riprovevole	blameworthy
risalire	to go up, to climb up
risapere	to come to know, to get to know
risata	laughter, laugh
riscaldato	heated, warmed
rischiare	to risk
riscoprire	to rediscover
risentito	resentful
riserva	reserve
riservare	to reserve, to keep
risiedere	to reside
risolvere	to resolve, to solve
risorsa	resource
risotto	risotto (rice speciality)
risparmiare	to save
rispettare	to respect
rispettato	respected
rispetto	respect
rispondere	to answer, to reply, to respond
risposare	to marry again
ristorante	restaurant
ristretto	narrow, limited
risultare	to result, to ensue
risultato	result
ritardato	delayed
ritardo	delay
ritenere	to think, to believe, to consider
ritirare	to withdraw, to retract
ritmico	rhythmic, rhythmical
ritmo	rhythm
rito	rite
ritornare	to return, to go back
ritorno	return
ritratto	n. portrait; adj. portrayed
ritrovamento	discovery
ritrovare	top find again, to recover
ritrovarsi	to find oneself, to meet again
ritto	upright, erect
riunirsi	to reunite, to unite, to meet
riuscire	to succeed, to be good at

riva	shore, bank
rivedere	to see again, to meet again, to return
rivelare	to reveal
rivelarsi	to reveal oneself, to turn out
rivista	magazine
rivolgere	to turn, to address
rivolgersi	to turn, to apply
rivolta	revolt
rivoluzionario	revolutionary (adj. and n.)
rivoluzione	revolution
robusto	strong, sturdy
rocca	fortress
roccia	rock
rock	rock (music)
romano	Roman (adj. and n.)
romantico	romantic
romanzo	n. novel
ronzio	buzzing
rosa	adj. pink, n. rose
rosso	red
rotto	broken
rovesciare	to upset, to overturn
rovina	ruin
rovinare	to ruin
rubare	to steal
rubrica	survey, column (newspaper), address book
rude	rough, severe; harsh
rudere	ruin, wreck
rumore	noise
rumorio	noise
ruolo	roll, list
ruotare	to rotate, to revolve
sabato	Saturday
sacco	sack
sacramento	sacrament
sacrificio	sacrifice
saggezza	wisdom
saggio	adj. wise; n. wise man; essay
saggista	essayist
sala	hall, room
salame	salame, salami
salario	wages, pay
sale	salt
saletta	small room
salire	to get on, to go up
salita	slope, ascent
salotto	drawing room, living room
salsa	sauce
salto	jump, leap
salutare	to greet, to say hello, to say good-bye
salute	health, safety
saluto	greeting, salutation
salvare	to save, to rescue
salve	hello! hi!
sanare	to heal
sangue	blood
sano	healthy, wholesome

santo	adj. holy, Saint, saintly; n. saint
sapere	to know, to know how, to hear about
sapore	taste, flavour
sbagliare	to make a mistake
sbaglio	mistake, error
sbalzo	leap, jump, bound
sbrigarsi	to hurry up
scacco	s.m. square; pl. chess
scala	staircase, stairs
scalino	step
scambiare	to exchange
scambio	exchange
scapolo	bachelor
scarpa	shoe
scarso	scarce
scatenare	to unchain; to rouse
scatola	box, tin, can
scaturire	to spring, to gush
scavo	excavation
scegliere	to choose, to select
sceicco	sheik
scelta	choice, selection
scena	scene
scenario	scenery
scendere	to go down, to descent
scenico	scenic
scenografo	scene designer
scheletro	skeleton
schema	scheme, plan
schermo	protection, screen
scherzare	to joke, to make fun, to kid
scherzo	joke, trick
schiamazzo	row, rowdiness, racket
schiavitù	slavery
schifo	disgust
sci	ski, skiing
scientifico	scientific
scienza	science
scienziato	scientist
sciocchezza	foolishness, silliness
sciopero	strike, walkout
scolaro	pupil
scolastico	adj. school, scholastic
scommessa	bet, wager
sconfiggere	to defeat
scontro	clash, collision, crash
scoperta	discovery, detection
scopo	aim, object, purpose, end
scoprire	to discover, to find out, to detect
scoprirsi	to discover
scorpione	scorpion
scorso	last, past
scritto	adj. written, n. writing
scrittore	writer
scrivere	to write
scudo	shield
scultura	sculpture, carving

scuola	school	serata	evening
scuotere	to shake, to stir	serie	series
scuro	dark	serio	adj. serious; n. seriousness
scusa	excuse, apology	serratura	lock
scusare	to excuse, to forgive	servire	to serve, to wait on
scusarsi	to apologize, to make one's excuses	servito	served
sdentato	toothless	servitore	servant
sdraio	lounge chair	servizio	service, set
se	whether, if	sessanta	sixty
sè	himself, herself, itself, oneself, themselves	sessantaquattro	sixty-four
		sessantuno	sixty-one
sebbene	though, although	sesso	sex
secco	dry, dried	sesto	sixth
secolo	century, age	seta	silk
seconda	second gear, second class	settanta	seventy
secondario	secondary	sette	seven
secondo	second (adj., pron., n.); prep. according to	settecento	seven hundred
		settembre	September
sede	center, seat	settimana	week
sedersi	to sit down, to be seated	settimanale	weekly
sedia	chair	settimo	seventh
sedicesimo	sixteenth	settore	sector, field
sedici	sixteen	sfilata	parade
seduta	sitting, session	sfondato	bottomless, insatiable
seduto	seated	sfondo	background, setting
seggiolone	high chair	sfortuna	bad luck
segnare	to mark, to note down	sfortunato	unlucky, unfortunate
segno	sign, mark, target, limit	sforzo	effort, strain, exertion
segretaria	secretary (f.)	sfrenato	unbridled, unrestrained
segretario	secretary (m.)	sfruttamento	exploitation
segreteria	registrar's office	sfruttare	to overwork, to exploit
segreto	secret	sfuggire	to escape
seguente	adj. following	sfumato	vanished, shaded, vague
seguire	to follow	sgombro	clear, free of, empty
seguito	n. following	sguardo	look, glance
sei	six	si	oneself, himself, herself, itself, themselves
selezione	selection		
selvaggina	game (in the wild)	sì	yes
selvaggio	adj. wild, savager; n. savage	sia	whether ... or, either ... or, each, other
sembrare	to seem, to appear		
semplice	simple	siccome	as, since, because
semplicemente	simply	siciliano	Sicilian
sempre	always	sicuramente	surely, certainly
senato	senate	sicurezza	certainty, safety, security
senatore	senator	sicuro	sure, certain, safe, secure
sensazione	sensation, feeling	siderurgico	adj. iron, metallurgic
sensibile	sensitive	sigaretta	cigarette
sensibilità	sensitiveness	significare	to mean
sensibilizzare	to sensitize	signora	lady, Mrs., woman, madam
senso	sense	signore	gentleman, Mr., man, Sir
sentimentale	sentimental	signorina	young lady, Miss
sentimento.	feeling	silenzio	silence
sentire	to feel	simbolo	symbol
sentirsi	to feel, to feel like	simile	alike, like, similar
sentitamente	heartily, sincerely	simpatia	liking, attraction
sepolcrale	sepulchral	simpatico	nice, likeable, pleasant, agreable
sepoltura	burial;sepulchre, tomb		
sequenza	sequence	sincero	sincere
sera	evening	sindacale	adj. trade union, labor union
		sindacato	n. trade union, labor union

sindaco	mayor
sinfonia	symphony
sinfonico	symphonic
singolare	singular
sinistra	left, left hand, (political) left
sintesi	synthesis
sistema	system, method, way
sistemare	to arrange, to settle
sistemarsi	to find accomodations, to find a job
sistemazione	arrangement, settlement
situare	to place, to site
situato	situated, placed, sited
situazione	situation, position
slancio	rush, enthusiasm, impulse
smettere	to stop, or to give up (doing something)
smilzo	thin, lean
socialdemocratico	adj. Social Democratic; n. Social Democrat
sociale	social
socialista	socialist
società	society
soddisfatto	satisfied
soddisfazione	satisfaction
sodo	solid, firm, hard-boiled
sofferenza	suffering, pain
soffrire	to suffer, to bear, to stand, to allow
soggetto	subject
soggiorno	stay
sognare	to dream
solamente	adv. only
soldato	soldier
soldi	money
sole	sun
solenne	solemn
solidarietà	solidarity
solito	usual, customary
solitudine	solitude
solo	adj. alone, only; n. only one; adv. only
soltanto	adv. only
soluzione	solution
somma	addition, sum, total
soporifero	soporific, boring
sopportare	to bear, to stand, to tolerate
sopra	prep. on, upon, above; adv. on, upstairs
soprattutto	above all
sopravvivenza	survival
sopravvivere	to survive
sorella	sister
sorgere	to rise, to arise
sorpassare	to exceed, to pass
sorpasso	passing
sorprendere	surprising, astonishing
sorpresa	surprise
sorpreso	surprised, amazed
sorridere	to smile
sorso	sip
sospendere	to suspend, to defer, to adjourn
sospetto	adj. suspicious; n. suspicion
sostanzialmente	substantially
sostare	to stop, to pause
sostegno	support, prop
sostenere	to support, to sustain
sottile	thin, fine, slender, slim
sotto	adv. and prep. under, below
sottolineare	to uderline
sottoscrizione	signature
sottrazione	subtraction
souvenir	souvenir
sovranità	sovereignty
sovrintendente	superintendent
spaghettata	spaghettata
spaghetti	spaghetti
spalla	shoulder
sparire	to disappear
spasimante	admirer, beau
spaventare	to frighten, to scare
spaventato	frightened, scared
spazio	space, room
specchio	mirror
speciale	special
specialista	specialist
specialistico	specialistic
specializzarsi	to specialize
specializzato	specialized
specializzazione	specialization
specialmente	especially, particularly
specie	kind, sort
spedire	to send, to ship
spedizione	dispatch, shipment, mailing
spendere	to spend
spento	extinguished, out, off
speranza	hope
sperare	to hope
sperimentare	to experiment
spesa	expense, cost; shopping
spesso	often, frequently
spessore	thickness
spettabile	respectable, honorable
spettacolo	performance, exhibition, show
spezzare	to break
spiaggia	beach
spicco	conspicuousness, prominence
spiegare	to unfold, to explain
spiegarsi	to explain oneself
spiegazione	explanation
spina	thorn
spinta	push, thrust, spur
spirituale	spiritual
splendido	wonderful, splendid
sporgersi	to lean out
sport	sport
sportello	teller's window, ticket window
sportivo	adj. sporting, sports; n. sportsman

sposalizio	wedding	subalterno	subordinate, subaltern (adj. and n.)
sposare	to marry	subire	to undergo
sposarsi	to get married	subito	at once, immediately
sposo	bridegroom, husband	sublime	sublime
spostare	to move, to shift, to change	succedere	to succeed, to follow; to happen
spray	spray	successivo	following, subsequent
sprecare	to waste	successo	success
sproporzionato	disproportionate	succhiare	to suck
spruzzare	to sprinkle	succo	juice
spumante	spumante	sud	south
spuntino	snack	sudato	sweaty
squadra	team, squad	sufficiente	enough, sufficient
squilibrio	lack of balance	suffragio	suffrage, vote
stabile	stable, steady, lasting	suggerire	to suggest
stabilire	to establish, to fix, to settle	suggestione	suggestion
stabilmente	stably	suo	his, her, hers, its, their, theirs
stagione	season	suocera	mother-in-law
stagno	pool	suonare	to play, to sound, to ring
stamattina	this morning	superare	to exceed, to overcome, to excel
stampa	printing, press		
stancare	to tire	superficiale	superficial
stancarsi	to get tired	superficie	area, surface
stanco	tired, weary	superiore	superior, upper, higher
stanza	room	supplicare	to beg
stare	to be; to stay, to remain; to suit	supporre	to suppose
		supporto	support
stasera	this evening, tonight	suscitare	to provoke, to cause, to stir up
stato	state, condition		
statuto	statute	suspense	suspense
stazione	station	svanire	to vanish
stereo	stereo	svegliarsi	to wake up
stesso	same; myself, yourself (etc.)	svelto	quick
stile	style	sviluppare	to develop
stimolare	to stimulate	svilupparsi	to develop, to expand, to grow
storia	history; story, tale; fib		
storico	adj. historical, n. historian	sviluppo	development, expansion, growth
strada	road, street, way		
straniero	adj. foreign, n. foreigner	svizzero	Swiss
strano	strange, odd, queer, funny	svolgere	to develop
straordinario	extraordinary	svolgersi	to happen, to occur, to take place
strato	layer, stratum		
straziante	tormenting, torturing, heartbreaking	tabaccheria	tobacconist's shop
		tacco	heel
strettamente	strictly	tacere	to be silent, to keep silent
stretto	narrow, tight; strict	tagliatelle	noodles
stringere	to press, to squeeze, to wring, to clasp	tale	such
		talora	sometimes
strumento	instrument, tool	talvolta	sometimes
struttura	structure	tana	lair, den
studente	student (m.)	tanto	adv. so, so much; adj. so much, so many
studiare	to study		
studio	study, course of study; study, office	tappo	plug, cap, cork
		tardi	late
studioso	adj. studious, n. scholar	tartina	open sandwich
stufo	fed up (with), sick (of)	tassa	tax
stupendo	wonderful, marvellous	tavola	table; board, plank, slab
stupito	amazed, astonished	tavolo	table
stupore	amazement, astonishment	tavolozza	palette
su	prep. on, upon, over, above; adv. upstairs		

tazzina	small cup	tifo	*fare il* - to support a team
te	you, to you, (familiar, singular)	tinta	dye, color, hue
		tipico	typical
tè	tea	tipo	type, kind, sort
teatrale	theatrical	tiranno	tyrant
teatro	theater, theatre	tirannosauro	tyranosaurus
tecnica	technique	titolo	title
tecnico	adj. technical, n. technician	toccare	to touch
tecnologia	technology	togliere	to take away, to take off
tecnologico	technological	tomba	tomb, grave
tedesco	German	tonnellata	ton
tela	cloth	tono	tone
telefonare	to telephone, to call, to ring up	tornare	to return, to go back, to come back
telefonata	telephone call	tortellini	tortellini
telefonico	adj. thelephone	toscano	Tuscan
telefono	n. telephone	totale	total (adj. and n.), complete
televisione	television	tra	between, among, amidst, in, within
televisore	television set		
tema	theme, composition, essay; fear	tradimento	betrayal, treachery
		tradizionale	traditional
temere	to fear, to be afraid of	tradizione	tradition
temibile	fearful	tradurre	to translate
temperatura	temperature	traduzione	translation
tempesta	storm, tempest	tragedia	tragedy
tempio	temple (building)	tramontare	to set, to wane, to die out
tempo	time, weather	tranne	prep. except, but, save
tenace	adhesive, tenacious	tranquillizzarsi	to calm down
tendenza	tendency, trend	tranquillo	adj. quiet, calm
tendenzialmente	fundamentally	transitorio	transitory
tendere	to stretch	trapano	drill
tenere	to keep, to hold	trascorrere	to spend, to pass
tenero	adj. tender	trasferire	to trasfer
tenersi	to keep oneself; to consider oneself	trasformare	to transform
		trasformarsi	to transform oneself, to change into
tennis	tennis		
tentativo	attempt	trasformazione	transformation
tentazione	temptation	trasmettere	to transmit, to broadcast
teorico	theoretical	trasmittente	adj. transmitting, n. transmitter
terminare	to end, to finish		
terno	tern	trattare	to deal
terra	earth, land, ground	trattarsi	to be a question of
terreno	ground, soil, land	trattato	treaty
terribile	terrible	traversata	crossing
terriero	adj. land	travestire	to disguise, to dress up
territoriale	territorial	tre	three
territorio	territory	tredicesimo	thirteenth
terrorizzante	terrorizing	tredici	thirteen
terzo	third	tremante	trembling, shaking, shivering, shuddering
tesi	thesis		
tesoro	treasure, treasury	tremare	to tremble, to shake, to shiver, to shudder
tessera	card, ticket, pass, membership card, identity card		
		tremendo	awful, terrible, tremendous
		treno	train
tessile	adj. textile, n. textiles	trenta	thirty
tessuto	cloth, fabric, material, stuff	trentuno	thirty-one
testa	head	triade	triad
testata	heading	triennale	triennal
testo	text	trionfo	triumph
ti	you, to you, yourself (fam. s.)	triste	sad

troppo	too much, too many, adv. too
trovare	to find, to find out
trovarsi	to be, to be situated
trovata	a great idea
tu	you (fam. s.)
tumulo	n. grave
tumultuoso	tumultuous, riotous
tuo	your, yours (fam. s.)
turco	adj. Turkish, n. Turk
turismo	tourism
turista	n. tourist
turistico	adj. tourist
turno	turn; duty, shift
tuttavia	but, yet, nevertheless
tutti	indef. pron. pl. all, everybody, everyone
tutto	adj. all, (the) whole, every; adv. all; pron. all, averything
ubbidiente	obedient
ubriacarsi	to get drunk
ubriaco	drunk (adj. and n.)
uccello	bird
uccidere	to kill
uffa	ugh!
ufficiale	adj. official, n. officer, official
ufficio	office, agency, department
uguaglianza	equality
uguale	equal
ultimo	last, latest, utmost
umanistico	humanistic
umanità	humanity
umano	human, humane
umbro	Umbrian
umido	adj. damp, humid; n. dampness, moisture
un	a, an, one
unanime	unanimous
undici	eleven
unico	only, one, sole, single; unique
unione	union
unire	to join together, to unite
unisex	unisex
unitamente	unitedly, jointly
unitariamente	unitarily, undividedly
unitario	unitary
unito	united, joined together
unità	unity, unit
universale	universal
universitario	adj. university
università	n. university
uno	a, an, one
uomo	man
uovo	egg
urbanizzare	to urbanize
usare	to use
uscire	to go out, to exit
uscita	exit
uso	use
utile	useful
utilità	utility, usefulness
utilizzato	utilized
uva	grape
vacanza	vacation, holiday
valere	to be worth
valido	valid
valigia	suitcase, luggage
vallata	valley
valle	valley, vale, dale
valore	worth, value
variare	to vary
varietà	variety
vario	various, varied
vaso	vase
ve	you (pl.), to you (pl.)
vastità	vastness
vasto	vast
vaticano	Vatican (adj. and n.)
vecchio	old
vedere	to see
vedersi	to meet
veloce	quick, rapid, fast
velocemente	quickly, rapidly
velocità	velocity, speed, quickness
vendere	to sell
venerdì	Friday
veneto	Venetian
venire	to come, to turn out
ventennio	period of twenty years
ventesimo	twentieth
venti	twenty
venticinque	twenty-five
ventidue	twenty-two
ventiduesimo	twenty-second
ventiquattresimo	twenty-fourth
ventiquattro	twenty-four
ventitreesimo	twenty-third
ventunesimo	twenty-first
ventuno	twenty-one
veramente	truly, really
verde	green
verdura	vegetables
vergine	virgin (adj. and n.)
vergogna	shame
verità	truth
vero	true, real
veronese	Veronese
verso	toward, near, about, around
vertice	top, summit
vescovile	episcopal, bishop's
vestire	to dress, to clothe
vestirsi	to get dressed
vestito	dress, suit
veterinario	veterinary
vetrina	shop window
vetro	glass
vi	you (pl.), yourselves (pl.), eachother; there
via	street, way; adv. away, scram

viaggiare	to travel
viaggiatore	traveller
viaggio	journey, trip, voyage, flight
vibrazione	vibration
vicenda	event
vicino	adj. near, close; n. neighbor; adv. near (by) close (by)
vie	paths, means
vietare	to forbid, to prohibit
vigliaccheria	cowardice, cowardliness
vigna	vineyard
vigneto	vineyard
vigore	strength, vigor
villa	villa
villaggio	village, hamlet
vincente	adj. winning, n. winner
vincere	to win, to beat, to overcome, to conquer
vino	wine
violenza	violence
virtù	virtue
visibile	visible
visita	visit, call; examination, check-up
visitare	to visit, to pay a visit
visitatore	visitor
vista	sight, view
vita	life, lifetime
vitale	vital
vite	vine
vitigno	vine
vittima	victim
vittoria	victory
vittorioso	victorious
viva	hurrah! hurray! long live!
vivacità	liveliness, vivacity
vivamente	heartily
vivente	adj. living; n. living being
vivere	to live
vivo	live, alive, living
vocabolario	vocabulary, dictionary
vocazione	vocation
voce	voice
voglia	wish, desire, longing, fancy, will
voi	you (pl.)
volentieri	gladly, willingly, with pleasure
volerci	to take
volere	to want, to wish, to like
volgare	vulgar, coarse, vernacular
volo	flight
volontà	will
volpacchiotto	fox-cub
volpe	fox
volta	tiime, turn
voltare	to turn
volto	face, visage, countenance
volume	volume
vostro	your, your own, yours (pl.)
votare	to vote
votazione	voting, poll
voto	vote, grade, mark
vuotare	to empty
vuoto	empty
zampa	leg, paw
zio	uncle
zitto	quiet, silent
zona	area, zone
zoo	zoo
zucchero	sugar

INDICE ALFABETICO   INDEX

INDICE ALFABETICO   INDEX

INDICE ALFABETICO   INDEX

INDICE ALFABETICO INDEX

INDICE ALFABETICO   INDEX

INDICE ALFABETICO   INDEX

INDICE ALFABETICO   INDEX

INDICE ALFABETICO INDEX

INDICE ALFABETICO   INDEX

INDICE ALFABETICO   INDEX

INDICE ALFABETICO   INDEX

INDICE ALFABETICO   INDEX

INDICE ALFABETICO   INDEX

NOTE

Stampa: Guerra guru s.r.l. - Via A. Manna, 25 - 06132 - Perugia - Tel. 075/5289090 - Fax 075/5288244